DATE DUE

NOV 2 9 2010	
APR 09 2012	
APR 2 4 2012	
NOV 18 2013	
DEC 0 6 2013	
AUG 0 8 2018	

BRODART, CO.   Cat. No. 23-221-003

PUNISHMENT AND INEQUALITY IN AMERICA

PUNISHMENT AND INEQUALITY IN AMERICA

Bruce Western

Russell Sage Foundation • New York

The Russell Sage Foundation

The Russell Sage Foundation, one of the oldest of America's general purpose foundations, was established in 1907 by Mrs. Margaret Olivia Sage for "the improvement of social and living conditions in the United States." The Foundation seeks to fulfill this mandate by fostering the development and dissemination of knowledge about the country's political, social, and economic problems. While the Foundation endeavors to assure the accuracy and objectivity of each book it publishes, the conclusions and interpretations in Russell Sage Foundation publications are those of the authors and not of the Foundation, its Trustees, or its staff. Publication by Russell Sage, therefore, does not imply Foundation endorsement.

Library of Congress Cataloging-in-Publication Data

Western, Bruce, 1964–
    Punishment and inequality in America / Bruce Western.
        p.   cm.
    Includes bibliographical references and index.
    ISBN 0-87154-894-1
    1. Imprisonment—Economic aspects—United States.   2. Imprisonment—Social aspects—United States.   3. Criminal justice, Administration of—Economic aspects—United States.   4. Criminal justice, Administration of—Social aspects—United States.   I. Title.

HV9471.W47   2006
365'.973—dc22

                                                                    2005055259

Text design by Genna Patacsil.

RUSSELL SAGE FOUNDATION
112 East 64th Street, New York, New York 10021
10 9 8 7 6 5 4 3 2

For Lucy, Miriam, and Grace

CONTENTS

ABOUT THE AUTHORS

Bruce Western is professor of sociology and faculty associate of the Office of Population Research at Princeton University.

Leonard Lopoo is assistant professor of public administration at The Maxwell School at Syracuse University.

Becky Pettit is assistant professor of sociology at the University of Washington, Seattle.

PREFACE

This book reports the main findings of an eight-year project investigating the scope and consequences of growth in the American penal population. Although a vast research literature had studied the evolution of penal institutions and their effects on crime, my research has tried to understand how prisons and jails in America have come to form part of a novel system of social inequality. Instead of seeing prisons chiefly as instruments for crime control, I examined how the penal system, for a generation of young men, came to reschedule the life course, influence economic opportunity, and shape family life. On the broader canvas of American society, this is a story as much about race and poverty as it is about crime and deviance.

The project was hatched, almost by accident, in conversations with my friend from graduate school, Katherine Beckett. Beckett was finishing work on her book *Making Crime Pay* (1997), a study of the politics of criminal justice in America. At that time, in the summer of 1995, the U.S. economy was on the brink of an historic expansion that would serve notice to the welfare capitalisms of western Europe. Unprecedented U.S. job growth, it seemed, could greatly help the disadvantaged if only government could avoid the European error of coddling the poor with welfare. Although the U.S. job machine of the 1990s brought prosperity to many, it appeared that the worst off had benefited the least. And, despite the end of welfare as we knew it, government had not withdrawn from the lives of America's poor: its role had simply changed. More punitive than limited, government had reached deeply into poor urban communities by sending record numbers of young men to prison and jail at a time when crime rates were at their lowest levels in thirty years. Beckett and I tried to make sense of these developments in a paper that viewed the penal system as a labor market institution—a systematic state influence on wages and employment.[1] That paper contained two ideas that are developed in greater detail in this book. First, large-scale imprisonment by the end of the 1990s concealed significant poverty and inequality from official statistics by locking up so many young men with little schooling. Second, the penal system deepened inequality by further diminishing the life chances of the disadvantaged.

The impact of the penal system on the labor market depended not just on the scale of incarceration, but also on the racial and economic cast of the prison population. Racial disparities had been studied extensively, but I could find little work on the economic situation of prison and jail inmates. I set out with Becky Pettit, then a graduate student at Princeton, to simply document incarceration rates for black and white men at different levels of education. The calculations were simple, but the results were startling. Among black male high school dropouts aged twenty to thirty-five, we estimated that 36 percent were in prison or jail in 1996. The U.S. Census Bureau's labor force survey, the Current Population Survey, estimated that 46 percent of young black male dropouts were employed, but this number dropped to 29 percent once prison and jail inmates were counted in the population.[2] We followed this up by estimating the chances a man would serve time in prison by his mid-thirties. By now we had learned to expect that young black dropouts were deeply involved in the penal system, but again the results were striking. Among black male dropouts born in the late 1960s, 60 percent had prison records by their early thirties. We also found that black men in their early thirties at the end of the 1990s were more likely to have been to prison than to have graduated from college with a four-year degree.[3]

What started as an effort to simply describe the extent of incarceration in different parts of the population had begun to reveal a picture of American race and poverty fundamentally transformed by the penal system. This book traces that story from conservative reaction to the Civil Rights Movement, through the historic drop in violence and other serious crime at the end of the 1990s.

My research would not have been possible without my superb collaborators. I am indebted to Katherine Beckett for helping me cross the bridge from my home base in comparative sociology to study American politics and society. I am also grateful to Becky Pettit, who co-authored chapter 1, for her sheer doggedness in the research process and sharp eye for quantitative detail. Both qualities have been invaluable for this project. Len Lopoo and Sara McLanahan rightly insisted on the importance of families and children in understanding the lives of men passing through the criminal justice system. Sara also generously made available advance releases of the Fragile Families Study of Child Wellbeing. Len Lopoo co-authored chapter 6. I have been fortunate to work with Meredith Kleykamp and Jake Rosenfeld, two excellent researchers offering their help from the ranks of the graduate program in sociology at Princeton. I also gratefully acknowledge the research assistance of Deborah Becher, Josh Guetzkow, Traci Schlesinger, Marylynne Hunt-Dorta, and Ogi Radic.

While writing this book, I had the opportunity to talk to prisoners, formerly incarcerated men, correctional officers, parole officers, and prosecutors. These conversations are not directly reported here, but they greatly shaped my thinking about mass imprisonment in America. My friends in New Jersey corrections and parole, Al Kandell and Lenny Ward, may not agree with everything I have written, but were kind enough to comment on several chapters and discuss numerous ideas in the book. I greatly appreciate their intelligence, compassion, and professionalism in what must be two of the most difficult jobs in the country. Patricia Gatling and Kevin Costin who developed the Brooklyn Distict Attorney's ComALERT program shared with me their great experience in the field of prisoner reentry. Will Whitaker convened several discussion groups with formerly incarcerated men who generously shared their time and life experience. I also thank the organizers of Hispanic Americans for Progress (HAP), Willie Garcia and Jesus Sanabria, and their collaborators at New Jersey State Prison. HAP organized several courses for me at the prison while I was working on the manuscript. I found these to be extraordinary teaching experiences and I am grateful to the students for their seriousness and acuity in commenting on early drafts of several chapters. My Princeton colleague, Patricia Fernandez-Kelly, was an indefatigable co-teacher at the prison and I am grateful for her support.

As this book was drafted, I benefited from the comments of a number of excellent readers and commentators. Parts of several chapters have earlier appeared in journals and I am grateful to my journal referees and editors. David Garland and Michael Hout provided detailed feedback on the full manuscript, and I have tried my best to do justice to their marvelous commentaries. Becky Pettit, Mitch Duneier, and Devah Pager also provided superb comments on the book as a whole and I thank them for their wisdom and generosity. My friend John McCormick indulged many conversations about the main themes and provided helpful comments as the project neared completion. At various stages of the writing process I also received invaluable criticism and assistance from Angus Deaton, David Ellwood, Deborah Garvey, Heather Haveman, Bob Jackman, Christopher Jencks, Jeff Kling, Steve Levitt, Ross Macmillan, Jo McKendry, Abigail Saguy, Rob Sampson, Jeremy Travis, Chris Uggen, and David Weiman. Hillard Pouncy graciously offered his class in Princeton's Woodrow Wilson School as a testing ground for several chapters.

Research for this book was supported by Princeton University, the Russell Sage Foundation, and National Science Foundation grant SES-0004336. Eric Wanner at the Russell Sage Foundation provided sustained support and encouragement, without which much of this research would not have been possible.

Although most of the empirical analysis of the book is new, parts of several chapters were published as "Black-White Wage Inequality, Employment Rates, and Incarceration," *American Journal of Sociology* 111: 553–78 (co-authored with Becky Pettit); "Incarceration and the Formation and Stability of Marital Unions," *Journal of Marriage and the Family* 67: 721–34 (co-authored with Leonard M. Lopoo); "Mass Imprisonment and the Life Course: Race and Class Inequality in U.S. Incarceration," *American Sociological Review* 69: 151–69 (co-authored with Becky Pettit); "The Impact of Incarceration on Wage Mobility and Inequality," *American Sociological Review* 67: 477–98; and "How Unregulated is the U.S. Labor Market? The Penal System as a Labor Market Institution," *American Journal of Sociology* 104: 1030–60 (co-authored with Katherine Beckett).

Introduction

In 1831, Alexis de Tocqueville and Gustave de Beaumont were dispatched to America to study the penitentiary, a novel institution generating great discussion among the social reformers of Europe. At that time, two institutions—Auburn State Prison in New York and the Eastern Penitentiary in Philadelphia—offered leading examples of a new approach to the public management of criminals. The institutions were devised for moral correction. Rigorous programs of work and isolation would remedy the moral defects of criminal offenders so they might safely return to society. The penitentiary was billed as a triumph of progressive thinking that provided a humane and rational alternative to the disorderly prisons and houses of correction in Europe. Tocqueville and Beaumont were just two of many official visitors from Europe who toured the prisons in the 1830s, eager to view the leading edge of social reform.

Grand projects in crime control often spring from deep fissures in the social order. Tocqueville and Beaumont saw this clearly, despairing of "a state of disquiet" in French society. Writing in 1833, they traced the need for prison reform to a restless energy in the minds of men "that consumes society for want of other prey."[1] This moral decline was compounded by the material deprivation of the French working class, "whose corruption, beginning in misery, is completed in prison." Instead of deflecting vice and poverty, the

French prisons made things worse—aggravating immiseration and immorality.[2] America offered a fresh alternative.

Although the prisons that provided the pretext for Tocqueville's American tour did not figure in his observations on American democracy, democratic aspirations were faintly inscribed on the Auburn and Pennsylvania penitentiaries. The project of rehabilitation assumed an innate moral equality among men that could be restored to criminals through penal discipline. Rehabilitative institutions comprised part of a primitive social democracy that conferred not just the vote and freedom of association but also a minimal equality of life chances. Despite curtailing freedom (and applying corporal punishment), the prison posed no basic threat to democracy because the official ideology of rehabilitation promised to reestablish the social membership of those who had fallen into poverty and crime. In practice, of course, the rehabilitative ideal was regularly compromised and in the South it barely took hold at all. In conception at least, and sometimes in practice, the prison sat comfortably alongside an array of welfare institutions that included not only reformatories and asylums but also public schools, hospitals, and rudimentary schemes for social insurance. Like other welfare institutions, the prison was conceived to rescue the citizenship of the unfortunate, the poor, and the deviant.

The story of this book begins one hundred and forty years later, in the 1970s, when the American penal system embarked on another journey of institutional change. The latest revolution in criminal punishment followed some of the logic of its nineteenth-century predecessor. Shifts in the structure of society and politics forced changes in criminal justice, with large consequences for the quality of American democracy. Through the last decades of the twentieth century, the patchwork system of American criminal justice turned away from the rehabilitative project first attempted in New York and Pennsylvania. By the 1970s, policy experts were skeptical that prisons could prevent crime by reforming their inmates. Incarceration would be used less for rehabilitation than for incapacitation, deterrence, and punishment. Politicians vowed to get tough on crime. State lawmakers abandoned the rehabilitative ideals etched in the law of criminal sentencing and opted for mandatory prison terms, the abolition of parole, and long sentences for felons on their second and third convictions. Tough new sentences were attached to narcotics offenses as the federal government waged first a war on crime, then a war on drugs. Locked facilities proliferated around the country to cope with the burgeoning penal population. Prison construction became an instrument for regional development as small towns lobbied for correctional facilities and resisted prison closure.

Prisons themselves changed as a result of the punitive turn in criminal justice. Budgets tightened for education and work programs. But some social service function remained as the penal system assumed new responsibilities for public health, delivering treatment on a large scale for mental illness, tuberculosis, HIV/AIDS, and hepatitis C. High-risk inmates were gathered in supermax facilities that placed entire prison populations in solitary confinement. In a thousand ways, large and small, the democratic aspirations of rehabilitative corrections were erased and the coercive power of the state penetrated more deeply into the lives of the poor.

Most striking was the increase in the size of the correctional population. Between 1970 and 2003, state and federal prisons grew sevenfold to house 1.4 million convicted felons serving at least one year behind bars, and typically much longer. Offenders held in county jails, awaiting trial or serving short sentences, added another seven hundred thousand by 2003. In addition to the incarcerated populations, another 4.7 million people were under probation and parole supervision. The entire correctional population of the United States totaled nearly seven million in 2003, around 6 percent of the adult male population.[3]

Growth in the penal population signaled more than a change in public policy. Throughout the twentieth century, African American history has been entwined with the history of America's prisons. Blacks have been more likely than whites to go to prison, at least since the 1920s. Southern prisons operated quite transparently as instruments of racial domination, using forced labor to farm cotton and build roads.[4] The prison boom, growing quickly in the wake of the civil rights movement, produced a wholly new scale of penal confinement. The basic brute fact of incarceration in the new era of mass imprisonment is that African Americans are eight times more likely to be incarcerated than whites. Incarceration rates climbed to extraordinary levels among young black men, particularly among those with little schooling. The Bureau of Justice Statistics reports that in 2004, over 12 percent of black men aged twenty-five to twenty-nine were behind bars, in prison or jail.[5] Among black men born in the late 1960s who received no more than a high school education, 30 percent had served time in prison by their mid-thirties; 60 percent of high school dropouts had prison records.[6]

By the end of the 1990s, criminal justice supervision was pervasive among young black men. This was a historically novel development in American race relations. We need only go back thirty years, to 1970, to find a time when young black men were not routinely incarcerated. The betrayal of the democratic purpose of rehabilitation had diminished the citizenship of African Americans most of all.

How can we understand the fabulous growth in the American penal system and its effects on the poor and minority communities from which prison inmates are drawn and ultimately return? This book first details the changing scope of incarceration in America through the 1980s and 1990s, then accounts for the growth in incarceration rates. I then examine the effects of the prison boom on crime, and economic opportunity and the family life of the men who serve time in prison jail.

My main arguments rely on two basic insights of the sociology of politics and crime. First, for political sociology, state power flows along the contours of social inequality. From this perspective, the prison boom was a political project that arose partly because of rising crime but also in response to an upheaval in American race relations in the 1960s and the collapse of urban labor markets for unskilled men in the 1970s. The social activism and disorder of the 1960s fueled the anxieties and resentments of working-class whites. These disaffected whites increasingly turned to the Republican Party through the 1970s and 1980s, drawn by a law and order message that drew veiled connections between civil rights activism and violent crime among blacks in inner cities. For these conservative politics, rehabilitation coddled the criminals who had forfeited their rights to fairness and charity. The young black men of poor urban neighborhoods were the main targets of this analysis. Jobless ghettos, residues of urban deindustrialization, lured many young men into the drug trade and left others unemployed, on the street, and exposed to the scrutiny of police. The punitive sentiment unleashed in the 1970s by rising crime and civil rights activism in the 1960s, institutionalized what had become a chronically idle population of young men with little education. Their life path through adulthood was transformed as a result.

Second, for sociologists of crime, the life path through adulthood normalizes young men, so criminal behavior recedes with age. Adolescents are drawn into the society of adults by passing through a sequence of life course stages—completing school, finding a job, getting married, and starting a family. The integrative power of the life course offers a way out of crime for adult offenders. Men involved in crime who can find steady work and a stable marriage also become embedded in a web of social supports and obligations. These social bonds help criminally active men desist from further offending. Men coming out of prison, however, have little access to the steady jobs that usually build work histories and wages. Employers are reluctant to hire job seekers with prison records, and former inmates are generally poorly prepared for the routines of steady employment. Prison also disrupts families. By 2000, over a million black children—9 percent of those under eighteen—had a father in prison or jail. In around half of all cases, these fathers were living with their children at the time they were incarcerated. The forced separation of men from their families also takes a toll on conjugal bonds. For women with men in prison, married life is threatened by the strains of visitation and the temptations of free men who can help support a household. Few couples survive a term of imprisonment. Unmarried men stigmatized by a prison time can also pay a price. Serving time signals a man's unreliability and a prison record can be as repellent to prospective marriage partners as it is to employers.

A common logic underlies the negative effects of incarceration on a former inmate's job prospects and family life. Although the normal life course is integrative, incarceration is disintegrative, diverting young men from the life stages that mark a man's gradual inclusion in adult society.

The employment problems and disrupted family life of former inmates suggests that incarceration may be a self-defeating strategy for crime control. Although incarceration surely prevents those who are locked up from committing crime in society, inmates are ultimately released with few resources to lead productive lives. Without great hopes for job security or a good marriage, crime remains an inviting alternative. Skeptics will counter that through the 1990s, when incarceration rates reached their highest levels, crime rates fell to their lowest levels since the 1960s. Correlation, however, is not causation. There were many forces operating at the end of the 1990s to drive down crime rates. My empirical analysis shows that fully 90 percent of the decrease in serious crime from 1993 to 2001 would have happened even without the run-up in the incarceration rates. The prison boom contributed a little to the decline in crime through the 1990s, but this gain in public safety was purchased at a cost to the economic well-being and family life of poor minority communities.

Even more important than the effects of the prison boom on crime are its effects on American inequality. The repudiation of rehabilitation and the embrace of retribution produced a collective experience for young black men that is wholly different from the rest of American society. No other group, as a group, routinely contends with long terms of forced confinement and bears the stigma of official criminality in all subsequent spheres of social life, as citizens, workers, and spouses. This is a profound social exclusion that significantly rolls back the gains to citizenship hard won by the civil rights movement. The new marginality of the mass-imprisonment generation can be seen not only in the diminished rates of employment and marriage of former prisoners. Incarceration also erases prison and jail inmates from our conventional measures of economic status. So marginal have these men become, that the most disadvantaged among them are hidden from statistics on wages and employment. The economic situation of young black men—measured by wage and employment rates—appeared to improve through the economic expansion of the 1990s, but this appearance was wholly an artifact of rising incarceration rates.

To tell this story, I begin by charting the scope of the prison boom. Chapter 1 places the era of mass imprisonment in comparative and historical perspective, underlining the historic novelty of the current period. Chapter 2 explores the causes of the prison boom by relating the growth in incarceration rates to shifts in crime rates. I see little evidence that growth in the penal population is related to either rising crime, or that increased incarceration among young disadvantaged men is associated with increased offending. Chapter 3 continues the search for the causes of rising imprisonment by studying changes in economic and political conditions. Incarceration rates grew most in states that elected Republican governors and adopted punitive regimes of criminal sentencing. Analyzing rates of prison admission for black and white men at different levels of education shows that class inequalities in imprisonment increased as the economic status of less-educated men decreased.

The remaining four chapters study the consequences of the prison boom. Links between the labor market and the penal system are examined in chapter 4 that measures the hidden inequality in wages and unemployment due to high rates of incarceration. I find that young black men obtained no benefit—either in employment or relative wages—from the record-breaking economic growth in the late 1990s. The invisible inequality that burgeoned through the boom times of the 1990s challenges the claim that robust growth by itself, without the supports of social policy, could bring opportunity to the most disadvantaged. Chapter 5 follows prison and jail inmates from release into society to their experiences in the labor market. Survey analysis shows that incarceration significantly reduces the wages, employment, and annual earnings of former inmates, even though their economic opportunities are extremely poor to begin with. The family life of criminal offenders is studied in chapter 6 which analyzes marital disruption and domestic violence among men coming out of prison. Here I find that incarceration undermines marital relations and thus increases a woman's risk of violence at the hands of her partner. Finally, chapter 7 tests the claim that the prison boom drove the fall in crime at the end of the 1990s. I find that the large negative effects on crime that are often attributed to imprisonment are overstated: The growth in incarceration rates explains only one-tenth of the decline in serious crime at the end of the 1990s.

Although the prison boom undermined economic opportunity and split up families, it cannot explain all the unemployment and female-headed households that underpin much of America's racial inequality. Unemployment and broken homes are as much a cause of imprisonment as a consequence. The disadvantaged men who go to prison would still risk unemployment and marital instability even if they weren't incarcerated. Instead, the prison boom helps us understand how racial inequality in America was sustained, despite great optimism for the social progress of African Americans. From this perspective, the prison boom is not the main cause of inequality between blacks and whites in America, but it did foreclose upward mobility and deflate hopes for racial equality. Perhaps more than adding to inequality between blacks and whites, the prison boom has driven a wedge into the black community, where those without college education are now traveling a path of unique disadvantage that increasingly separates them from college-educated blacks.

The prison boom opened a new chapter in American race relations, but the story of race and class inequalities sustained by political institutions is an old one. The punitive turn in criminal justice disappointed the promise of the civil rights movement and its burdens fell heavily on disadvantaged African Americans. By cleaving off poor black communities from the mainstream, the prison boom left America more divided. Incarceration rates are now so high that the stigma of criminality brands not only individuals, but an entire generation of young black men with little schooling. Tocqueville and Beaumont might be surprised that the American prison had failed so completely to realize the promise of its democratic origins. Although the growth in imprisonment was propelled by racial and class division, the penal system has emerged as a novel institution in a uniquely American system of social inequality.

PART I

The Scope and Causes of the Prison Boom

CHAPTER 1

Mass Imprisonment

If prisons affected no one except the criminals on the inside, they would matter less. But, after thirty years of penal population growth, the impact of America's prisons extends far beyond their walls. By zealously punishing law-breakers—including a large new class of nonviolent drug offenders—the criminal justice system at the end of the 1990s drew into its orbit families and whole communities. These most fragile families and neighborhoods were the least equipped to counter any shocks or additional deprivations.

We normally relate the prison boom to the problem of crime in America. Some say that we have more prisoners today because there is more crime. Others say that crime rates have fallen because we've locked up so many dangerous criminals. This book studies the prison boom, but crime is not the main focus. I argue that the prison boom is significant, mostly for its effects on social inequality. Indeed, the penal system has become so large that it is now an important part of a uniquely American system of social stratification.

This is an extravagant claim in many ways. In any given year in the last century, only one in a thousand Americans could be found in prison. Even at the height of the prison boom, in the early 2000s, less than 1 percent of the U.S. population was behind bars. These tiny incarceration rates should not be surprising: Prisons and jails are criminal justice institutions. Their constituents are the small number of criminals who break the law, not the vast majority of law-abiding citizens. If we are interested in the institutions that affect inequality in America, perhaps we should look at schools, or labor unions, or welfare programs.

By 2000, however, the U.S. incarceration rate was unparalleled in the economically developed democracies and unprecedented in U.S. history. Although prison and jail inmates are only a small fraction of the entire population, this chapter will show that the prison boom transformed the institutional landscape traveled by poor black males as they grew out of childhood and became young adults. Imprisonment became commonplace among young black men, more common than military service or college graduation. For black men who dropped out of high school, prison time became a modal event, more common than not. The concentration of imprisonment among young black men, particularly those with little schooling, provides the first piece of evidence for the generalized institutional significance of the American penal system. Empirical evidence for large-scale incarceration justifies the term mass imprisonment—an incarceration so vast as to draw entire demographic groups into the web of the penal system.

INCARCERATION IN HISTORICAL AND COMPARATIVE PERSPECTIVE

Before the prison boom, incarceration was the backstop of the criminal justice system. After school suspension, juvenile hall, warnings from police, arrest, commitment to the adult courts, conviction, and probation, came the county jail and then state prison. The many layers of criminal punishment ensured prison was rarely used, and only then for violent offenders or career criminals who cycled in and out of jail.

The penal system itself is divided among local, state, and federal jurisdictions. County jails account for about a third of the penal population. Jails hold defendants awaiting trial and misdemeanor offenders serving less than a year. John Irwin describes the jail as an instrument for managing "the rabble," mostly disreputable petty offenders who live under the close eye of the police.[1] State and federal prisons—home to about two-thirds of the penal population—typically hold felony offenders serving a year or more. Most prisoners are serving time for violent, property, or drug crimes. Nine out of ten prison inmates are housed in state facilities. One-third of these, in 1997, had committed homicide, rape, or robbery, and the remainder are mostly property and drug offenders. In the federal system, three out of five prisoners

Figure 1.1   Incarceration Rates and Prison Populations

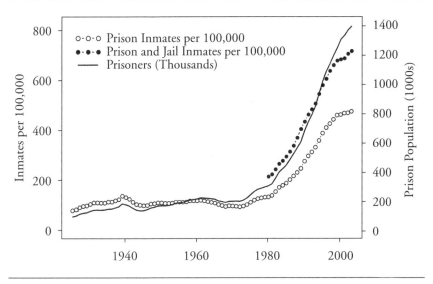

Source: Maguire and Pastore (1996, table 6.22); Beck and Glaze (2004).
Note: Incarceration rates are shown on the left-hand axis. The prison population is shown on the right-hand axis.

by 1997 were drug offenders.[2] Nearly all prisoners serve at least one year, but most serve much longer sentences. In 1996, state drug offenders averaged just over two years in prison, compared to eleven years for murderers. In federal prison the same year, the average time for drug offenders was forty months.[3]

The great scale of the penal system in the early 2000s is new. On any day for fifty years from 1925 to 1975, about a hundred Americans out of a hundred thousand—just one-tenth of 1 percent of the U.S. population—were in prison (figure 1.1). From 1975, the imprisonment rate began to rapidly increase. By 2003, the share of the population in prison had increased every year for twenty-eight years, standing at nearly half of 1 percent at the beginning of the new century. If we add jail inmates to the count of the incarcerated population, seven-tenths of 1 percent of the U.S. population was locked up by 2003. This incarceration rate reflects a penal population of 2.1 million inmates. After more than a quarter of a century of growth, the scale of incarceration exceeded its historic average by a factor of nearly five.

The extent of incarceration in the United States is also unusual by inter-

Figure 1.2   Incarceration in the United States and Western Europe

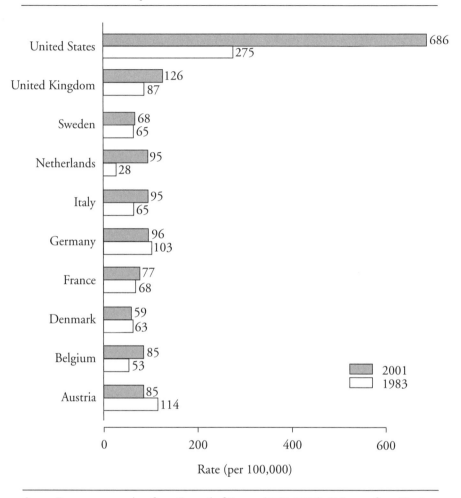

Rate (per 100,000)

Source: European rates taken from Council of Europe (1983, 2002); U.S. rates from Harrison (2000) and Pastore and Maguire (2003, 486).

national standards. In 1983, the rate of 275 per hundred thousand was about four times higher than in western Europe (figure 1.2). Only Britain's penal population approached American levels, and even in this case the U.S. rate was more than twice as high. By 2001, the imprisonment gap between Europe and the United States had widened. The U.S. incarceration rate had climbed to 686 per hundred thousand, and European remained close to 1983 levels—around a hundred per hundred thousand and less. In 2001, Britain still recorded the highest incarceration rate in western Europe, but the American imprisonment rate was more than five times greater. Indeed, to find close competitors to the American penal system we must look beyond the longstanding democracies of western Europe, to Russia (628 per hundred thousand) and South Africa (400).[4]

INEQUALITY IN INCARCERATION: SEX, AGE, RACE, AND EDUCATION

By 2000, the U.S. incarceration rate was comparatively and historically large but the scale remained small in absolute terms. Even at the height of the prison boom, less than 1 percent of the population was incarcerated. Can an institutionalization of this size possibly have large effects?

The broad significance of the penal system for American social inequality results from extreme social and economic disparities in incarceration. More than 90 percent of all prison and jail inmates are men, and throughout this book I focus on men's incarceration. Women's incarceration rates have increased more quickly than men's in the twenty years after 1980, but the main effect of the prison boom on gender relations is due precisely to the approximate fact that men go to prison, and women are left in free society to raise families and contend with ex-prisoners returning home after release. Incarceration is also concentrated among the young. About two-thirds of state prisoners are over eighteen years old but under thirty-five. With this age pattern, only a small number of people are incarcerated at any time, but many more pass through the system at some point. Age and sex disparities in incarceration magnify the influence of the penal system. In a gendered world like ours, institutions that shape the lives of men or women alone have great consequences for the other sex. The effects of institutions that entangle young adults may be sustained over a lifetime.

Gender relations and the life course amplify the effects of a penal system that locks up mostly young men, but race and class disparities in incarceration are significant for inequality in another way. Incarceration is concentrated among the disadvantaged and large race and class disparities in imprisonment reinforce lines of social disadvantage. High incarceration rates among less educated, less skilled, financially disadvantaged, and minority men are unmistakable. The 1997 survey of state and federal prisoners shows that state inmates average fewer than eleven years of schooling. A third were not working at the time of their incarceration, and the average wage of the remainder is much lower than that of other men with the same level of education. African Americans and Hispanics also have higher incarceration rates than whites. Blacks and Hispanics together account for about two-thirds of the state prison population. The black-white disparity in imprisonment is especially large. Black men are six to eight times more likely to be in prison than whites.

The demographic contours of imprisonment produced large differences in incarceration rates across the population (table 1.1). Through the last two decades of the twentieth century the national incarceration rate of the United States grew from about one-fifth of 1 percent of the population to seven-tenths of 1 percent. Because nearly all prison and jail inmates are men of working age, the incarceration rate in this group is nearly three times the national average. Incarceration rates for minority men are much higher. By 2000, more than 3 percent of Hispanic men and almost 8 percent of African American men of working age were in prison or jail.

The black-white difference in incarceration rates is especially striking. Black men are eight times more likely to be incarcerated than whites and large racial disparities can be seen for all age groups and at different levels of education. The large black-white disparity in incarceration is unmatched by most other social indicators. Racial disparities in unemployment (2 to 1), nonmarital childbearing (3 to 1), infant mortality (2 to 1), and wealth (1 to 5) are all significantly lower than the 8 to 1 black-white ratio in incarceration rates.[5] If white men were incarcerated at the same rate as blacks there would be more than six million people in prison and jail, and the incarceration rate would include more than 5 percent of the male working-age population.

Age, race, and educational disparities concentrate imprisonment among the disadvantaged. White men aged twenty to forty saw their incarceration rates rise from .6 to 1.6 percent between 1980 and 2000. The incarceration rate for young Hispanic men in 2000 was three times higher. Large black-white differences in the incarceration rate can also be seen for men under age forty. Three out of every two hundred young white men were incarcerated in 2000, compared to one in nine young black men. Incarceration of the poor is deepened by the severe educational disadvantage of prison and jail inmates. Among young men who had never been to college, 5.5 percent of Hispanic and 17 percent of black men under age forty-one were in prison or

Table 1.1   Percentage in Prison or Jail

	1980 (1)	2000 (2)	2000–1980 Ratio (2)/(1)
All U.S. residents	.2%	.7%	3.5
Men age eighteen to sixty-five			
All	.7	2.1	3.0
White	.4	1.0	2.5
Hispanic	1.6	3.3	2.1
Black	3.0	7.9	2.6
Men age twenty to forty			
White	.6	1.6	2.7
Hispanic	2.1	4.6	2.2
Black	4.8	11.5	2.4
Noncollege men age twenty to forty			
White	.9	3.2	3.6
Hispanic	2.6	5.5	2.1
Black	6.0	17.0	2.8
High school dropout men age twenty to forty			
White	2.1	6.7	3.2
Hispanic	3.2	6.0	1.9
Black	10.7	32.4	3.0

Sources: The incarceration rate for all U.S. residents in 1980 is based on data from Beck and Glaze (2004); the incarceration rate for all U.S. residents in 2000 are from Pastore and Maguire (2003, 486). All other rates are author's estimates.

jail in 2000. At the very bottom of the education distribution, among high school dropouts, about 7 percent of young whites were in prison or jail in 2000. The black male population as a whole shares, in this respect, the same status as less-educated whites.

The stratification of incarceration by race and education produced extraordinary incarceration rates for young black male dropouts by the end of the 1990s. Nearly a third were in prison or jail on a typical day in 2000, three times their incarceration rate just twenty years earlier. The growth in incarceration among less-educated blacks has also drawn a sharp line between the black underclass and the middle class. In 1980, black dropouts were around four times more likely to be incarcerated than their college-educated counterparts. Twenty years later, the difference was more than eight times. In 2000, one in three black dropouts were locked up, compared to just one in twenty-five of their college-educated counterparts.

In sum, disparities in incarceration produced astonishing rates of penal confinement among less-educated and minority men. Among the most socially marginal men—African Americans in their twenties and thirties who had dropped out of high school—incarceration rates were nearly fifty times the national average.

INCARCERATION AS INSTITUTIONAL MEMBERSHIP

Studies of social inequality usually cast working-age men in the roles of worker or job seeker. For workers and job seekers, the key institutional influences on economic well-being are labor unions and the welfare state. By raising the wages of union members and paying out unemployment benefits, labor organization and social policy significantly modify and augment the distribution of rewards in the labor market. Prisons and jails, on the other hand, aren't usually treated as labor market institutions. Instead, they lie on the horizon of social life, separating the deviant few from the mainstream. Because prisons and jails regulate deviance, incarceration is usually thought to mark a criminological, not an economic, status. In any case, formal controls on deviance have not been extensive enough to broadly influence economic opportunity. The scale of imprisonment in the 1990s challenges us to view penal institutions as significant economic influences on the men who serve time in prison or jail. Is the reach of the penal system sufficiently extensive to justify its comparison to other institutions that we normally see as shaping young men's labor market experiences?

I address this question by comparing involvement in the penal system to labor union membership and enrollment in government social programs, and later study the economic effects of imprisonment more directly. To begin, however, if men's involvement in the penal system rivals their involvement in unions and social programs, we are challenged to count incarceration as a major institutional presence in the economic lives of young men.

Table 1.2 compares incarceration rates among young men to rates of

Table 1.2   **Men Incarcerated (2000), in Unions, or in Social Programs (1996)**

	Whites	Hispanics	Blacks
All men, age twenty to forty			
In prison or jail	1.6%	4.6%	11.5%
In labor union	9.7	10.7	11.5
On welfare	1.7	1.4	2.3
In any program (including welfare)	6.7	4.9	10.8
Male high school dropouts, age twenty to forty			
In prison or jail	6.7	6.0	32.4
In labor union	6.3	8.1	2.3
On welfare	6.2	1.7	3.7
In any program (including welfare)	17.9	6.3	24.0

Source: Incarceration rates are based on author's estimates. Union membership, welfare, and other government program enrollment figures are calculated from the Survey of Incomes and Program Participation (1996). All figures are author's estimates.

Note: Welfare programs include Aid to Families with Dependent Children and Food Stamps. Any program includes welfare programs, supplemental security income, medicaid benefits, unemployment insurance, veteran's assistance, and any job-related support.

union membership and participation in government welfare and other social programs. Although unions and social programs are important institutions for young whites, their reach is at least equaled by the penal system for young blacks. Among whites, union membership (9.7 percent) and social program participation (6.7 percent) are far more common than incarceration (1.6 percent). Hispanic men show a similar pattern, though they are less likely to participate in government programs. Black men under age forty have an incarceration rate of 11.5 percent, and are just as likely to be in prison or jail as in a labor union, and about twice as likely to be incarcerated, as to receive government benefits. High school dropouts participate at high rates in welfare and other government programs, but white and Hispanic dropouts are at least as likely to be incarcerated as to be in a union or receive some assistance from a welfare program. Their black counterparts also participate heavily in government programs, but a third are in prison or jail. The incarceration rate for these blacks exceeds any support they receive for health care, training, and income maintenance through the welfare state.

These figures indicate that by the end of the 1990s, penal confinement had become common for African American and less educated men, compared to involvement in labor unions and social programs. The economic institutions that we normally associate with the welfare of young men was being eclipsed in the era of the prison boom, especially among the most disadvantaged—African American youth who had dropped out of high school.

INCARCERATION OVER THE LIFE CYCLE

Incarceration rates offer a snapshot of the extent of penal confinement. Time series of incarceration rates tell us how the extent of penal confinement has shifted historically. We can also study not the level of incarceration at a particular time, but how the risk of incarceration accumulates over an individual's life. This kind of life course analysis asks what is the likelihood an individual will go to prison by the time he is twenty-five, thirty, or thirty-five. Instead of providing a snapshot of the risk of incarceration, the life course analysis tries to characterize a typical biography.

The life course perspective provides more than just a way of thinking about the risks of incarceration; it also provides a comprehensive social analysis. For students of the life course, the passage to adulthood is a sequence of well-ordered stages that affect life trajectories long after the early transitions are completed. Today, arriving at adult status involves moving from school to work, then to marriage, to establishing a home and becoming a parent. Completing this sequence without delay promotes stable employment, marriage, and other positive life outcomes. The process of becoming an adult thus influences success in fulfilling adult roles and responsibilities.

As an account of social integration, life course analysis has attracted the interest of students of crime and deviance.[6] Criminologists point to the normalizing effects of life course transitions. Steady jobs and good marriages build social bonds that keep would-be offenders in a daily routine. They enmesh men who are tempted by crime in a web of supportive social relationships. Strong family bonds and steady work restrict men's opportunities for antisocial behavior and offer them a stake in normal life. For persistent lawbreakers, the adult roles of spouse and worker offer a pathway out of crime.[7] Those who fail to secure the markers of adulthood are more likely to persist in criminal behavior. This idea of a normalizing, integrative, life path offers a powerful alternative to claims that criminality is a stable trait present in some, but absent in others. Above all else, the life-course account of crime is dynamic, describing how people change as their social context evolves with age.

Imprisonment significantly alters the life course. In most cases, men entering prison will not be following typical life trajectories. Time in juvenile incarceration and jail and weak connections to work and family divert many prison inmates from the usual path followed by young adults. Spells of imprisonment—thirty to forty months on average—further delay entry into the conventional adult roles of worker, spouse, and parent. Diversions from the normal life course are not always negative. Military service, for example, has been identified as a key event that redirects life trajectories. Glen Elder describes military service as a "legitimate timeout" that offered disadvantaged servicemen in World War II an escape from family hardship.[8] Similarly, imprisonment can provide a chance to reevaluate life's direction.[9] Typically, however, imprisonment has negative effects. In contrast to the legitimate time out of military service, imprisonment is an illegitimate timeout that confers an enduring stigma. Employers of less-skilled workers are reluctant to hire men with criminal records. The stigma of a prison record also creates legal barriers to skilled and licensed occupations, rights to welfare benefits, and voting rights.[10] Later chapters will show that ex-prisoners earn lower wages and suffer more unemployment than similar men who have not been incarcerated. Former prisoners are also less likely to get married or live with the mothers of their children. By eroding opportunities for employment and marriage, incarceration may also lead former inmates back to a life of crime. The volatility of adolescence may last well into midlife for men serving prison time. In short, imprisonment is a turning point to fewer opportunities and attenuated citizenship. The life course significance of incarceration motivates analysis of the evolving probability of prison incarceration as young men age through their twenties and thirties.

THE HISTORICAL SIGNIFICANCE OF THE PRISON BOOM FOR THE LIFE COURSE

Biographies unfold in particular historical contexts. To choose a famous example, boys growing up through the Great Depression started their working lives young, in adolescence, to help support their families. Having seen the depredations of mass unemployment, they valued economic security, often at the expense or more lucrative employment in later life. They also delayed marriage and fatherhood as they struggled to establish themselves economically before starting a household. The imprint of history on this birth cohort of depression era boys makes a generation—a cohort of children whose collective coming of age is shaped decisively by historic forces of social change.[11]

These youth were to become the "Greatest Generation," as familiar in the public imagination as they were to professional demographers. World War II drew nearly all of the able-bodied among them into the military. For those from poor families or with histories of delinquency, military service was a turning point. As servicemen, the children of the Great Depression often received additional schooling, and those who survived the war with mind and body intact could also take advantage of the GI Bill. The GI Bill massively subsidized the collective mobility of the American working class, through its support for college education and home ownership. After the war, even the most needy and troublesome youth who attended school under the GI Bill would come to enjoy good jobs and higher incomes as they moved into midlife. The Greatest Generation, forged as much by the GI Bill as wartime, escaped the constraints of family background and personal history to share in the great social and economic benefits of the first decades of the postwar period.[12]

Throughout the twentieth century, history has left its mark on generations through great programs in social improvement. The GI Bill is the leading example, but the hundred-year emergence of mass public education also transformed the passage to adulthood. For successive cohorts since the 1900s, the expansion of public education contributed to an increasingly orderly and compressed transition to adulthood.[13] We might also think of a Civil Rights Generation, African Americans growing up after school desegregation, and under the umbrella of antidiscrimination protections. These black men and women, growing up through the 1960s and 1970s, enjoyed great gains in schooling and employment, significantly closing the gap with whites.[14] These examples show how individual lives, confronted with the transformative force of military service and education, have been redirected to produce significant episodes of collective mobility.

The prison boom, too, can be viewed as a major social change that has reordered the biographies of those growing up through the 1980s and the 1990s. In the historic context of the prison boom, incarceration has reshaped adulthood for entire birth cohorts. In this way, the growth of America's prisons is similar to other social transformations that precipitated major shifts in life trajectories.

Of course, prison time is not chosen in the same way as school attendance or military service. Men must commit crime to enter prison. Despite this qualification for imprisonment, the penal system has no necessary monopoly over young men involved in crime. A variety of institutions compete for jurisdiction over the life course.[15] Criteria for entry into prison, the military, or school are historically variable. During World War II, the scale of the U.S. war effort ensured that all able-bodied young men were potential servicemen, and most were drafted. As the number of college places expanded during the 1960s and 1970s, young men became potential college students qualifying less on the basis of social background, and more through academic achievement. The prison emerged through the 1980s and 1990s as a major institutional competitor to the military and the educational system, at least for young black men with little schooling. Much more than for older cohorts, the official criminality of men born in the late 1960s was determined by race and class.

In the past, going to prison was a marker of extreme deviance, reserved for violent and incorrigible offenders. Just as the threshold for military service was lowered during World War II, the threshold for incarceration was lowered by the forces driving prison boom. We will see how incarceration became more common for convicted felons, and how the criminalization of the drug trade swept up large numbers of small-time offenders. These trends suggest the novel normality of criminal justice sanction in the lives of recent cohorts of disadvantaged minority men. Richard Freeman, for example, writes that "participation in crime and involvement in the criminal justice system has reached such levels as to become part of normal economic life for many young men."[16] John Irwin and James Austin echo this observation: "For many young males, especially African Americans and Hispanics, the threat of going to prison or jail is no threat at all but rather an expected or accepted part of life."[17] David Garland similarly observes that for "young black males in large urban centers . . . imprisonment . . . has come to be a regular, predictable part of experience."[18] All these claims of pervasive imprisonment suggest a wholly new experience of adult life for recent cohorts of disadvantaged, minority men.

The widely claimed significance of mass imprisonment in the lives of young African American men suggests two hypotheses. First, imprisonment by the 1990s became a modal life event for young black men with little education. Second, the prevalence of imprisonment among African American men in the 1990s rivals in frequency more familiar life events such as military service and college graduation.

LIFETIME RISKS OF IMPRISONMENT

To place the risks of imprisonment in the context of the life course, I calculated the likelihood that a man would go to prison by age thirty-five. Imprisonment by that age provides a good estimate of the lifetime risk, because very few are incarcerated for the first time after their mid-thirties. Although a number of different incarceration statistics are reported in tables 1.1 and 1.2, it is important to remember that the following figures describe the deep end of the penal system for which there are lengthy terms of confinement for a felony conviction. By focusing on prison and bracketing jail, these figures understate the full reach of the penal system.[19]

Two birth cohorts of black and white men are contrasted to judge the effects of the prison boom. The older cohort is born just after World War II, from 1945 to 1949, and reaches their early thirties in the late 1970s. The older cohort passes through their twenties and early thirties before the most rapid increase in imprisonment rates. The younger cohort is born during the Vietnam War, from 1965 to 1969, and reaches their early thirties at the height of the prison boom. How much have the risks of imprisonment changed from one birth cohort to the other?

I answered this question using life-table methods that calculate the probability that a man with a clean record will go to prison for the first time at age twenty, then at twenty-one, twenty-two, and so on. Adding up these probabilities at each age, and adjusting for mortality, gives an estimate of the probability that a man has ever been to prison by age thirty-five. To make these calculations, I assembled a variety of data sources, including prison inmate surveys, administrative data on state and federal prison populations, household survey data on the noninstitutional population, and vital statistics on mortality. More information about the analysis and some checks on the quality of the estimates are reported later this chapter.

Life table estimates show how the risk of ever being imprisoned grows as men get older (figure 1.3). For white men born in the late 1940s, the probability of going to prison for the first time by age twenty was relatively small, less than half of 1 percent. By the time they were in their late twenties, this

Figure 1.3   Cumulative Risks of Incarceration

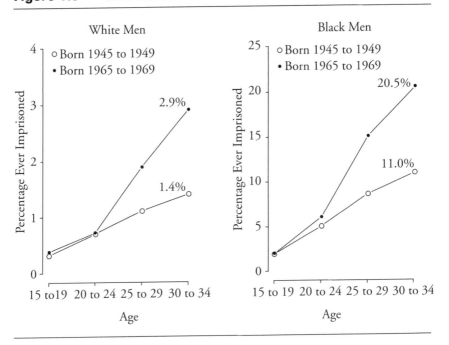

Source: Author's estimates.

probability had climbed to over 1 percent, that is, just over one in a hundred. Growth in the risk of imprisonment slows a little by the time these men were in their mid-thirties to 1.4 percent. For the younger birth cohort, born in the late 1960s and growing up through the prison boom, the risks of imprisonment until age twenty-five are similar to those of the older cohort. The effect of the prison boom on the path through young adulthood can be seen from age twenty-five to thirty-five. From their mid-twenties onwards, white men who have never been to prison became much more likely through the 1990s to serve time. Indeed, by their early thirties, the cumulative risk of imprisonment in the younger cohort of white men was more than double that of those born twenty years earlier.

The changing risk of imprisonment over the life course is strikingly parallel among black men. The imprisonment risk is so much higher than for the earlier generation, in fact, that we might of think of the prison boom as transforming young adulthood for black men. For black men born in the late

1940s, around one in ten served time in prison by their early thirties, in 1979. Those born twenty years later were more than twice as likely to go to prison. Changes in imprisonment over the life course help us understand how the adulthood of black men has been transformed by the prison boom. Most obviously, prison has become commonplace for African American men born since the late 1960s. More than twenty percent have spent at least a year—and typically two—locked up for a felony conviction. As for whites, the chances of incarceration have also increased for those in their early thirties. This may be because repeat offenders, on their second and third convictions, became more likely to be sentenced to prison. The growing likelihood of imprisonment for those entering midlife suggests that incarceration has become more disruptive. As they reach their late twenties most men are beginning to establish and support a household. For black men born in the late 1960s, much more than for their counterparts born twenty years before, this pathway to manhood is increasingly blocked as the penal system reaches deeper into the life course.

Calculating lifetime risks of imprisonment for high school dropouts, graduates, and the college-educated shows how the lives of the disadvantaged have been changed by rising incarceration rates. Imprisonment has become relatively common for white high school dropouts (figure 1.4). By 1999, one in nine would go to prison by their early thirties. The lifetime risks of imprisonment decline as we go up the educational ladder. White high school graduates were only 3.6 percent likely to go to prison by their early thirties in 1999, less than half the risk faced by white dropouts. College-educated whites were largely spared from the prison boom, their lifetime risk of imprisonment growing from just .5 to .7 of 1 percent from 1979 to 1999.

The cumulative risks of imprisonment for black men at the end of the 1990s are extremely high. Incredibly, a black male dropout, born in the late 1960s had nearly a 60-percent chance of serving time in prison by the end of the 1990s. At the close of the decade, prison time had indeed become modal for young black men who failed to graduate from high school. The cumulative risks of imprisonment also increased to a high level among black high school graduates. Nearly one out of five black men with just twelve years of schooling went to prison by their early thirties. Among all noncollege blacks—the bottom half of the education distribution—nearly a third had gone to prison in the younger cohort compared to just one in eight, two decades earlier.[20] As for whites, virtually all the increase in the risk of impris-

Figure 1.4   Cumulative Risks of Imprisonment by 1979

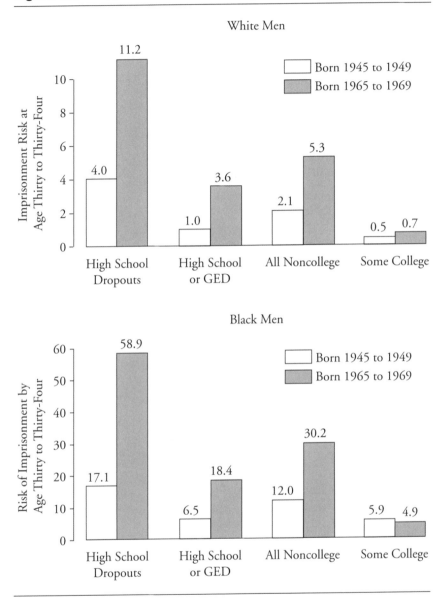

Source: Author's compilations.
Note: All noncollege men include high school dropouts and high school graduates.

onment among blacks fell on those with just a high school education. In fact, my estimates indicate that the lifetime risk of imprisonment actually declined slightly for college-educated blacks through the last decades of the twentieth century.

IMPRISONMENT AND OTHER LIFE-COURSE MILESTONES

Just as we can compare incarceration rates to labor union membership and participation in government programs, the cumulative risk of imprisonment can be compared to other life experiences that mark the transition to adulthood. College graduation, military service, and marriage are all important markers of progress through adult life. Each of these milestones moves young men forward in life to establishing a household and a steady job. Comparing imprisonment to these other life events indicates how the pathway through adulthood has been changed by the prison boom.

Table 1.3 shows the chances, for men born 1965 to 1969, of experiencing different life events by their early thirties in 1999. The risks of each life event are different for blacks and whites, but racial differences in imprisonment greatly overshadows any other inequality. Whites by their early thirties are more than twice as likely as blacks to hold a bachelor's degree. Blacks are about 50 percent more likely to have served in the military. However, black men in their early thirties are about seven times more likely than whites to have a prison record. Indeed, recent birth cohorts of black men are more likely to have prison records (22.4 percent) than military records (17.4 percent) or bachelor's degrees (12.5 percent). The share of the population with prison records is particularly striking among men with less than a college education. Whereas few such whites have prison records, nearly a third of black men with less than a college education have been to prison. Black men in their early thirties in 1999 without college were more than twice as likely to have served time in prison than to have served in the military. By 1999, imprisonment had become a common life event for black men that sharply distinguished them from white men.

MASS IMPRISONMENT

David Garland coined the term "mass imprisonment" to refer to the high rate of incarceration in the contemporary United States. In Garland's definition, mass imprisonment has two characteristics. First, he writes, "mass im-

Table 1.3   Percentage Non-Hispanic Men, Born 1965 to 1969, Life Events by 1999

Life Event	Whites	Blacks
All men		
Prison incarceration	3.2	22.4
Bachelor's degree	31.6	12.5
Military service	14.0	17.4
Marriage	72.5	59.3
Noncollege men		
Prison incarceration	6.0	31.9
High school diploma or GED	73.5	64.4
Military service	13.0	13.7
Marriage	72.8	55.9

Source: Author's estimates. The incidence of all life events except prison incarceration were calculated from the 2000 census.

Note: To make the incarceration risks comparable to census statistics, the estimates are adjusted to describe the percentage of men, born 1965 to 1969, who have ever been imprisoned and who survived to 1999.

prisonment implies a rate of imprisonment. . . that is markedly above the historical and comparative norm for societies of this type."[21] Indeed, this chapter has shown that the rate of incarceration in America by the late 1990s was far higher than in western Europe and without precedent in U.S. history. Second, Garland argues, the demographic concentration of imprisonment, produces not the incarceration of individual offenders, but the "systematic imprisonment of whole groups of the population."[22] The empirical markers of mass imprisonment are more slippery in this case. When will the incarceration rate be high enough to imprison, not the individual, but the group?

The picture painted by the statistics here help us answer this question. Not only did incarceration become common among young black men at the end of the 1990s, its prevalence exceeded that of the other life events we usually associate with passage through the life course. More than college graduation or military service, for example, incarceration typified the biographies of African American men born since the late 1960s.

Because of the nature of imprisonment, as an official sign of criminality, the collective experience of incarceration is as much a relational as a biographical fact. The mass imprisonment generation—black men without college education born since 1965—is set apart from the mainstream by official criminality. Through its extent, concentration, and designation of deviance, mass imprisonment converts young black men with little schooling from a demographic category into a social group. As such, they share the same life chances and are ascribed the same social status by state officials, employers, and others in power. In the era of mass imprisonment, to be young, black, and male, even if never having gone to prison, is to arouse suspicion and fear. To go to prison, even if not young, black, and male, is to acquire something of that identity. The idea of mass imprisonment as constitutive of a social group, shares something with Loïc Wacquant's idea of Jim Crow and the ghetto as "race-making" institutions.[23] Mass imprisonment, however, makes not the whole race. Instead, it divides the race, as the real experience of pervasive incarceration is confined just to those without college education. Imprisonment of the group, mass imprisonment, results not just from a high level of incarceration but from a high level of incarceration, unequally distributed.

CONCLUSION

The empirical evidence in this chapter supports three claims. First, the last two decades of the twentieth century produced a penal system that is without precedent in American history, and unlike any other in the advanced democracies. The growth in imprisonment has been sustained over the three decades from 1975 and incarceration rates in the early 2000s were five times higher than the incarceration rates that prevailed for most of the twentieth century. Although the U.S. incarceration rate had long been higher than in most western European countries, the imprisonment gap between Europe and the United States widened significantly in the period of the prison boom.

Second, race and class disparities in imprisonment are large, and class disparities have grown dramatically. From 1980 to 2000, black men were about six to eight times more likely to be in prison or jail than whites and Hispanics, about three times more likely. Some researchers claim that racial disparity has grown as incarceration increased, but I found no strong evidence for this trend. Class inequality increased, however, as a large gap in the prevalence of imprisonment opened between college-educated and noncollege men in the

1980s and the 1990s. Indeed, the lifetime risks of imprisonment roughly doubled for all men from 1979 to 1999, but nearly all of this increased risk was experienced by those with just a high school education.

Third, imprisonment has become a common life event for recent birth cohorts of black men without college education. In 1999, about 30 percent of these had gone to prison by their early thirties. Among black male high school dropouts, the risk of imprisonment had increased to 60 percent, establishing incarceration as a normal stopping point on the route to midlife. Underscoring the historic novelty of the prison boom, these risks of imprisonment are about three times higher in 1999 than twenty years earlier.

The criminal justice system has become so pervasive that we should count prisons and jails among the key institutions that shape the life course of recent birth cohorts of African American men. By the end of the 1990s, black men with little schooling were more likely to be in prison or jail than to be in a labor union or enrolled in a government welfare or training program. Black men born in the late 1960s were more likely, by 1999, to have served time in state or federal prison than to have obtained a four-year degree or served in the military. For noncollege black men, a prison record had become twice as common as military service.

Although the great institutional interventions in the life course of the twentieth century had progressive effects, mass imprisonment threatens the reverse. The growth of military service during World War II and the expansion of higher education exemplify projects of "administered mobility"—that detached the fate of disadvantaged groups from their social backgrounds. Inequalities in imprisonment indicate the opposite effect, in which the life path of poor minorities was cleaved from the well-educated majority and disadvantage was deepened, rather than diminished. More strikingly than patterns of military enlistment, marriage, or college graduation, prison time differentiates the young adulthood of black men from that of most others. Convict status inheres now, not in individual offenders, but in entire demographic categories.

Why did incarceration rates rise so greatly, particularly among black men with little schooling? Two main explanations have been offered. One suggests that crime has increased. Although aggregate crime rates did not rise steadily through the 1980s and 1990s, some have claimed that urban street crime proliferated as joblessness increased in inner-city communities. Against this argument, others say that the growth in incarceration rates was due largely to the changes in politics and policy. In this scenario, a crackdown on crime, beginning in the 1970s, intensified criminal punishment even though criminal offending did not increase. In the next two chapters, I weigh evidence for both these explanations of mass imprisonment.

APPENDIX: CALCULATING RATES AND RISKS OF INCARCERATION

Detailed incarceration rates for age-race education groups are estimated using data from the *Survey of Inmates of State and Federal Correctional Facilities* (1974, 1979, 1986, 1991, 1997),[24] and the *Survey of Inmates of Local Jails* (1978, 1983, 1989, 1996).[25] These figures are combined with counts of the noninstitutional population from the Current Population Survey and counts of military personnel to determine the size of the population.

The life table calculations reported in figures 1.3 and 1.4 are described in detail by Becky Pettit and Bruce Western.[26] The cumulative risks of imprisonment use the surveys of inmates of state and federal correctional facilities (1974 to 1997), to calculate age-specific risks of prison admissions for five-year birth cohorts from 1945 to 1949 to 1965 to 1969.

To help assess the accuracy of these estimates, I compared the cumulative risks to two other statistics. First, the Bureau of Justice Statistics has reported lifetime risks of imprisonment using data from 1991 survey of prison inmates.[27] These imprisonment risks are not defined for any particular birth cohort, nor are they calculated at different levels of education. Still, they do offer a rough guide to the prevalence of imprisonment in recent birth cohorts. The second source of data is a panel survey, the National Longitudinal Survey of Youth (NLSY), that interviewed a national sample of young men every year until 1994, and then every other year after that (Center for Human Resource Research 2004). The survey recorded men's levels of education and whether they were interviewed in prison. The NLSY only provides data for one birth cohort, born 1957 to 1964, and a small sample of incarcerated men. Still, like the BJS estimates, it provides a check that my estimates agree with other data sources and methodologies.

Table 1A.1 reports the cumulative risk of ever having been to prison by 1979 for men born between 1945 and 1949, and by 1999 for men born between 1965 and 1969. Reassuringly, for all black and white men, my figures

Table 1A.1   Cumulative Risk of Imprisonment

	All (1)	Less than High School (2)	High School or GED (3)	All Noncollege (4)	Some College (5)
White men					
BJS	3.0	—	—	—	
NLSY	4.3	11.3	3.7	5.1	1.5
Born 1945 to 1949	1.4	4.0	1.0	2.1	.5
Born 1965 to 1969	2.9	11.2	3.6	5.3	.7
Black men					
BJS	24.6	—	—	—	
NLSY	18.7	30.9	18.8	19.3	7.2
Born 1945 to 1949	10.5	17.1	6.5	12.0	5.9
Born 1965 to 1969	20.5	58.9	18.4	30.2	4.9

Sources: BJS figures reported by Bonczar and Beck (1997) using synthetic cohort from the 1991 Survey of Inmates of State and Federal Correctional Facilities (BJS 1993). NLSY figures give percentage of respondents interviewed in a correctional facility by age thirty-five (whites N = 2171, blacks N = 881). NLSY cohort was born between 1957 and 1964.

are close to those calculated by the BJS and similar to the risks of incarceration measured by the NLSY. Like the NLSY data, my figures also capture the steep stratification of the risks of incarceration by education, although the NLSY tends to underestimate imprisonment at very low levels of education, compared to my figures.

CHAPTER 2

Inequality, Crime, and the Prison Boom

Extraordinary incarceration rates among young, less-educated black men at the end of the 1990s have a seemingly obvious explanation: black youth with little schooling commit a great deal of crime. Indeed, criminologists report high rates of serious violence among young black men, with strong indications that violence is concentrated among the poorest.[1] Even more suggestively, the emergence of mass imprisonment coincided with a twenty-year rise in economic inequality that stalled the economic progress of less-educated black men during the 1980s and 1990s. Unemployment and stagnant wages may have driven these men to crime. The story is more complicated than these patterns suggest, however, because trends in incarceration haven't tracked trends in the crime rate. The incarceration rate has steadily grown since the 1970s, through waves of violence in the late 1980s, and major gains in public safety through the late 1990s. Looking at race or class differences in crime at a point in time suggests that crime and incarceration are closely linked. Looking at changes in overall rates of serious offending suggests that trends in imprisonment and crime are unrelated.

Although the prison boom was not obviously driven by mounting crime rates, crime may have become more serious in poor communities while declining among the middle class. Under these conditions, the incarceration rate may not follow trends in aggregate crime rates, but increased crime among the poor could raise rates of arrest and prison admission. The key empirical question, which few researchers have examined directly, asks if poor young men were more involved in crime at the height of the prison boom in 2000 than twenty years earlier.

Here I examine the connections between social inequality, crime, and imprisonment. I begin by asking why socially marginal groups, like the poor and racial minorities, might be more involved in crime. Although many studies describe links between race, class, and crime, I know of no empirical test that simply records whether crime increased among low-status young men in the period of the prison boom. I provide several such tests and find that young, poor men—black and white—were much less involved in crime in 2000 than in 1980, despite a large increase in their chances of incarceration. How can crime go down while incarceration goes up? To answer this question, I go on to look at the stages of criminal processing from offending to arrest, conviction, and imprisonment. This analysis shows that the criminal justice system became more punitive in the two decades from 1980, increasing the risk of imprisonment for those who are arrested and increasing the time served of those locked up.

CRIME AND INEQUALITY

If the prison boom reflected trends in crime, we would expect that poorly educated and African American men were breaking the law more at the end of the 1990s than twenty years earlier. Certainly, sociologists and economists have often argued that crime flourishes amid poverty and racial division. Robert Merton famously claimed that frustration at blocked opportunities drives the poor to crime so they might obtain the material success enjoyed legally by the middle class.[2] Economists make similar claims from a cost-benefit perspective. Gary Becker argued that temptations of crime will be strongest when its benefits—the income from robbery or drug dealing, say—are high and its costs are low. Severe punishment can raise the costs of crime, but so can the legitimate job opportunities that provide alternatives to illegal activity.[3] In addition to the influence of economic rewards, steady work subjects daily life to supervision and routine. Continuously employed men have fewer opportunities to get involved in crime. Young unemployed men can spend more time with their idle friends and may be more weakly committed to the roles of worker and provider.

These explanations emphasize the motives that push the poor into crime, but the home life and neighborhoods of the middle class can also erect barriers to criminal behavior. A stable marriage, like a steady job, creates everyday routines for husbands who might otherwise be on the street, getting into trouble. The social bonds of orderly, closely knit, neighborhoods also inhibit delinquency and crime. Communities lacking these social connections—in which families are weakly tied to employers, voluntary organizations, and friends—risk high rates of violence and other crime.[4]

Unemployment, family instability, and neighborhood disorder combine to produce especially high rates of violence among young black men. Although black men made large economic strides between 1940 and 1970, their unemployment rate has been double that of whites since the 1970s. High rates of black unemployment accompany large numbers of female-headed households and neighborhoods of concentrated poverty. Because of low marriage rates among African Americans, and because black adolescents are more likely to grow up in female-headed households than whites, black youth are more loosely tied by the family bonds that prevent criminal offending. Poor black neighborhoods, in which poverty and its demographic correlates are highly concentrated, also lack the web of social networks that can supervise children after school, watch the street, and quickly seek help if it's needed.

Several statistical studies have found close links between violent crime and economic and racial inequality. Usually examining cities or states, these studies uncover high rates of homicide and other violence in areas of severe poverty, with large numbers of female-headed households. One of the most thorough studies of this kind, by Kenneth Land and his colleagues, finds that between 1960 and 1980, in central cities, broader metropolitan areas, and states, the highest rates of homicide are found in localities with the highest rates of poverty, unemployment, and divorce.[5] We also see the effects of family structure and the neighborhood environment when the focus is on urban violence. The large number of female-headed black families in metropolitan areas has been found to explain a significant share of the homicide rate among black adolescents.[6] Poor segregated neighborhoods with weak community ties and concentrated disadvantage have also been found to have more homicides, robberies, and burglaries.[7] Although the quantitative studies find strong evidence that criminal violence is stratified by race and class, they provide little sense of the role of crime in the everyday life of the poor.

Ethnographies of poor urban areas offer a more vivid picture of the pervasive presence of crime and its close connection to incarceration. The inner-city drug trade occupies a special place in this research, providing economic opportunity for young men in neighborhoods with high rates of unemployment. In his ethnography of Hispanic drug gangs in New York, Philippe Bourgois argues that "the insult of working for entry-level wages amidst extraordinary opulence is especially painful" for Spanish Harlem youths.[8] This inequality drives young Puerto Rican men "deeper into the confines of their segregated neighborhood and the underground economy."[9] Sudhir Venkatesh and Steven Levitt analyze the economic significance of drug dealing for Chicago's "outlaw capitalism." Drug trafficking thrived in the vacuum of legitimate employment in Chicago's Southside neighborhoods. Chicago youth spoke to Venkatesh and Levitt of their "gang affiliation and their drive to earn income in ways that resonated with representations of work in the mainstream corporate firm. Many approached [gang] involvement as an institutionalized path of socioeconomic mobility for down-and-out youth."[10] In Elijah Anderson's account, violence follows the drug trade as crime becomes a voracious force in the poor neighborhoods of Philadelphia:

> Surrounded by violence and by indifference to the innocent victims of drug dealers and users alike, the decent people are finding it harder and harder to maintain a sense of community. Thus violence comes to regulate life in the drug-infested neighborhoods and the putative neighborhood leaders are increasingly the people who control the violence.[11]

The picture drawn by the ethnographic research is of poor neighborhoods, chronically short of legitimate work and embedded in a violent and illegal market for drugs.

The perils of the drug trade and other street crime include not just the threat of violence, but also the risk of incarceration. The seemingly mechanical connection between crime and incarceration is captured by Sullivan's account of how knifepoint robberies by Hispanic youth led progressively from arrest, to jail time, to imprisonment. The inevitability of incarceration, Sullivan reflects, illustrates the "limits of confrontational street crime as a source of income. One, two, even several crimes may be perpetrated with impunity, but continued involvement in such visible and violent crime does lead to serious sanctions."[12] The great prevalence of incarceration in high-crime neighborhoods is probably most extreme in Washington, D.C. Donald Braman observes the experiences of Londa, a twenty-year-old mother of three living in the heart of the District. In the two-block radius of Londa's residence, Braman counted sixty-four arrests for drug possession and distribution over the course of a year. During that period, 120 men living within that two-block radius were admitted to the D.C. correctional system. Talking about the children in the neighborhood, Londa says, "I look around here and none of these kids have fathers. It's a mess what's happened."[13] Qualitative observations, like these, match in their details my statistical finding of pervasive incarceration among young men, particularly black men, with little schooling.

CRIMINAL ACTIVITY AMONG DISADVANTAGED MEN

It is often observed that trends in incarceration are, at best, only loosely related to trends in crime.[14] Figure 2.1 compares the imprisonment rate to the index crime rate from 1970 to 2000. The index crime rate is calculated from the FBI's Uniform Crime Reports—serious crimes reported to the police, including murders, rapes, robberies, aggravated assaults, burglaries, larcenies, motor vehicle thefts, and arsons. The imprisonment rate grew steadily through periods of increasing crime in the 1970s, and declining crime in the 1990s. The correlation between incarceration and crime is a statistically insignificant, −.2. Statistics like these have led some commentators to discount any relationship between crime and punishment. Nils Christie points the point bluntly: "The explosion in the number of prisoners in the USA cannot be explained as 'caused by crime.' It has to do with penal policy."[15]

This disposes of the issue too quickly. For recent ethnographies of urban poverty, incarceration is an occupational hazard of street crime, and crime—particularly drug dealing—has been an important part of the ghetto economy at least since the 1980s. In this context, crime and incarceration appear closely related. But if crime among the ghetto poor were the main driver of the rise in incarceration rates, we would expect to see that young black men with little schooling were more involved in drug dealing and other crime in 2000 than in 1980. To test this hypothesis, I now turn to an empirical examination of crime among disadvantaged male youth.

There is surprisingly little empirical work examining trends in crime among poor young men. I provide a simple analysis using data on self-reported offending and criminal victimization. The 1979 and 1997 cohorts of

Figure 2.1   Trends in Index Crime Rate and Imprisonment

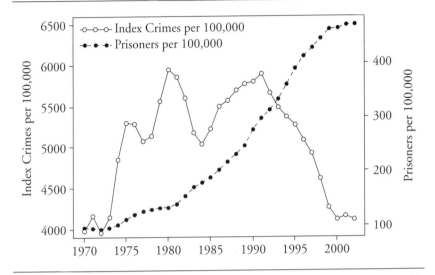

Sources: Crime in the United States (1977, 1991, 2004); Pastore and Maguire (2005, table 628).

the National Longitudinal Surveys of Youth (NLSY) are unusual in providing data on self-reported criminal activity at different points in time. The NLSY asked two national samples of young men and women in 1980 and 2000 about their criminal activity over the past year. I analyzed crime among male NLSY respondents, aged fifteen to eighteen. Because the NLSY respondents are younger than adult prisoners, the survey data do not provide direct evidence on those at risk of imprisonment. Still, juvenile and adult crime rates move roughly together and virtually all adult felons have a history of juvenile offending. If increased criminality among lower-class men increased the prison population, we would also expect to see increased criminality among lower-class youth.

Data on juveniles also have important advantages for studying trends in crime. Some writers attribute a large decline in adult crime between 1980 and 2000 to the rise in imprisonment.[16] Juvenile incarceration, however, has not increased nearly as much as adult incarceration. In 1979, the juvenile incarcerated population numbered 71,922 compared to 108,931 in 1999.[17] As the juvenile incarcerated population increased by about 50 percent, the adult prison population increased by 430 percent.[18] If we observe large declines in juvenile crime, as we have for adults, it is much less likely that these are explained by rising incarceration.

Table 2.1 describes criminal activity among male youth in the NLSY. Respondents were asked to report whether they had attacked someone, vandalized property, stolen something, or sold drugs in the past year. I calculated crime rates for all male youth, and for those whose household incomes fell below the poverty line.

Consistent with broader trends, older teenagers in the NLSY were much less involved in crime in 2000 than in 1980. Rates of crime declined significantly in all offense categories. Property crime fell the most as the number of youth who reported vandalism or larceny (stealing) dropped by between 65 and 75 percent. The decline in violent assaults is smaller but still substantial. In 1980, 15 percent of male youth said they had attacked someone with the intention of seriously hurting them, or killing them, compared to fewer than 11 percent in 2000.

If mushrooming criminality among the poor drove the prison boom, we would expect to see rising crime among poor youth. In fact, like the rest of the population, youth from poor families were less involved in delinquency in 2000 than in 1980. Property crime was halved among poor whites, and fell by even more among the poor minority youth, whom many writers saw as drawn to crime by the decline of inner-city economies. Although research claims that drug dealing replaced legitimate economic opportunity in ghetto neighborhoods, poor black and white youth in the NLSY survey were selling drugs far less in 2000 than in 1980. For example, 16 percent of black teenagers from poor families said they sold drugs in 1980, compared to just 5 percent in 2000. Only violent crime did not fall substantially. Poor juveniles were getting into serious fights about as often in 2000 as they were twenty years earlier. In short, data on self-reported crime among young men from poor families look very similar to aggregate crime rates. Levels of crime at the end of the 1990s were much lower than in the early 1980s. There is no evidence here that disadvantaged youth have become more involved in crime. Indeed, they are much less involved in crime at the peak of the prison boom in 2000, that at the beginning in 1980. What's more, because juvenile incarceration rates have not greatly increased, the decline in crime shown in the survey data is unlikely to be an artifact of rising incarceration.

The NLSY data provide no evidence of rising crime among needy youth,

Table 2.1   Male Youth, Age Fifteen to Eighteen, Involved in Crime

	1980	2000	Percentage Change
Attacked someone to seriously hurt or kill them			
All youth	15.0	10.6	−29
Poor whites	18.5	17.0	−8
Poor blacks	17.5	13.8	−21
Poor Hispanics	11.8	12.8	8
Purposely damaged or destroyed property			
All youth	32.8	11.3	−66
Poor whites	31.0	14.6	−53
Poor blacks	26.2	8.5	−68
Poor Hispanics	31.1	9.4	−70
Stolen something from a store, house, or person			
All youth	45.5	12.4	−73
Poor whites	39.8	17.3	−57
Poor blacks	40.1	12.9	−68
Poor Hispanics	39.6	7.9	−80
Sold drugs, including marijuana, cocaine, or heroin			
All youth	17.8	10.0	−44
Poor whites	18.0	8.8	−51
Poor blacks	16.1	5.0	−69
Poor Hispanics	9.7	9.9	2

Source: Author's compilations.
Note: Self-reported crime is taken from NLSY 1979 and 1997 cohorts. Sample sizes, 1980: 2,958 (all youth), 740 (poor youth). Sample sizes, 1997: 3,375 (all youth), 563 (poor youth).

but self-report data are subject to errors in which respondents may underreport very serious crime. Another approach looks at victimization data. Victimization is typically recorded by surveys, in which individuals are asked if they have been assaulted, had property stolen, and so on. Because a great deal of crime happens among acquaintances and neighbors, victimization data for poor men will also be informative about their levels of criminal activity. The

Table 2.2   Criminal Victimization Among Men Age Twenty-Two to Thirty

	1980 to 1983	1997 to 2000	Percentage Change
Victimizations per 1000			
All men	568	179	−68.7
White dropouts	541	215	−60.3
Black dropouts	466	132	−71.7
Hispanic dropouts	433	101	−76.6
Victimizations per 1000, adjusting for imprisonment			
All men	671	242	−63.9
White dropouts	640	293	−54.2
Black dropouts	550	180	−67.3
Hispanic dropouts	512	138	−73.0

Source: Author's compilations.
Note: The adjustment for imprisonment forms an index of by dividing total prison admissions by arrests. Assuming each imprisonment reduces victimizations by ten, the index is multiplied by ten to obtain a multiplier for the victimization rates. This adjustment increases the 1980 to 1983 rates by 18.25 percent, and 1997 to 2000 rates by 36.3 percent.

National Crime Victimization Survey annually asks a national sample, twelve years and older, about their experiences of household, property, and violent crime. I calculated property and violent victimization rates for young men, aged twenty-two to thirty, and for young male high school dropouts, the group who have experienced the largest increases in incarceration. Because sample sizes are quite small for dropouts, I pooled data for 1980 to 1983 and for 1997 to 2000.

Table 2.2 reports victimization rates for the two periods for all young men and for those who dropped out of high school. Between the early 1980s and the late 1990s there was a large decline in rates of criminal victimization. In the mid-1980s, one of two men in their twenties was a victim of property crime or violence. By the late 1990s, fewer than one in five was, a decline of about 70 percent. Men with little education also shared in the gains in public safety. Victimization rates for young dropouts declined by between 60 and 75 percent, in line with national trends.

Unlike the earlier analysis of juvenile crime, victimization figures among young men may reflect the effects of growing imprisonment. Men may be safer by the end of the 1990s because prisons had taken most of the criminals off the streets. I adjusted for this effect by taking account of the growing punitiveness of the criminal justice system. This can be measured by the number of prison admissions for every arrest. In the early 1980s, admissions accounted for about 1.8 percent of all arrests. By the late 1990s, that figure was about 3.6 percent. By this measure, punitiveness between 1980 and 2000 has doubled. Assuming each person imprisoned would otherwise be responsible for ten crimes against men aged twenty-two to thirty, I can adjust victimization rates to reflect the growth in criminal punishment.

The second panel of table 2.2 reports adjusted victimization rates that take account of the rise in imprisonment. Although the declines in rates are smaller once growing imprisonment is accounted for, they are still substantial. Among young white dropouts, victimization has fallen by nearly 50 percent and fallen even more among young and less-educated minorities.

These data leave us with a puzzle. Between 1980 and 2000, self-reported crime fell significantly among disadvantaged youth. Teenagers from poor households in 2000 were less involved in violence and drug dealing than twenty years earlier. Declines in vandalism and theft were especially large and were mirrored by large declines in criminal victimization among young less-educated men. High school dropouts in their twenties, whose incarceration rates are now extraordinarily high, are 60 to 70 percent less likely to be victimized by crime in 2000 than in 1980. How have large reductions in crime among disadvantaged young men become associated with large increases in incarceration?

LINKING CRIME TO PUNISHMENT

We can understand how reduced crime is associated with increased imprisonment by following each stage of criminal processing. Table 2.3 compares the number of crimes to rates of arrest and prison admission. About one million violent crimes are reported to the police each year. The number of violent crimes increased from over nine hundred thousand to 1.36 million from 1980 to 1990. But from 1990 to 2001 the level of violence fell. Just under half of the complaints to police resulted in an arrest. However, the chances that an arrest would result in prison roughly doubled, from 13 to 28 percent.

Time served in prison by violent offenders also increased significantly, from thirty-three months in 1980 to fifty-three months on average by 2001. Because time served and the rate of prison admission both increased, the incarceration rate for violent crime rose from seventy-six to 208 per hundred thousand, despite the decline in the level of violence.

Property offenders, mostly burglars and car thieves, show a similar pattern. About eight times more property crime is reported to police than violent crime. Like violent crime, property crime increased from 1980 to 1990, but then fell over the next ten years. Fewer than one in five property crimes result in an arrest, much lower than the rate for violence. From 1980 to 2001, the property offender's chances of imprisonment nearly doubled, from 6 to 11 percent. Time served for property crime also increased by 75 percent. The increasing chances of imprisonment given an arrest and increasing time in prison more than doubled the incarceration rate.

Finally, figures on drug crimes show a similar pattern of intensified law enforcement. Unlike violent and property offenses, there are no crime statistics on levels of drug use and trafficking, neither in victimization surveys nor in the police reports of the Uniform Crime Survey. The numbers of drug arrests, however, are recorded. Unlike arrest trends for other crime types, drug arrests increased by 170 percent in the two decades from 1980. The prison admissions for each arrest increased sixfold, from two to 12 percent. Many drug offenders who were admitted to prison in the 1990s were parolees readmitted not for new offenses, but for violating the conditions of their parole. Failing a drug test, for example, is a common parole violation. In the 1990s, parole revocation doubled for drug offenders, increasing the number of people reentering prison and not convicted of new crimes. Time served also increased sharply so that by 2001, released drug offenders had served about two years in state prison. These factors—the large increase in drug arrests, the growing likelihood of imprisonment given arrest, the increased risk of parole revocation, and increasing time served—produced more than a tenfold increase in the drug crime incarceration rate from 1980 to 2001.

These figures on arrest, prison admission, parole revocation, and time served explain why trends in crime bear only a slight relationship to the scale of imprisonment. At every stage of criminal processing, from policing, to the court hearing, to parole, criminal justice officials decide on the disposition of offenders and these effects on the scale of imprisonment far overshadow fluctuations in the level of crime.

Table 2.3   Offending, Arrests, and Incarceration, Violent, Property, and Drug Crimes

	1980	1990	2001
Violent crime			
Number of offenses	914,576	1,364,705	1,131,923
Arrests per offense	.44	.46	.47
Prison admissions per arrest	.13	.17	.28
Parolees per admission	.17	.18	.19
Average time served (months)	33	38	53
Violent crime incarceration rate	76	125	208
Property crime			
Offenses known to police	8,228,506	10,759,757	8,235,013
Arrests per offense	.17	.18	.17
Prison admissions per arrest	.06	.10	.11
Parolees per admission	.21	.24	.23
Average time served (months)	16	24	28
Property crime incarceration rate	39	69	81
Drug crime			
Arrests	580,900	1,361,700	1,579,600
Prison admissions per arrest	.02	.10	.12
Parolees per admission	.11	.11	.22
Average time served (months)	14	17	24
Drug crime incarceration rate	8	59	86

Source: Author's compilations.

Note: Data on offending and arrests were compiled from the *Sourcebook of Criminal Justice Statistics* (various years). Offending data refer to crimes known to police recorded in the Uniform Crime Reports. Data on prison admissions, parolees per admission, and time served were tabulated from the National Corrections Reporting Program (1983, 1990, 2001). Time served and admissions data in the first column are from 1983.

DRUG USE AND DRUG ENFORCEMENT

How do we interpret the large increase in the number of drug arrests from 1980 to 2001? Propelled by policy initiatives of first the Nixon and then the Reagan administration, drug enforcement escalated dramatically through the 1970s and 1980s. I'll have more to say about America's war on drugs in the

Figure 2.2   Drug Offenses and Arrest Rate Ratio

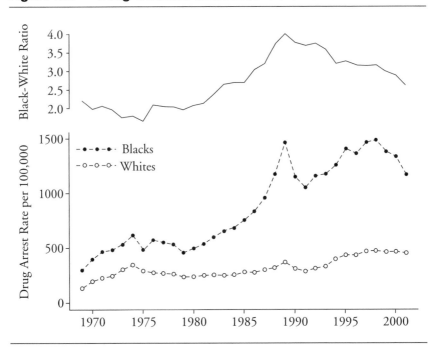

Source: Federal Bureau of Investigation (1993, 2003).
Notes: Bottom panel shows arrests for drug offenses per 100,000, 1970 to 2001, blacks and whites. Top panel shows black-white ratio of drug arrest rates, 1970 to 2001.

following chapter, but for now we can see its quantitative extent reflected in the fourfold growth in drug arrest rates from the late 1960s to 2001 (see figure 2.2). Drug arrests had always shown a large racial disparity. In the early 1970s, blacks were about twice as likely as whites to be arrested for a drug offense. The great growth in drug arrest rates through the 1980s had a large effect on African Americans. At the height of the drug war in 1989, arrest rates for blacks had climbed to 1,460 per hundred thousand compared to 365 for whites. Throughout the 1990s, drug arrest rates remained at these historically high levels. These trends may be related to trends in drug use or to trends in drug enforcement. Because there are no crime statistics on drug use, we cannot systematically compare offending rates to arrest and imprisonment rates. However, we can look further at the link between drug use and drug arrests trends in drug use by examining social surveys and hospital reports of drug-related emergency room visits.

Figure 2.3   High School Seniors Reporting Drug Use

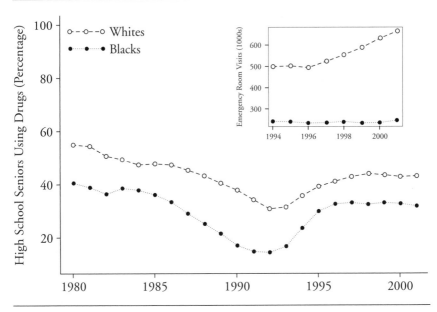

Sources: Johnston et al. (2004), Office of Applied Studies SAMHSA, Drug Abuse Warning Network (2003).

Figure 2.3 shows trends in drug use with data from the Monitoring the Future Survey and the Drug Abuse Warning Network. The survey asked a national sample of high school seniors whether they had ever used drugs in the past year. In 1980, just over 50 percent said they had, compared to around 40 percent in 2000. White high school students consistently reported more drug use than black students. National samples of adults, studied by the National Survey on Drug Abuse (NSDA), similarly show that drug use among adults declined from 20 to 11 percent from 1979 to 2000. Like the high school survey, the NSDA shows that levels of drug use do not differ much between blacks and whites.

The survey responses may not provide a good indication of trends in serious drug use. A shorter time series is available from the Drug Abuse Warning Network that records the number of drug-related emergency room visits from hospitals in twenty-one cities. Whites had roughly twice to three times the number of drug-related emergency room visits than blacks. Whites increased their share of drug-related emergency care through the 1990s. Although data on drug use are patchy, there is little evidence that mounting drug use or relatively high rates of drug use among blacks fueled the increase in drug arrests during the 1990s.

CRIME AS CONTEXT RATHER THAN CAUSE

We have seen that there is no consistent, positive relationship between crime and incarceration rates through the prison boom period. Still, several writers claim that trends in crime are not the cause but the context for the rise in incarceration rates.[19] In this account, the growth in crime in the 1960s before the prison boom exposed middle-class whites to serious risks of victimization for the first time. The growth in crime contributed to new feelings of vulnerability among the affluent and created a political opening for a change in crime policy that ultimately increased the incarceration rate.

How much did crime really increase? Crime rates were not measured very accurately until the Census Bureau began its victimization survey in 1972. Still, before 1972, murder rates were measured more accurately than other crime statistics.[20] From 1965 to 1980, the annual number of murders in the United States increased from about ten thousand each year to more than twenty thousand, an increase from 5.1 to 9.6 deaths per hundred thousand residents. Although measured less accurately, the overall violent crime rate—which includes rapes, robberies, and assaults as well as homicides—increased threefold between 1965 and 1980, from 200 to 597 crimes per hundred thousand.[21] The large growth in crime rates predated the explosion of the penal population.

Although the incarceration trends have not tracked trends in crime, the largest increases in the 1960s and 1970s are in states with the largest increases in incarceration rates twenty years later (figure 2.4). Southern states such as Louisiana, Mississippi, Oklahoma, and Texas all experienced big increases in their homicide rates. By the end of the 1990s, these four had the highest rates of incarceration. At the other end of the scale, small Midwestern and New England states saw only modest increases in serious violence through the 1970s, and incarceration rates increased only a little in subsequent decades.

This empirical pattern provides a clue. Crime rates themselves may not have driven the prison boom, but long-standing fears about crime and other social anxieties may form the backdrop for the growth in imprisonment. While crime was rising in the late 1960s, urban riots, racial tensions, and

Figure 2.4   Murder and Incarceration Rates

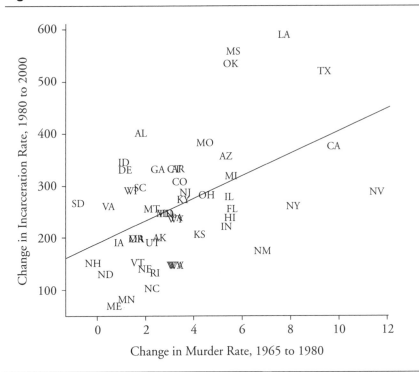

Source: Author's compilations.
Note: A regression line indicates the trend.

economic recession closed a chapter in American postwar social history. This period of rapid social change ushered in a new economy, characterized by urban deindustrialization, and a new politics, characterized by law-and-order appeals to white suburban voters. We turn to these trends, and their effects, in the next chapter.

CONCLUSION

The research and data I have presented so far help us untangle the links between social inequality, crime, and the growth of imprisonment among disadvantaged men. In trying to understand why so many less educated and minority men are going to prison, we should carefully distinguish the two parts to this story.

First, there is good evidence that disadvantaged men are, at any given time, highly involved in crime and that this is closely associated with the high rate of their imprisonment. Quantitative studies and field observation in poor neighborhoods show that poor young men are greatly involved in violence and other crime. Black homicide offending offers the clearest example. Several studies have shown that blacks are roughly seven times more likely to be imprisoned for murder than white men, but are also seven times more likely to be arrested for murder and to be murdered than whites. High rates of homicide among black men fully explain the parallel high rates of imprisonment for murder. However, for less serious offenses, race differences in incarceration are not well explained by high crime rates. Black men are much more likely than whites to be arrested for a drug offense, and go to prison if arrested, even though they are no more likely to use drugs than whites. Criminologists estimate that about 80 percent of black-white difference in imprisonment rates is due simply to the high involvement of black men in crime.[22] This number has likely declined with growth in the share of drug offenders in prison. We also have seen research showing that economically disadvantaged men are also more involved in crime than middle-class men. It seems reasonable that a large fraction of the class inequality in incarceration is also attributable to class differences in offending, but there is little direct evidence on this point.

Second, although high crime rates among the disadvantaged largely explain their incarceration at a given time, trends in crime and imprisonment are only weakly related over time. Poor and minority men were much less involved in crime in 2000 than twenty years earlier, matching declines in crime in the population as a whole. Although disadvantaged men became much more law-abiding, their chances of going to prison rose to historically high levels. Statistics on criminal processing showed that there were three main causes of the growth in imprisonment, each of which is unrelated to trends in crime. First was a significant increase in the use of imprisonment for those who are convicted of a crime. Second was that those who go to prison are now serving longer sentences. Third was a dramatic increase in the prosecution and incarceration of drug offenders. Indeed, 45 percent of the increase in the state prison population is explained by the rising incarceration among drug offenders.[23] The increased risk of imprisonment given arrest, and increased time served, show that courts are treating drug and other offenders more harshly than before. What's more, crime statistics do not measure the level of drug offending so most crime statistics shed little light on a key area of state prison population growth.

Crime is not consistently related to imprisonment trends in the 1980s and 1990s, but states that experienced the largest increases in serious violence through the 1960s and 1970s, also experienced the largest gains in imprisonment decades later. These trends lead us to look at the politics of crime policy and the economic context in which criminal justice is administered.

CHAPTER 3

The Politics and Economics of Punitive Criminal Justice

The American penal system is now the largest in the world. For young black men in inner cities, government presents itself mostly as the policeman, the prison guard, or the parole officer. By the end of the 1990s, criminal justice authorities had become a constant presence in poor urban neighborhoods. As recently as the late 1970s, however, the penal population was only one-quarter as large and young male ghetto residents did not routinely go to prison. Growth in the prison population was not directly related to a rise in crime. National crime trends did not track prison population growth. At the individual level, imprisonment became common for less-skilled blacks, but these men were less involved in crime in 2000 than in 1980. If the young men who fill the nation's prisons and jails aren't committing more crime than they used to, why are they setting records for incarceration?

Going beyond crime to explain the prison boom requires a theory of punishment, one that tells us why some acts are criminalized and carry the penalty of incarceration. Such a theory should help explain why the risks of imprisonment increased for those who were arrested, why time served in prison increased, and why the prosecution of drug crimes escalated so sharply. As we just saw, it was these developments in criminal processing, rather than trends in crime, that account for the rise in imprisonment rates in the 1980s and 1990s.

This chapter traces increasing imprisonment to economic and political causes. Economic theories of punishment relate the scale of imprisonment to the standing of the underprivileged. From this viewpoint, rising economic inequality in America and the failure of urban labor markets to provide good jobs for young unskilled men in the 1970s and 1980s precipitated mass imprisonment in the 1990s. For political theories of punishment, the scale of imprisonment is shaped by conflicts over the definition and status of society's outsiders. In the 1960s and 1970s conservative politicians, mostly in the Republican Party, honed a law-and-order message that dramatized the problem of street crime and broadly hinted at black criminality. More suited to retribution than rehabilitation, criminals were targeted by tough new penalties for drug crimes, violence, and recidivism.

Underlying these political and economic explanations of mass imprisonment is a broader account of political reaction to the upheaval in American race relations through the 1960s and the collapse in urban labor markets for less-skilled men. The social turbulence of the 1960s—a volatile mixture of rising crime, social protest, and the erosion of white privilege—sharpened the punitive sentiments of white voters. The economic demoralization of less-skilled urban blacks in the 1970s presented a vulnerable target for the punitive turn in criminal justice. These were the basic preconditions for mass imprisonment.

These ideas about the sources of mass imprisonment are not new, but they have not been rigorously tested. Several studies have related differences in state imprisonment rates to differences in state politics, but this research has typically compared just a few points in time. Here I present a statistical analysis of state imprisonment with data on forty-eight states in every year from 1980 to 2000. These detailed data allow a stronger test of political effects, the effects of the Republican Party and criminal sentencing law. State-level studies do a good job of describing political differences, but a poor job of describing race and class inequalities in incarceration. I thus go on to examine inequality in prison admission rates for black and white men at different ages and levels of education. This analysis offers a strong test of the hypothesis that growth in the level of imprisonment is a by-product of increasing race and class inequality in imprisonment.

THE ECONOMIC ORIGINS OF THE PRISON BOOM

The pioneering research of Frankfurt School sociologist Georg Rusche viewed crime as a product of economic necessity, deterred only when the severity of punishment exceeded the ravages of poverty. Quoting George Bernard Shaw, Rusche observed that "if the prison does not underbid the slum in human misery, the slum will empty and the prison will fill."[1] Historic forms of punishment—fines, torture, imprisonment—were shaped by historic variation in the economic situation of the dispossessed. The unemployed, representing the most wretched and crime-prone workers, occupied a special place in the theory. Lawmakers and judges were more lenient when labor was scarce and workers were fully employed. Punishment intensified and became more wasteful of labor when the economy slowed and workers were idle. Rusche's innovation was to show that property owners and state officials responded, not to the criminality of individual offenders, but to the threat posed by the entire propertyless class. In this sense, the criminal justice system embodied a social conflict that pitted the forces of property against the lower classes.

The modern descendants of Rusche broadened his idea by arguing that the idle poor are not just a criminal threat: they also challenge the social order in a more basic way.[2] They may refuse to work, reject the dominant values of hard work and achievement, and advocate revolutionary change. Steven Spitzer described young crime-prone men at the bottom of the social ladder as "social dynamite," evoking volatility more than chronic disadvantage.[3] Perceiving this broader threat, authorities use crime control as part of a larger project to enforce conformity and maintain order among socially marginal groups that have come to include minority youth as well as the poor and unemployed.[4]

In the abstract, this description of punishment as a social conflict sounds conspiratorial. Would public officials really direct the state's legitimate violence against those who are powerless? Research on criminal punishment suggests that this happens in three ways. First, legislators perceiving poor and marginal populations as dangerous or threatening may write criminal law to contain the threat. Laws against vagrancy offer a clear historical example of the criminalization of poverty. Markus Dubber argues that criminal possession has replaced vagrancy as the main statutory control on the poor. Like vagrancy, possession offenses—which cover not just drugs, but drug paraphernalia, weapons, stolen property, and a host of other items—require no criminal intent. Possession punishes only the threat, rather than actual victimization. The abstract notion of regulating social threat is thus concretely expressed in the law of criminal possession.[5]

Second, police may scrutinize and arrest the poor more frequently than the affluent. They concentrate on poor urban communities in part because more daily life, and illegal activity, transpires in public space. Ethnographers suggest that the purchase and consumption of drugs, drunkenness, and domestic disturbances are more likely to take place in public in urban areas, but in private homes in the suburbs. Consequently, poor urban residents are more exposed to police scrutiny and risk arrest more than their suburban counterparts.[6] The great social distance between the police and poor urban minorities also contributes to distrust on both sides. Police tend to view disadvantaged blacks and Hispanics and the communities in which they live as unsafe.[7] The poor are treated with more suspicion as a result.

Third, judges may treat poor defendants harshly once in court. Tough sentences for the disadvantaged needn't imply that judges are acting out of animus. Such defendants may be considered with less empathy, and as being more blameworthy. Judges may also see poor defendants as having fewer prospects and social supports, thus as having less potential for rehabilitation.[8] Studies of criminal sentencing that control for legally relevant factors like the seriousness of the crime and the defendant's criminal history have found the highest chances of incarceration among socially disadvantaged— either minorities or those living in high unemployment areas.[9]

Skeptics will say that the poor are arrested and incarcerated more than the rich because they commit more crime. But this misses the argument in two ways. First, if only the poor committed crime, we would still need to explain why they are punished more harshly at some times than others. Second, inequalities in punishment are not fully explained by inequalities in crime. In some cases, the law is enforced more aggressively against the disadvantaged. As we saw earlier, blacks and whites use drugs at similar levels, but the police have arrested proportionately more blacks than whites.[10] In other cases, the marginal are clearly more involved in crime than the mainstream. The high rate of homicide and the high rate of incarceration for homicide among young African American men is probably the most important example. Real differences in criminality between blacks and whites influence authorities' perceptions of the threat blacks may pose. But authorities' perception of blacks as threatening is sharpened by the low social and economic status of the black community. Like any organized social activity—run according to rules and routines—law enforcement and punishment are blunt instruments; they fail in the impossible task of meting out justice in a highly individualized way. Perceptions of black criminality—partly based on fact, partly colored by social disadvantage—are woven into the rules and routines of the police and the courts. In this way, law enforcement and court officials magnify inequalities in crime into larger disparities in punishment.

If the scale of punishment is produced by social conflict rooted in economic disadvantage, the growth in U.S. income inequality in the decades after 1970 was a potent force for prison expansion. The great economic losers of the new inequality were men with only a high school education. Without a college degree, these less-skilled men missed out on the technical and white-collar jobs that retained their value through the 1970s and 1980s. Young black men in urban areas were hit the hardest. As urban labor markets buckled under the loss of industrial jobs, minority neighborhoods in the Northeast and the Midwest descended into poverty and chronic joblessness. These trends suggest that income inequality, the unemployment rate, and perhaps black unemployment rates specifically are all associated with higher levels of imprisonment.

The economic decline of the ghetto, well under way by the mid-1970s, coincided with the take-off of the prison boom. Loïc Wacquant provides a historical and institutional analysis that views mass imprisonment as the latest of an evolving variety of social institutions confining and dominating African Americans.[11] In his analysis, slavery and Jim Crow in the South were succeeded by the northern ghetto. Through the first seven decades of twentieth century, the ghetto—the black city within the white—maintained racial separation, preventing blacks from fully participating in white society. The economic collapse of the ghetto and retrenchment of the welfare state ushered in a new institutional form of racial domination—the "prison hyperghetto." For Wacquant, the prison in the era of the jobless ghetto functions to warehouse a population made superfluous by urban deindustrialization, but radicalized by the social movements of the 1960s.[12] Young black men drift back and forth between the prison and the ghetto, putting the stamp of custodial supervision on street life, and drawing the life of the street into the institution. In this setting, the prison is "race-making"—an institution that contributes to a distinctively stigmatized collective experience among poor African Americans.[13]

There are flaws in this story, to be sure. White supremacy is more an assumption of the analysis than a contingent historical achievement of the agents of racial conservatism. We see little sign, then, of the concrete political forces driving institutional change. Still, the historical perspective is valuable and, even better, suggests a hypothesis. If mass imprisonment is a stage in the institutional evolution of American racial domination, the prison boom will likely have fallen most heavily on the most economically disadvantaged blacks. Not only would imprisonment have increased, but race and class inequality in imprisonment would have deepened. This is the sense in which mass imprisonment is race-making, attaching the marker of moral failure to the collective experience of an entire social group.

THE POLITICS OF THE PRISON BOOM

The economic account that couples labor market trends to prison growth is provocative but incomplete. The jobless ghetto supplied a pool of potential inmates, but policy makers had also to decide that crime, and street crime in particular, deserved imprisonment. In the early 1970s this decision was by no means obvious. Indeed, criminal justice experts had begun to doubt the utility of imprisonment. Advocates for prisoners' rights protested the inhumanity of incarceration and the abuses of a justice system marked by large racial disparities.[14]

For most of the twentieth century, the main official objective of criminal justice was correction.[15] Correction was served by tailoring sentences to individual cases. This system of indeterminate sentencing began with legislatures who gave judges wide latitude in determining whether an offender should go to prison. Conviction would not often result in incarceration. Instead, criminal offenders were assigned to community supervision under the charge of a probation officer. If sentenced to prison, the offender's release was typically decided by a parole board that would consider the circumstances of an individual's crime, criminal history, and measure the potential for rehabilitation. Parole supervision itself was intended to reintegrate criminal offenders into society.[16] Traditionally, parole officers functioned partly as social workers, connecting their parolees to social services and job opportunities. David

Garland described this combination of indeterminate sentencing, corrections, and community supervision as "penal welfarism."[17] For the vast majority of convicted offenders, the criminal justice system was an extension of the welfare state—a government-sponsored effort to provide opportunity and lift society's failures back into the mainstream.

In practice, judges and prison wardens adapted the ideals of penal welfarism to the administrative realities of criminal processing, and the goal of rehabilitation was regularly compromised.[18] American prisons could be disorderly, understaffed, and poorly managed.[19] In the South, the rehabilitative project was never fully accepted and prisons often remained instruments of racial domination and forced labor. Southern chain gangs that built the roads and prison farms that cultivated cotton demonstrated little of the rehabilitative philosophy officially adopted elsewhere in the country.[20] Still, the principles of individualized treatment and rehabilitation were engraved in the formal institutions of indeterminate sentencing and parole. Prison was not yet the default punishment for convicted felons, and penal confinement was reserved for the most dangerous and incorrigible.

The 1970s was a transitional decade in the history of American criminal justice. The official philosophy of rehabilitation was replaced by a punitive approach. Two political projects—the war on crime and the war on drugs—conceived of a new role for prisons, and a new array of offenses and procedures for criminal processing. In a time of rising crime and academic skepticism about rehabilitative programs, prisons were enlisted for a more modest purpose. They would incapacitate criminals who would otherwise be on the streets and deter those who might be tempted to offend. Drug users and the drug trade were seen as major sources of violent crime.[21] If drug treatment could not prevent addiction, government must focus on reducing the drug supply by cracking down on drug trafficking. Although drug use was not increasing, the rate of drug arrests increased by about 250 percent from 1980 to 1996, driven by a sharp increase in arrests among minorities.[22] By the end of the 1990s, nearly 60 percent of all federal prisoners were drug offenders, and the share of drug offenders in state prison had more than doubled.[23] No longer an extension of the welfare state, the new penal system of the 1990s fortified society against incursions by the criminal class.

The transformation of American criminal justice, through the wars on crime and drugs, needed an agent of change and a method for implementing the new punitive philosophy. The main agent was the Republican Party. The key method for expanding the scale of imprisonment was a new regime of criminal sentencing that repudiated the philosophy of rehabilitation and its accompanying methods for individualized sentencing.

The Politics of Law and Order

Although the prison boom moved into high gear in the 1980s, its political origins are often traced to Barry Goldwater's presidential run in 1964.[24] Goldwater, in accepting the Republican nomination, warned of the "the growing menace in our country. . . to personal safety, to life, to limb, and property." Crime and disorder, he observed, were threats to human freedom and freedom must be "balanced so that liberty lacking order will not become the license of the mob and of the jungle." At the time, Goldwater's appeal had little basis in crime trends or public opinion. The murder rate in 1964 was no higher than five years earlier and fewer than 4 percent of Americans counted crime among the country's most important problems, compared to large majorities concerned with foreign affairs and civil rights.[25] Still, the Republican campaign of 1964 had linked the problem of street crime to civil rights protest and the growing unease among whites about racial violence. Although Goldwater was roundly defeated by Lyndon Johnson, conservatives within the Republican Party had taken a significant step to introducing a new kind of politics. Historically, responsibilities for crime control were divided mostly between state and local agencies. The Republicans had placed the issue of crime squarely on the national agenda. What's more, by treating civil rights protest as a strain of social disorder, veiled connections were drawn between the crime problem on the one hand, and black social protest on the other.

Despite Goldwater's defeat, the law and order message later resonated, particularly among southern whites and northern working-class voters of Irish, Italian, and German descent who turned away from the Democratic Party in the 1970s.[26] The social problem of crime became a reality as rates of murder and other violence escalated in the decade following the 1964 election. Through the 1960s, urban riots in Los Angeles, New York, Newark, Detroit, and dozens of other cities provided a socially ambiguous mixture of disorder and politics. Progressives saw in the riots disappointed aspirations for racial equality. Conservatives, however, decried the agitation of black militants intent on inciting violence.[27] Urban violence through the 1960s fanned the racial fears of whites, already discomfited by desegregation, black voting rights, and other civil rights victories.

Elevated crime rates and the realigned race relations of the post–civil rights period provided a receptive context for the law-and-order themes of the national Republican Party. The message was refined and sharpened by Republican presidential candidates in each electoral season over the next twenty years. In his 1970 State of the Union address, Richard Nixon declared war on "the criminal elements which increasingly threaten our cities, our homes, and our lives." In 1982, Ronald Reagan extended the campaign against crime to a war on drugs that would introduce mandatory federal prison sentences for drug offenders.[28] In the 1988 contest, Republican candidate George Bush declared his strong support for the death penalty and charged his opponent Michael Dukakis with placating dangerous criminals. Bush's Willie Horton campaign commercial signaled the dangers of black criminality and Democratic complicity in the threat. The penal welfare orthodoxy, and the Democrats, came under fire for offering more sympathy to criminals than crime victims: "There are some. . . who have wandered off the clear-cut path of commonsense and have become lost in the thickets of liberal sociology. . . when it comes to crime and criminals they always seem to 'Blame Society First'. . . [Criminal justice under Dukakis is] a 'Twilight Zone' world where prisoners' 'right to privacy' has more weight than a citizen's right to safety."[29] Rooted in reaction to civil rights social protest, and fueled by rising violent crime rates, the presidential politics of law and order had largely rejected the possibility, and perhaps even the desirability, of rehabilitation.

National politics illustrate the hardening of Republican crime policy, but governors and state legislators led the effort to rebuild the penal system. The law-and-order politics of the state Republican parties can be seen in Joseph Davey's comparison of imprisonment trends in adjacent states in the 1980s and early 1990s. Five out of six states with the highest rates of imprisonment growth were governed by Republicans when state prison populations were growing most rapidly. Republican governors presided in fewer than half of the comparison states where incarceration rates changed little.[30] The clearest examples of aggressive law-and-order politics were provided by Governors John Ashcroft of Missouri and Carroll Campbell of South Carolina. From 1985 to 1993, when Ashcroft was governor, the Missouri imprisonment rate increased by 80 percent. During his two terms, Ashcroft cut state services by over $1 billion, but spent $115 million on new prisons and increased the annual correctional budget from $87 million to $208 million. The Missouri legislature passed a range of severe penalties and Ashcroft pursued steep sentence enhancements for drug offenders.[31] In South Carolina, Governor Campbell oversaw a 39-percent increase in imprisonment from 1986 to 1990. Like Ashcroft, Campbell supported harsh sentences for drug offenders. No-parole and mandatory minimum prison sentences for drug crimes were also adopted during Campbell's tenure.

Although Republican politicians promoted prison expansion and tough new criminal sentences, Democrats also supported an increasingly punitive criminal justice policy. Liberals had opposed the death penalty since its resumption in 1976, but by the early 1990s congressional Democrats were introducing bills carrying dozens of capital offenses. In 1991, Democratic Senator Joe Biden would boast: "The Biden crime bill before us calls for the death penalty for 51 offenses. . . . The President's bill calls for the death penalty on 46 offenses." Biden also voiced his support for the death penalty "without the racial justice provision in it," referring to a proposal to prevent capital punishment where there is statistical evidence of racial disparity.[32] President Clinton's 1994 Violent Crime Control and Law Enforcement Act authorized funding for local police and imposed a ban on assault weapons—popular measures among big-city mayors—but also earmarked $9.9 billion for prison construction and added life terms for third-time federal felons.[33] At the state level, Mario Cuomo, the liberal Democratic governor from New York conducted a massive increase in prison capacity. In Texas, incarceration rates grew more quickly under Democratic Governor Ann Richards than under her Republican successor, George W. Bush.[34] In short, Democrats also joined in the rejection of the penal welfarism, although they may have come later and with less enthusiasm to punitive criminal justice policy.

Anecdotes linking parties to crime policy can be marshaled on both sides. More systematic evidence is needed to weigh the influence of Republicans and Democrats on the prison boom. David Jacobs and Ronald Helms analyzed national time series and found that imprisonment rates grew quickly under Republican presidents, but slowly under Democrats.[35] National data are suggestive, but a stronger test studies the large political and penal differences between states. Jacobs and Jason Carmichael estimated the effects of Republican electoral strength on state incarceration rates.[36] They found that incarceration rates were higher in states with Republican legislatures and governors, more so in the 1990s than the 1980s. The issue remains unsettled, however. David Greenberg and Valerie West using similar data from the

1970, 1980, and 1990 censuses were unable to find any significant effects of Republican governors on state incarceration rates.[37]

Criminal Sentencing

The legal framework for criminal processing—the system of sentencing and parole release—was a visible and vulnerable target for the new law-and-order politics. Before the mid-1970s, indeterminate sentencing let judges decide whether an offender would be sent to prison and the maximum time they might serve. The length of time actually served was not generally set at the trial but was instead determined in prison by a hearing of the parole board. In principle, the wide discretion of judges and parole boards enabled correctional treatment that could be tailored to individual cases. Although this permitted the indefinite incapacitation of prisoners viewed as dangerous or incorrigible, it also allowed the early release of those identified as having great potential for rehabilitation.

By the end of the 1960s, the discretion of judges and parole boards was assailed from the left and the right. Left-wing critics charged that police and judicial discretion enabled racial and class bias.[38] The American Friends Service Committee argued in their report *The Struggle for Justice* that "many distortions and corruptions of justice—such as the discriminatory use of penal sanctions . . . depend on the existence of wide margins of discretionary power."[39] To remedy the abuse of discretion, they recommended short fixed sentences, the abolition of parole, and unsupervised street release.

Although activists on the left were concerned that judicial discretion led to excessive incarceration, conservatives feared that incarceration was not used often enough. In his book *Thinking About Crime*, policy analyst James Q. Wilson argued that criminals were not made in the poor and broken homes that dotted traditional criminology; they were born into the world wicked and covetous. Rehabilitation was a sentimental delusion for this tough-minded analysis. Incarceration could reduce crime only by locking away the hard cases and by deterring the opportunists.[40] To deter, punishment had to be certain and not left to the vagaries of the sentencing judge and the parole hearing.

Opposition to indeterminate sentences set in motion a wave of legislative activity that limited judicial discretion in criminal punishment.[41] In 1978, in an effort to reduce race and gender disparities, lawmakers in Minnesota and Pennsylvania established the first sentencing commissions that developed guidelines for judges. Twenty more states adopted sentencing guidelines over the next fifteen years. Arbitrary punishment was to be minimized by a grid that determined an offender's sentence by considering only the crime and the offender's criminal history. In at least nine states, guidelines were intended to help control prison growth, and imprisonment did grow more slowly through the late 1980s in these cases.[42] Guidelines, however, may also have had the opposite effect of increasing the severity of punishment. The "psychology of the two-dimensional grid" leads to a more punishing approach to sentencing because the defendant's social context is eliminated from consideration.[43] The zeal for uniform treatment prevents judges from considering mitigating factors such as employment, education, and family situation—factors that would reduce sentences under an indeterminate scheme. Criminal history is also weighed relatively heavily, so repeat offenders may serve more time.[44]

Sentencing guidelines were sometimes introduced as one piece of a two-part reform that also abolished early release through parole. The hearing that monitored an offender's conduct and rehabilitative potential was conceived as part of the correctional model of individualized treatment. Parole abolitionists were sometimes motivated to reduce discretion to prevent unfair treatment particularly for minority defendants. Often, however, parole was abolished as part of a tough-on-crime project that rejected rehabilitation and individualized treatment.[45] Maine disbanded its parole board first, in 1976 and fifteen states followed over the next twenty years. Another five states eliminated parole release just for violent or personal crimes.[46] Where parole was abolished, prisoners could earn early release by accumulating time off for good conduct. Like sentencing guidelines, parole abolition may increase prison populations. By applying broader standards for release than good conduct, parole release might reduce prison growth. Parole boards might also operate as a safety valve, adjusting release decisions to conditions of prison crowding.[47] The evidence for these effects is mixed, however. Thomas Marvell and Carlisle Moody found higher imprisonment rates in only one of the ten states they studied with mandatory release.[48] Violent offenders also spend more time in prison in states with discretionary parole release.[49]

New mandatory minimum sentences also affected prison release. Mandatory minimums require offenders to serve a fixed period before the possibility of early release. Although mandatory minimum sentences were on the books in many states before 1970, they were disliked by judges and few appeared to comply with the mandate.[50] From the 1970s, mandatory sentencing became popular among lawmakers eager to show their tough-on-crime credentials. The new generation of mandatory minimums was first adopted by New York Governor Nelson Rockefeller. A moderate Republican, Rockefeller had supported some of the country's leading drug treatment programs in the 1960s. By the early 1970s, he had become disillusioned by the failure of New York's drug treatment programs to stem the flow of new drug addicts. In 1973, he proposed mandatory life prison sentences for anyone selling or conspiring to sell heroin, amphetamines, LSD, or other hard drugs. Life sentences were not confined to drug dealers. Possession of more than an ounce of heroin or cocaine could also earn life in prison.[51] The Rockefeller drug laws passed the state legislature in May 1973. High level drug dealers have served long prison sentences under the laws, but their broad scope has also swept up many small-time dealers. Jennifer Gonnerman tells the story of Elaine Bartlett, a twenty-six-year-old hairdresser and mother of four, who was offered $2,500 to take four ounces of cocaine from New York City for sale in upstate Albany. A novice drug mule, Bartlett was caught in a sting operation and sentenced in 1984 to twenty years to life. She was released after sixteen years on a grant of clemency.[52] Although the New York laws remained among the nation's harshest, by the mid-1990s, thirty-five other states had adopted mandatory minimums for drug possession or trafficking.[53]

Mandatory minimum sentences were also widely adopted for repeat offenders. California's three-strikes law, passed in 1994, is the best-known example. Three-strikes, however, is a misnomer. The Californian law doubles sentences for serious second-time felony offenders. The third strike carries life in prison. The clearest case for disproportionate punishment arises for third-strike nonviolent felons. Sasha Abramsky's *Hard Time Blues* describes the third strike for Billy Ochoa, a lifelong heroin addict who supported his habit mostly by burglary and welfare fraud. After thirty-one arrests and six burglary convictions, Ochoa was on parole at age fifty-three and caught supplying false identities for food stamps and emergency shelter vouchers. The welfare fraud, valued at $2,100, earned a sentence of 326 years at the New Folsom supermax prison.[54] The third-time enhancements, like Ochoa's, were the most severe, but the main burden of the Californian law falls on second-time offenders. A year after three-strikes was passed, 65 percent of those eligible—about ten thousand Californian prisoners—were estimated to be sentenced under the second-strike provision.[55] By adding time to the sentences

Table 3.1 Limited Judicial Discretion in Criminal Sentencing

States that Have:	1980	1990	2000
Sentencing guidelines[a]	2	10	17
Abolished or limited parole[b]	17	21	33
Three-strikes laws	0	0	24
Truth-in-sentencing laws[c]	3	7	40

Source: Author's compilations.
[a]Includes states with voluntary and presumptive guidelines.
[b]Includes states that limit parole release only for violent offenders.
[c]Includes states that mandate at least 50 percent of sentences be served for some offenses.

of large numbers of defendants with a single felony conviction, the California three-strikes law is probably the most severe in the country. Many other states also adopted some version of these provisions and by the mid-1990s, forty states had passed mandatory sentences for repeat offenders.

Mandatory minimums reduced an ostensibly dishonest feature of indeterminate sentencing: potentially severe sentences were allowed by law but seldom imposed by judges. So-called truth-in-sentencing measures sought greater transparency through greater severity, requiring offenders to serve a majority of their prison sentence. Truth-in-sentencing was applied mostly to violent crimes, although in Florida, Mississippi, and Ohio it applied to all prisoners.[56] The earliest truth-in-sentencing scheme was introduced in Washington state in 1984. The measures proliferated after federal law in 1994 authorized funding for additional prisons and jails for states mandating 85 percent of time served for serious violent crimes. By 1998, twenty-five states had adopted the 85-percent standard. Another seven require that at least half the sentence be served.[57]

To gauge trends in criminal sentencing, I measured the presence of sentencing guidelines, parole release, three-strikes laws, and truth-in-sentencing laws in every state between 1980 and 2000. By these measures, the sentencing and release of offenders changed fundamentally through the two decades of the prison boom (table 3.1). Parole was widely abolished at an early stage, in seventeen states by 1980. Innovations like three-strikes and truth-in-sentencing were widely adopted only in the 1990s. State legislatures, by mandating minimum prison sentences and limiting the role of judges and parole boards, increasingly asserted control over the punishment of criminals. In the courtroom, much of the power to incarcerate moved from judges to prosecutors. By choosing which charges to bring, prosecutors largely controlled a defendant's chances of going to jail.

I have so far described two main explanations for the growth in imprisonment in the thirty years after 1970. An economic explanation points to the steady rise in American economic inequality and high unemployment among poor urban blacks. A political explanation points to the influence of the law-and-order politics of the Republican party and the adoption of a tough new system of determinate sentencing. Researchers have studied these explanations empirically by examining times series of national incarceration rates and variation across states and over time. The state-level research capitalizes on large differences in penal systems across jurisdictions. The data sets of earlier research, however, were often sparse, examining only decennial census years and providing only coarse measures of changes in criminal sentencing. These limitations of data and measurement produced little agreement among the statistical studies. Some found strong evidence of the effects of economic inequality and political forces. Others did not.[58] I next provide a more comprehensive empirical test that examines incarceration in the states using annual data from 1980 to 2000. The analysis also introduces a detailed measure of changes in criminal sentencing.

INCARCERATION IN FIFTY STATES

There is more variation in imprisonment across the fifty states than between the United States and Europe. Figure 3.1 shows the distribution of state imprisonment rates each year from 1970 to 2003. Each box shows the incarceration rates spanning the middle twenty-five states (the 25th to the 75th percentiles). The median incarceration rate is marked by the line in the middle of each box. The whiskers extending from the box roughly span the first and last percentiles, with outliers marked beyond the whiskers. State imprisonment rates become more dispersed over time. State prison populations increased everywhere, but in some states more quickly than others. Louisiana, Mississippi, and Texas stand out for their extraordinary growth. Imprisonment rates in these three states increased by more than five hundred per hundred thousand from 1980 to 2003. By 2003, Louisiana's incarceration rate of 801 per hundred thousand was nearly two-thirds higher than the national average. Texas accounted for 7.5 percent of the U.S. population, but housed 13.1 percent of its state prisoners.

Figure 3.1   Annual Rates of State Imprisonment

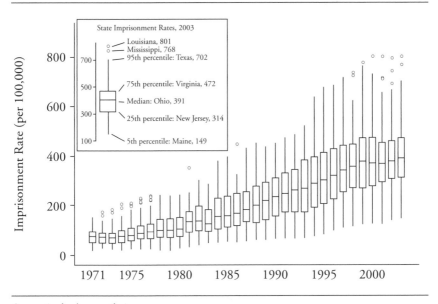

Source: Author's compilations.
Note: Data are for all fifty states.
Inset: Boxplot for state imprisonment rates, fifty states in 2003.

Variation in imprisonment across the states between 1980 and 2000 helps us understand the effects of changing political and economic conditions. If mass imprisonment grew out of a bad labor market for black men, incarceration rates would likely have increased most in states with the largest increases in unemployment and income inequality. If law-and-order politics and tough-on-crime sentencing swelled prison populations we would expect to see incarceration rates rise in states that elected Republican lawmakers and installed determinate sentencing.

Table 3.2 lists socioeconomic conditions and political and legal factors that might affect a state's imprisonment rate. Many different labor market conditions may affect imprisonment, but researchers have focused on unemployment and income inequality.[59] Income inequality—measured by the Gini index of individual incomes—increased through the 1990s and may reflect the economic status of disadvantaged men better than unemployment. If the prison boom stems from joblessness, black men's unemployment rates

Table 3.2 Means of Imprisonment Rates and Predictors, Fifty States

	1980	1990	2000
State-level incarceration			
Imprisonment per 100,000	120.1	241.6	388.2
Socioeconomic predictors			
Unemployment rate (percentage)	6.8	5.4	3.8
Unemployment rate, black men (percentage)	12.4	11.0	7.0
Young jobless noncollege men[a] (percentage)	1.2	1.6	1.5
Gini index of incomes	45.2	44.6	46.2
Percentage black in state population	9.4	10.1	10.9
Legal and political predictors			
Determinate sentencing index (0 to 4 points)	.3	.6	2.0
Percentage Republican governors	37.5	43.8	66.7

Source: See Appendix.

[a]Noncollege men age nineteen to forty-five not in labor force as percentage of noninstitutional men age nineteen to forty-five.

may also be a better predictor of incarceration than the overall unemployment rate. Unemployment rates go up and down with the business cycle and do not capture the chronic joblessness associated with ghetto poverty. To tap this more enduring unemployment, I also measured the proportion of men under forty-five in the population who have only a high school education and who have dropped out of the labor force.

Viewing punishment as a social conflict led a number of researchers to study not only the economic status of outsiders but also their race. States with large black populations have been found to have high rates of imprisonment.[60] The proportion of African Americans varies more across states than over time. Still, recent changes in the geographic distribution of the black population reflect an important trend. Declining employment in the manufacturing centers of the Midwest and Northeast in the 1960s and 1970s reversed a northern migration that dated from the early decades of the twentieth century. Blacks returned to the South in the two decades after 1980, increasing their populations in states such as Georgia, North Carolina, and Florida.[61]

Two kinds of measures tap the changing political context of criminal processing. First, the Republican realignment is indicated by changes in the number of Republican governors. More than half of all governors were Democrats in 1980, but this number had fallen to a third by 2000 (table 3.2).[62] Determinate sentencing proliferated as Republicans gained power. A four-point scale combining information on sentencing guidelines, parole abolition, truth-in-sentencing laws, and three-strikes laws, increases from a mean of .3 to 2.0 between 1980 and 2000. Whereas determinate sentencing measures were uncommon in 1980, most states had adopted at least two kinds of limits on judicial discretion by 2000.[63]

The economic and political sources of incarceration may be confounded with the effects of crime, urbanization, the growth in spending on police. I therefore control for all these factors in the data analysis. I also take account of citizens' political liberalism, which may lead states to implement more lenient criminal justice policy and elect Democratic governors and legislators.

Panel data like these, which vary across time and space, allow a strong empirical test of causal claims. In addition to the predictors that may influence imprisonment, the analysis can adjust for enduring, but unobserved, traits of states that do not vary over time. These state effects account for all factors that do not change over time but have been left out of the study and may be related to the predictors. For example, incarceration rates may have been historically high in some southern states like Georgia and Mississippi because of a southern culture of violence that urges retribution against law-breakers.[64] The culture of violence is a relatively fixed characteristic of southern states and its influence is absorbed by the state effects. We can take the analysis a step further by adjusting for factors that vary over time but not across states. These year effects can adjust, for example, for the nationwide trend to rising incarceration. The state and the year effects together provide a stringent empirical test of the effects of the political, legal, and socioeconomic sources of state imprisonment.

Table 3.3 reports the regression results. The data analysis provides uneven evidence for the effects of the labor market on the scale of imprisonment. When state effects are accounted for, the negative effects of the unemployment rate and black men's unemployment rate indicates that rising joblessness is associated with a falling incarceration rate (table 3.3, column 1). The negative effects of unemployment are due to the tight labor market at the end of 1990s: imprisonment rates increased while joblessness was falling.

Table 3.3   Regression Analysis of Imprisonment Rates, 1980 to 2000

	Effect on State Imprisonment (Percentage)	
	(1)	(2)
Socioeconomic effects		
1 point rise in unemployment rate	−4.1*	1.1*
1 point rise in black men's unemployment rate	−1.0*	.2
1 per 1,000 rise in share of young jobless noncollege men	2.3*	4.6
1 unit rise in Gini index of incomes	−1.4*	−.7
1 point rise in black population share	1.6*	−.3
Legal and political effects		
Change from Democratic to Republican governor	13.8*	5.7*
1 point rise in 4-point determinate sentencing scale	12.8*	−4.8*
Including state effects?	Yes	Yes
Including year effects?	No	Yes

Source: Author's compilations.
Note: Estimates are for forty-eight states, from a regression of log state imprisonment rates on murder, nonlethal violent crime, property crime, noncollege joblessness, percentage black, percentage urban, determinate sentencing scale, Republican governor, state spending on police, and citizen's liberal ideology (N = 1008, R^2 = .86 with state effects, R^2 = .96 with state and year effects). Other estimates are obtained by replacing noncollege joblessness with unemployment, black men's unemployment, or the Gini index. All predictors except the sentencing index are lagged one year.
*p < .01

Adding year effects removes from the analysis these nationwide trends in unemployment and incarceration (table 3.3, column 2). Because states with high unemployment rates have high incarceration rates, adjusting for year effects brings the expected result: slack labor market conditions are associated with increased criminal punishment. The more fine-grained measure of joblessness among young noncollege men yields stronger evidence for the link between unemployment and incarceration. If the fraction of jobless, less-skilled young men in the population increases by a tenth of a percentage point, the imprisonment rate is estimated to rise by between about 2 and 4 percent. In Texas, for example, this population increased by half a percentage point between 1980 and 2000, producing an estimated rise in state imprisonment between 10 and 20 percent. Because the Texas imprisonment rate increased by more than 200 percent in the two decades from 1980, the effect of less-skilled jobless population is in fact quite small.

The remaining socioeconomic effects—the Gini index of income inequality, and the size of a state's black population—are not strongly supported by the data analysis. The estimated effect of income inequality on incarceration is very close to zero. The state effects model indicates that, where the black population grew, incarceration rates tended to rise. This suggests that the return of blacks from the rustbelt cities of the Northeast and the Midwest to states such as Georgia, Louisiana, Maryland, and Mississippi contributed to growth in those prison populations. When year effects are added, however, the effect is estimated to be negative rather than positive and is not statistically significant.

The socioeconomic effects are only modestly supported by the statistics, but evidence is stronger for the effects of political parties. There is strong evidence that imprisonment rates have grown faster under Republican governors. Accounting for state effects shows that imprisonment rates are about 14 percent higher under Republicans than under Democrats. The estimated effect is only a third as large when year effects are added, but the results remain statistically significant.

In the state effects model, the twenty-year reduction in judicial discretion in sentencing and release is closely associated with prison growth (table 3.3, column 1). Low-incarceration states like Maine and Minnesota led in adopting determinate sentencing, but those that followed this path experienced the largest increases in imprisonment. For example, a state that abolishes its parole board (a 1-point increase in the sentencing scale) undergoes an estimated 13-percent rise in its imprisonment rate. Because indeterminate sentencing was adopted early by states with low-incarceration rates, adding year effects yields a negative relationship between indeterminate sentencing and the imprisonment rate (table 3.3, column 2). The quantitative data thus fails to provide a clear signal that determinate sentencing raised the state imprisonment rate.

The data on state imprisonment strongly indicates the effects of Republican lawmakers and joblessness among less-skilled men. If the share of noncollege young men without jobs and the number of Democratic governors had remained at 1980 levels, would the incarceration rate have been much lower through the 1980s and 1990s? We can predict the trend in incarcera-

Figure 3.2   Reduction in Imprisonment if Partisanship and Percentages Are Unchanged

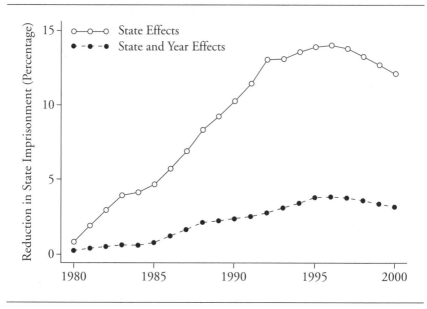

Source: Author's compilations.

tion, assuming that 1980 political and labor market conditions endured over the following twenty years. Figure 3.2 shows the percentage reduction in the state imprisonment rate attributable to the political and labor market conditions for the state effect and state-year effect models. The statistical analysis indicates that by 2000 the imprisonment rate would be between 4 and 12 percent lower had the Democrats maintained their electoral advantage and the share of less-skilled jobless men in the population remained at its low 1980 level. These effects are quite modest and suggest that much of the rise in imprisonment would have occurred even without the growing dominance of the Republican party and the deteriorating labor market situation of less-skilled young men.

Many of the measures of labor market conditions failed to show a strong relationship to the scale of punishment. Various measures of unemployment and the Gini index of income inequality were not consistently related to state imprisonment rates. Other research has produced similarly weak results. Several recent papers have estimated the effects of unemployment rates, income inequality, and poverty, but report weak evidence of the effects of these economic conditions on state imprisonment.[65] This is partly a problem of research design. The state-level analysis focuses on aggregate incarceration rates and labor market indicators, not on the incarceration and economic status of the most disadvantaged. The aggregated approach of the state analysis thus misses a central implication of labor market theories of incarceration: economic inequality expands criminal punishment among the disadvantaged by increasing inequality in incarceration.

DISAGGREGATING INCARCERATION RATES

To study whether economic inequality is related to the level of imprisonment through its effects on inequality in imprisonment, we need a different kind of research design. Instead of examining aggregate imprisonment rates, we calculate the risk of imprisonment for white and black men at different ages and levels of education. These disaggregated prison admission rates are related to disaggregated measures of wages and employment.

The aggregate statistics studied so far conceal large race and class disparities. To analyze race and class disparities in imprisonment, I constructed detailed figures using the annual census of prison admissions, the National Corrections Reporting Program (NCRP). The data, available from 1983 to 2001, record the age, education, and race of every prisoner released in thirty-eight states, covering 80 to 90 percent of the total prison population.[66] I estimated prison admission rates separately for black and white men at ages twenty to twenty-four, twenty-five to twenty-nine, thirty to thirty-four, and thirty-five to thirty-nine, for high school dropouts, high school graduates, and those with at least some college. The steep educational inequalities in prison admissions among young men are shown in figure 3.3. Regardless of race, high school dropouts are five times more likely to go to prison than high school graduates. Prison admission rates rose significantly for less-educated men from the early 1980s to the late 1990s but little among the college-educated. The combination of racial and educational inequality strikingly affects young black male dropouts. One in six black male dropouts per year went to prison in the late 1990s. The protective effects of college education are also clear; fewer than 1 percent of college-educated black men were admitted to prison in the late 1990s.

To isolate the effects of social control directed at the disadvantaged, analysis of these prison admission rates must also account for the effects of crime. I

Figure 3.3   Noninstitutional Men Annually Entering Prison

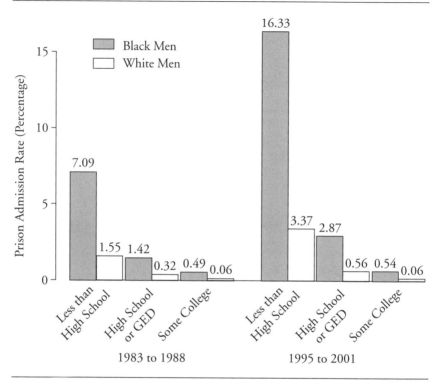

Source: Author's compilations.

measure crime with disaggregated data on victimization. Because violent crime usually involves victims and perpetrators with similar social status, crime among blacks and whites at different levels of education can be tapped with victimization data from the National Crime Victimization Survey (NCVS). The NCVS annually asks respondents about their exposure to violence over the past year. The data can be used to construct violent victimization rates—the number of victims of violence divided by the population—for different offenses and for different subgroups.[67] As in the state analysis, I also sometimes use fixed effects, in this case to capture the propensity to crime that varies by age, race, and education. Analyzing disaggregated admission rates and adjusting for fixed effects introduces far more detailed information about the risks of incarceration than in earlier research. If increased inequality influences imprisonment by raising incarceration most among the disadvantaged, this disaggregated analysis is more likely to detect the effect.

Figure 3.4   Inequality in Admission Rates

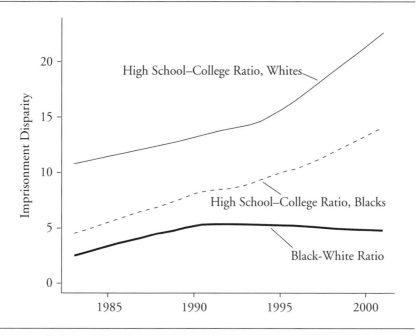

Source: Author's compilations.

To describe how inequality in imprisonment has changed over time, I begin by calculating for each year, the chances of imprisonment among blacks compared to whites, and among the high school educated (graduates and dropouts) compared to the college educated, controlling for age and violent crime. We can think of these ratios as measures of race and class inequality in imprisonment. Figure 3.4 plots the trends in race and class inequalities in U.S. state prison admission between 1983 and 2001 for men aged twenty to thirty-nine. Racial inequalities in prison admission increased a little in the 1980s, but for most of the period blacks were around five times more likely to go to prison than whites. Class inequality in imprisonment increased significantly. Whereas high school–educated blacks were five times more likely to go to prison in 1983, by 2001 the relative disparity in imprisonment had grown threefold. Although prison admission rates are five times lower for whites than blacks, class inequality in imprisonment is higher among whites. By 2001, whites with only a high school education were more than twenty

Figure 3.5   Prison Admission Rates

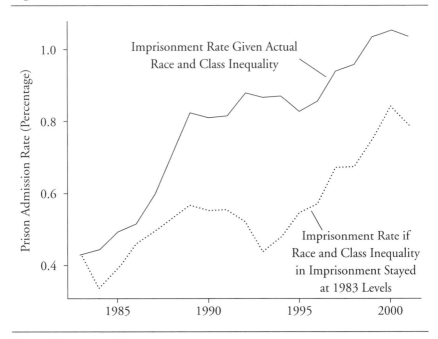

Source: Author's compilations.

times more likely than their college-educated counterparts to go to prison, controlling for age and educational differences in violent crime.

With rising levels of education, the high school educated may be less able, and more marginal, than in the past. Trends in educational inequality in imprisonment may just reflect increasing criminal propensity in a shrinking pool of low achievers. Shifts in carceral inequality are unlikely to be an artifact of rising education, however. Although the number of dropouts fell between 1983 and 2001, the share of graduates increased, meaning that the proportion of high school educated has not fallen much, certainly far too little to account for the large increases in educational inequality. College, too, has become less selective over time. We might therefore expect rising incarceration among men with higher education. All the increase in prison admission, however, is concentrated among noncollege men.

Part of the growth in prison admission rates is attributable to the large increase in class inequality indicated by the escalation of imprisonment among men with little schooling. What if prison admission among high school graduates followed its actual path, roughly a twofold increase, but educational inequality in prison admission remained at its 1983 level. How much did the increase in inequality in imprisonment add to the overall growth of prison admission? Figure 3.5 answers this question by showing prison admissions, given observed trends in educational inequality, and assuming educational inequality in imprisonment was unchanged since 1983. By 2001, the prison admission rate for all men, aged twenty to thirty-nine, would be 20 percent lower if the relative risk of imprisonment had not increased so much among high school dropouts.

We can take the analysis a step further by relating inequality in imprisonment to trends in the labor market. The rise in the risk of imprisonment among less-educated men may be related to trends in their earnings and employment. I studied the link between men's labor market status and their risk of going to prison by calculating the median weekly earnings and employment rates of black and white men at different ages and levels of education.[68]

Estimates of the effects of earnings and employment on prison admission are shown in table 3.4. When data for black and white men are analyzed together, a $100 increase in weekly pay—roughly the earnings gap between

Table 3.4　Regression of Admission Rates, 1983 to 2001

	Effect on Prison Admission (Percentage)
All men	
$100 increase in weekly pay	−31.6*
10 percentage point increase in employment	−10.4
White men	
$100 increase in weekly pay	−41.1*
10 percentage point increase in employment	17.5
Black men	
$100 increase in weekly pay	−25.9*
10 percentage point increase in employment	−15.6*

Source: Author's compilations.
Note: Regression for all men also includes controls for violent crime and race-age-education effects. Results for black and white men control for violent crime and age-education effects.
*Statistically significant at p < .01 level.

dropouts and high school graduates—is associated with a 32-percent decline in the chances of imprisonment. A 10-percent increase in employment rates—roughly equal to the dropout-graduate employment gap among whites—is associated with a 10-percent reduction in prison admissions, though this result is not statistically significant.

There are clear race differences in the effects of labor market status on incarceration. Among whites, the growing chances of going to prison are only significantly associated with wages, not employment. A $100 increase in wages is estimated to lower the chances of imprisonment by about 40 percent. Among blacks, both wage and employment trends are significantly associated with incarceration. A $100 increase in pay is estimated to reduce the chances of going to prison by about one-quarter. The $30 drop in pay among black dropouts between the mid-1980s and the late 1990s is estimated to have raised prison admissions by about 8 percent. Employment trends were not significantly related to incarceration among whites, but among blacks, a 10-percentage-point increase in the employment rate is associated with a 15-percent increase in the chance of imprisonment. Between the mid-1980s and the late 1990s, employment rates for black dropouts fell 7 percentage points, increasing their chances of going to prison by 11 percent. The declining wage and employment rates of young less-skilled black men through the 1980s and 1990s is thus estimated to have increased their chances of imprisonment by about 20 percent. In sum, there is strong evidence that deteriorating labor market status is closely associated with increasing risks of imprisonment.

CONCLUSION

This chapter provides evidence that the prison boom is the product of fundamental economic and political changes in American society. Rapid growth in incarceration among young, black, noncollege men closely followed the collapse of urban labor markets and the creation of jobless ghettos in America's inner cities. The traditional research method, looking at differences in incarceration across states, offered little suggestion that the prison boom was fueled by the poor job prospects of less-skilled blacks. Shifting the focus to race and class inequality in imprisonment, however, showed that incarceration had increased most among those whose jobless rates were highest. Class inequality in imprisonment increased dramatically from 1983 to 2001, contributing about 20 percent to the rise in risk of prison admission. By the early 2000s, the chances of imprisonment were more closely linked to race and school failure than at any other time in the previous twenty years.

The political context for the shifting demography of imprisonment is provided by a resurgent Republican party and a fundamental reform of criminal sentencing. Republicans' law-and-order politics grew out of reaction to the gains of the civil rights movement and anxieties about rising crime among white voters. Republican governors rejected rehabilitation, expanded prison capacity, and turned the penal system to the twin tasks of incapacitation and deterrence. Indeterminate sentences were discarded as legislators worked to limit the discretion of judges and parole boards. The quantitative evidence offered mixed evidence that determinate sentencing raised imprisonment rates. The effects of partisanship were less ambiguous: there is a strong quantitative indication that Republican governors promoted the growth of the penal system.

Of course, these political and economic accounts of the prison boom are closely connected. The political and economic causes of the prison boom are vitally implicated in the disappointed promise of the civil rights movement. The growth in violence among the ghetto poor through the 1960s and 1970s stoked fears of white voters and lurked in the rhetoric of law and order. Crime, however, did not drive the rise in imprisonment directly, but formed the background for a new style of politics and punishment. As joblessness and low wages became enduring features of the less-skilled inner-city economy, the effects of a punitive criminal justice system concentrated on the most disadvantaged.

APPENDIX: ANALYSIS OF STATE IMPRISONMENT

Variables used in the regression analysis of state imprisonment included:

PRISON ADMISSION RATES State prisoners per hundred thousand residents were assembled from BJS data on incarceration rates for prisoners under state jurisdiction.[69]

MURDER, VIOLENT, AND PROPERTY CRIME RATES Offending rates are taken from the Uniform Crime Reports.

LABOR MARKET MEASURES Unemployment jobless rates and Gini indexes were estimated using the Outgoing Rotation Group Files of the Current Population Survey.[70]

DETERMINATE SENTENCING INDEX Information on parole abolition, truth in sentencing, and sentencing guidelines was compiled from the Bureau of Justice Assistance, Paula Ditton and Doris Wilson, Michael Tonry, and Tamasak Wicharaya.[71]

REPUBLICAN GOVERNORS Data were collected from Carl Klarner[72] and state sources.

With panel data and a large number of possible covariates, the number of plausible models is very large. The reported results were estimated with least squares. Smaller standard errors can be obtained by adjusting for heterogeneity in the error variances. Larger standard errors are obtained by adjusting for autocorrelation. Residual autocorrelation in the regressions average .63 across states. A first difference specification eliminates autocorrelation and yields significant, though smaller, effects for Republican governors and indeterminate sentencing.

APPENDIX: ANALYSIS OF THE DISAGGREGATED INCARCERATION RATES

PRISON ADMISSION RATES The prison admission rate is defined as the number of people annually entering the custody of state or federal prison as a percentage of the noninstitutional civilian and military population. Annual age-race-education cell proportions were calculated from the NCRP.[73] These cell proportions were then multiplied by aggregate counts of male admissions obtained from the National Prisoner Statistics Series (NPS-1) of the Bureau of Justice Statistics. The NCRP data yield similar age-race distributions to the *Survey of Inmates of State and Federal Correctional Facilities*. However, levels of schooling in the NCRP tended to be lower than in the inmate survey. The denominator of the admission rate—the population at risk of going to prison—was calculated from the Outgoing Rotation Groups files of the CPS, and counts of military personnel obtained from the Department of Defense.

EARNINGS Earnings are measured annually by the median weekly earnings of each age-race-education cell for all male workers, deflated by the CPI-U. Earnings are earnings-weighted figures from the Outgoing Rotation Group files of the CPS. Additional analysis examined earnings for full-time full-year workers, and measures of earnings relative to different percentiles of the earnings distribution, but these alternative specifications yield results identical to those reported in the paper.

EMPLOYMENT Employment is measured by the employment to population ratio of each age-race-education cell for the male noninstitutional and civilian and military population. Employment rates are calculated from survey-weighted data in the Outgoing Rotation Group files of the CPS and counts of military personnel from the Department of Defense.

VIOLENT CRIME Violent crime is measured by the total number of personal crimes suffered as a proportion of the civilian noninstitutional population. The number of criminal victimizations is given by the incident-based files of National Crime Victimization Survey.[74] Victimizations are calculated separately for blacks and whites, aged twenty to fifty, at different levels of education. Denominators for the victimization rates were taken from the Outgoing Rotation Groups files of the CPS.

PART II

The Consequences of Mass Imprisonment

CHAPTER 4

Invisible Inequality

Although numerous, the poor are invisible in America's affluent society. The everyday hardships of low-income families are unfamiliar to those who are economically comfortable. Poor people are seldom depicted in the popular culture, in movies, or on television. The poor are especially invisible during periods of economic prosperity. At the end of the 1990s, unemployment rates dropped to historically low levels, yet large numbers of workers remained poor in their minimum-wage jobs. In the context of a booming stock market and rising incomes among the rich, growth in the numbers of low-income workers fell outside everyday understanding of the major economic trends. The working poor, wrote Katherine Newman, "have attracted very little attention. They do not impinge on the national conscience."[1] David Shipler sounds a similar theme, observing that low-wage workers "blend into familiar landscapes and are therefore overlooked. They make up the invisible silent America that analysts casually ignore."[2] Cyclical affluence, it seems, erases the poor from public consciousness.

A strong economy also concealed the poor from public view in the early 1960s. The unemployment rate was then extremely low, and the United States was enjoying a period of sustained economic growth in which the wages of even unskilled workers grew strongly. The mood of economic optimism was sobered when Michael Harrington pulled back the curtain on

U.S. poverty with the publication in 1962 of *The Other America*. During that earlier economic expansion, Harrington also found that the poor had disappeared from the outlook of policy makers and the middle class. In the affluent society of the early 1960s, "the millions who are poor in the United States tend to become increasingly invisible. Here is a great mass of people, yet it takes an effort of the intellect and will even to see."[3] Why are the poor invisible? Harrington observes "poverty is often off the beaten track."[4] *The Other America* thus spanned rural Appalachia, the rented rooms and boarding houses of the elderly, and the urban ghettos of the big cities to document the lives of millions of Americans without steady work or subsistence.

In part because *The Other America* invigorated antipoverty policy in the 1960s, the demography of the poor has changed significantly. Between 1959 and 1998, the poverty rate among the elderly declined from 35 percent to 10 percent in response to a large increase in Social Security benefits. Structural changes in the economy reduced the numbers of the rural poor as farm employment declined significantly over the last four decades of the century. As in the early 1960s, however, the invisibility of today's poor remains rooted in the physical and social distance between whites and blacks. Residential segregation, dividing neighborhoods along racial lines, resisted legally mandated integration and black economic progress.[5] Poor urban blacks are the most isolated. The most recent data from the 2000 census showed that blacks were most segregated in cities where racial inequality in incomes was highest.[6] The underclass, the master concept for a generation of poverty researchers, pinpoints the profound separation of poor blacks from the American mainstream. The underclass, being chronically jobless, is outside the class structure. Not just poor, the underclass appears behaviorally deviant, mired in crime and family disruption. The underclass is thus defined by its social remoteness, its invisibility, as much as by its deprivation. This remoteness has a physical reality (the poor live separately from the middle class), and a social reality (the everyday routines and experiences of the poor are unlike those of the middle class).

The invisibility of the poor results not from immiseration but from inequality. The poor are invisible not because they are in desperate straits, but because they are beyond the horizon of middle-class social experience. If poverty and unemployment were commonplace, as they were during the Great Depression, middle-class families would also know the anxieties and deprivations of job loss and the dole queue. Under mass unemployment, economic misfortune is palpable and more commonly attributed by the middle class to the failures of society, not to individual deficiency. Orwell, for example, writing *The Road to Wigan Pier* in 1937, was struck not by the social isolation and hyper-segregation that marks today's urban poverty, but by the vast ubiquity of idleness in northern England. "Even the middle classes," he writes, "are beginning to realize that there is such a thing as unemployment."[7] Sociologists of the life course see the Great Depression as forging an entire birth cohort. Poverty in that case was formative, imprinted on the collective biography of a generation reaching midlife after the second world war. The generation of the Great Depression in some ways experienced a more disorderly path through the life course. The pressure of economic circumstances often delayed marriage but adolescence was cut short by the necessity of finding a job.[8] Contemporary poverty, however, is a by-product of inequality that redirects economic losers away from the social mainstream.

The prison boom makes a new contribution to the invisibility of the poor in a profound way. Imprisonment conceals criminal offenders by removing them from the poor communities that feed the penal system. These inmates occupy a shadowy status that affects a variety of official statistics that record the economic well-being of the population. In many cases, prison and jail inmates are not counted in government measures of economic activity, joblessness, or poverty. The invisibility of the penal population in our official accounts underlines the depth of inequality generated by incarceration. The task of this chapter is to render the penal population visible in our assessment of economic trends and inequalities over the last twenty years. As we'll see, much of the optimism about declines in racial inequality and the power of the U.S. model of economic growth is misplaced once we account for the invisible poor, behind the walls of America's prison and jails.

INCARCERATION AND OFFICIAL STATISTICS

Imprisonment makes the disadvantaged literally invisible because the penal population is omitted from the data sources used to track economic trends. Government statistics like poverty rates, unemployment rates, and wage levels are compiled from large surveys run regularly by the Census Bureau. The surveys draw from a large list of American households. People who live in any kind of institution, such as an old age home or army barracks, are excluded. The most common institutionalization among young men, as might be expected, is incarceration in prison or jail. These prison and jail inmates, as we have seen, are overwhelmingly minority men with low levels of schooling. When we count the poor or the jobless, vast numbers of young disadvantaged men are overlooked because they are incarcerated.

At one level, this is unremarkable. Employment rates, for example, are defined only for the noninstitutional population. Prison and jail inmates fall outside the definition, and outside the official statistics of the labor market. However, statistics on employment and wages are useful because they tell us something in general about the economic status of the population, not just the officially defined population. The demographer Clifford Clogg made this observation in relation to the unemployment rate. Although official unemployment refers only to the nonworking labor force actively seeking work, the unemployment rate is also an important but imperfect indicator of labor utilization—the degree to which the population is productively engaged.[9] It is relatively straightforward to measure the unemployment rate, but a more complete measure of labor use would gauge the economic self-sufficiency and well-being of the entire population.

The penal system dramatically influences the distribution of labor. Prison and jail inmates, mostly young able-bodied men, are not in paid employment. Beyond the reach of household surveys, prison and jail inmates have no economic status, either productive or unproductive. How should we classify the economic status of the penal population? Some might say that prison work programs are a type of employment and that inmates in work programs should therefore be counted as employed. Work in prison industries, however, confers none of the rights or economic independence we associate with paid employment. Prison work programs are not covered by minimum wage or industrial relations laws, an inmate's standard of living is not improved by work in prison industries, and inmates of course are not free to quit their jobs and search elsewhere. Thus the Census Bureau rightly regards the incarcerated population as not working, reserving the employment classification for those in paid jobs on the open labor market.

If the penal population is classified as jobless, the penal system reallocates labor, rendering prison and jail inmates invisible in official statistics. We can more accurately measure the economic status of the population and the labor-allocative effect of the penal system by calculating alternative figures that include the incarcerated population.

How much difference does it make to simply count these incarcerated men when we assess the economic status of the population? One simple approach compares a common measure of employment, the noninstitutional employment-to-population ratio, to an alternative figure that includes the prison and jail inmates in the population. Less obviously, the penal population also affects measured wage inequality by removing low-wage workers from the lower tail of the wage distribution. The employment and wage data reported in this chapter show that mass imprisonment generated substantial invisible inequality through the 1990s, when it appeared that strong economic growth was broadly improving the living standards of all Americans.

INCARCERATION AND HIDDEN JOBLESSNESS

Employment in the population is usually measured by an unemployment rate or an employment-to-population ratio. The unemployment rate is too restrictive for studying socially marginal groups because it does not count the long-term jobless who are discouraged from seeking work. The employment-to-population ratio is a simpler measure counting only those with jobs, indicating them as a fraction of the population. Because my interest centers on those out of work, I report a jobless-to-population ratio—one minus the typical employment ratio. If we rely on the usual labor force surveys, the jobless consist of the unemployed and those not in the labor force for a variety of reasons, including invalids, students, and others who are not seeking work. I make two adjustments to standard statistics based on household survey data to provide a more complete account of the population. First, to measure the share of the population who are gainfully employed, I include the military. Second, I add prison and jail inmates to the count of those who are not employed.

The share of the penal population among the jobless increased with the incarceration rate. Figure 4.1 shows jobless rates for white, Hispanic, and black men aged twenty-two to thirty in 1980 and 2000. The shaded portion of each bar in the figure represents the incarcerated fraction of the jobless population. In 1980, ninety thousand prison and jail inmates accounted for only about one in twenty jobless young white men. By 2000, the number of young white males behind bars had climbed to 185,000 and one out of every eight of those out of work was incarcerated. In 2000, the conventional jobless rate for young white men was 10.6 percent; the figure rises to 12.0 percent once the penal population is counted.

The contribution of incarceration to joblessness is larger for Hispanics and blacks. Between 1980 and 2000, the number of young incarcerated Hispanic men grew from 25,000 to 130,000. By 2000 the penal population ac-

Figure 4.1   Jobless Men

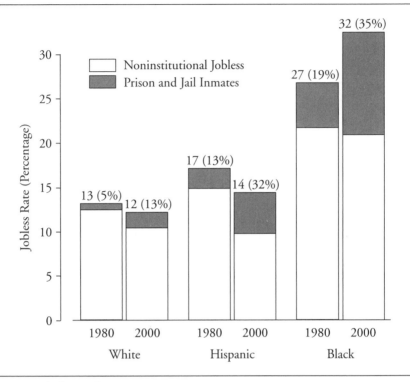

Source: Author's compilations.
Note: Figures in parentheses are the percentage of inmates among the jobless.

counted for 30 percent of all joblessness among Hispanic males aged twenty-two to thirty. This level of incarceration lifts the conventional jobless rate from 10.3 to 14.3 percent in 2000. Overall rates of employment are lowest for African Americans, regardless of whether prison and jail inmates are counted among those not working. In 1980, in the noninstitutional population alone, 22.9 percent of young black men were out of work, roughly double the jobless rate for whites at that time. Joblessness among young blacks rises to 26.7 percent in 1980 once prison and jail inmates are added to the population. Between 1980 and 2000, the population of young black incarcerated men increased from 110,000 to 285,000. One out of every three young black men out of work in 2000 was in prison or jail. Household survey data indicated that joblessness stood at 23.7 percent of young black men in 2000, but adjusting for incarceration raised the true rate to 32.4 percent.

Young black men were the only group to experience a steep increase in joblessness between 1980 and 2000, and this was due to the increase in the penal population.

EDUCATIONAL INEQUALITY IN HIDDEN JOBLESSNESS

The contribution of the penal system to low rates of employment among young black men is larger if we focus just on men who have never been to college, that is, on the dropouts and high school graduates. Figure 4.2 shows, among young men for the year 2000, jobless rates and the fraction of prison and jail inmates among the jobless. Joblessness is reported only among those without a college education and high school dropouts. (As before, military personnel are also counted in all these figures.) Accounting for the penal population adds little to our understanding of the prevalence of employment among noncollege white men. The conventional jobless rate is 12 percent, and 15 after the penal population is counted. The discrepancy is a little larger for Hispanics. Conventional statistics tell us that 10 percent of all young noncollege Hispanic men were out of work in 2000. This figure rises to 15 percent once we account for joblessness attributable to incarceration. The jobless rates for blacks are remarkably high. Although standard data sources show that joblessness among young noncollege black men stood at 30 percent in 2000, the true jobless rate in the population, including prison and jail inmates, was 42 percent. Among young less-skilled black men, two out of five of those not working were incarcerated.

At the very bottom of the education ladder, among young male high school dropouts, the share of concealed joblessness in the penal system is larger still. Figures for young black male dropouts indicate that the noninstitutional jobless rate increased from 34 to 49 percent in the twenty years from 1980. If we include prison and jail inmates among those out of work, the true jobless rate increases from 41 to 65 percent. Only by counting the penal population do we see that fully two out of three young black male dropouts were not working at the height of the 1990s economic expansion. Of those not working, nearly half were in prison or jail.

Differences between conventional jobless rates and adjusted rates that include prison and jail inmates point to the large biases in employment estimates based on household surveys. To put these biases in perspective, the household surveys are designed to produce accurate estimates of employ-

Figure 4.2   Jobless High-School Educated Men in 2000

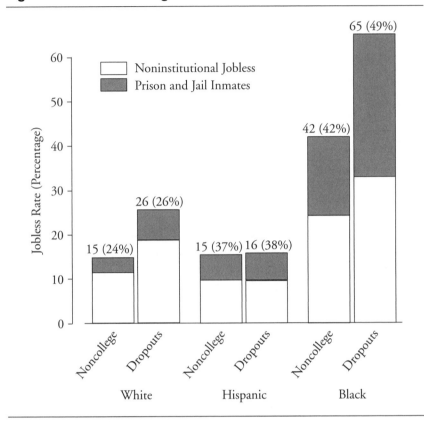

Source: Author's compilations.
Note: Figures in parentheses are the percentage of inmates among the jobless.

ment, to within fractions of a percentage point. By omitting the penal population, standard estimates underestimate the true jobless rate by as much as 24 percentage points for less-educated black men.

These statistics tell us several things. First, standard labor force data significantly overestimate the prevalence of employment among young black men, particularly those without higher education. Rates of joblessness among young black men, already high in official statistics, are really one-fifth to one-quarter higher, given so many men in prison and jail. Second, because of the large racial disparity in incarceration, racial inequality in employment is significantly understated by standard data sources.

Figure 4.3   Black-White Ratio in Jobless Rates, Noncollege Men

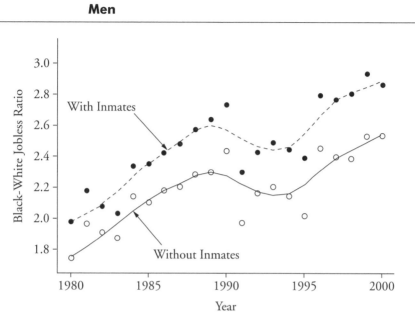

Source: Author's compilations.

RACIAL INEQUALITY IN JOBLESSNESS

Inequality can be measured with the ratio of black to white jobless rates. To study how incarceration conceals inequality, we focus just on the employment situation of noncollege men aged twenty-two to thirty. Figure 4.3 shows the trend in the black-white ratio in jobless rates for the noninstitutional population and for the corrected rate that includes prison and jail inmates. The trend lines indicate that racial inequality in employment increased significantly, both in the noninstitutional population and in the general population that includes prison and jail inmates. Standard statistics suggest that the black-white ratio increased to around 2.5 by 2000; that is, young black noncollege men are 2.5 times more likely to be out of a job than their white counterparts. Including prison and jail inmates raises the ratio to 2.9, indicating that standard data sources understate racial inequality by about one-fifth among young men with only a high school education.

THE 1990S EXPANSION REVISITED

Including the penal population in our estimate of the jobless rate also provides a more accurate understanding of the link between the economic status of socially marginal men and trends in the economy as a whole. In a famous remark that became a hypothesis for countless poverty researchers, President Kennedy observed that a "rising tide lifts all boats." A strong economy, he suggested, would provide economic benefits to even the most disadvantaged. For most of the postwar period until the early 1970s, this appeared to be true. Strong economic growth was associated with increased wages for less-skilled workers with little education. The rising tides hypothesis appeared to break down following the recession of 1973. For the next twenty years, through the ups and downs of the business cycle, income inequality increased steadily and workers at the bottom of the income distribution increasingly lost ground.

The rising tides hypothesis was reprised during the 1990s economic boom. From 1992 to 2000, the United States enjoyed its longest and largest peacetime economic expansion. The unemployment rate dropped from 7.5 percent in 1992 to 4 percent in 2000, and the economy added about eighteen million new jobs. These effects were widely celebrated not least because of the beneficial effects at the margins of the labor market among less-skilled workers. Strong economic growth and low unemployment, it seemed, could significantly improve living standards for the most disadvantaged in society. In February of 1999, the *Washington Post* sounded a familiar theme: "Unemployment rates among blacks and Hispanics fell last month to the lowest levels since the federal government began tracking them in the early 1970s, as the nation's booming economy created more jobs than expected, lifting many of the unemployed who have been left behind during other good times."[10] The *New York Times* similarly reported that "after nearly eight years of growth, the tightest labor market in decades is having a noticeable effect on [young black men's] participation in the work force and on employers' willingness to hire them." In an otherwise buoyant assessment of the labor market, the *Times* added cautiously, "the employment figures do not reflect the growth in the percentage of young black men who are in jail or prison, so it is unclear whether things have improved quite as much as the jobs data show."[11] Indeed, the penal population was invisible in the government jobs data, and no figures counting inmates among the jobless were published in official statistics or by the media.

Did the surging labor market of the 1990s improve employment among young and less-skilled men? The most common barometer for the performance of the labor market as a whole is the unemployment rate. We can study whether the boats of young minority men were lifted by the rising tide of job growth by comparing the overall unemployment rate of the labor force to jobless rates for young noncollege men. Figure 4.4 plots national unemployment rates against the noninstitutional and incarceration-adjusted jobless rates for white, Hispanic, and black men in their twenties who had not been to college, the top left-hand panel shows the jobless rate among young white noncollege men in the noninstitutional population. There is a clear positive relationship between overall unemployment and joblessness among young less-skilled whites. The regression line indicates that a 1-point fall in overall unemployment is associated with a 1-point fall in the jobless rate for white male youth in the noninstitutional population. Counting prison and jail inmates among those out of work slightly weakens the relationship, so that a 1-point fall in unemployment accompanies .7-point fall in the jobless rate for young noncollege whites. Employment rates among young Hispanics are more tightly linked to overall unemployment. Regardless of how joblessness is measured, falling unemployment rates in the late 1990s is associated with increasing employment rates for noncollege Hispanics in their twenties.

The connection between overall unemployment rates and jobless rates for young, black, less-skilled men is very weak, however (figure 4.4). If we look just at noninstitutional men, the trend line slopes upwards, indicating that a 1-point fall in the total unemployment rate has been associated with .6-point fall in the jobless rate among young noncollege black men. If prison and jail inmates are counted among the jobless, the trend line slopes downwards, indicating that the economic prospects of young black men largely became detached from the path of the labor market as a whole. Joblessness significantly increased among young noncollege black men at the end of the 1990s when economic conditions were generally improving for the rest of the population.

In sum, prison and jail inmates are invisible in the official labor statistics that describe the economic well-being of the population. Once the penal population is added to statistics on joblessness, the prevalence of employ-

Figure 4.4   **Unemployment and Jobless Rates for Noncollege Men, Age 22 to 30, 1980 to 2000**

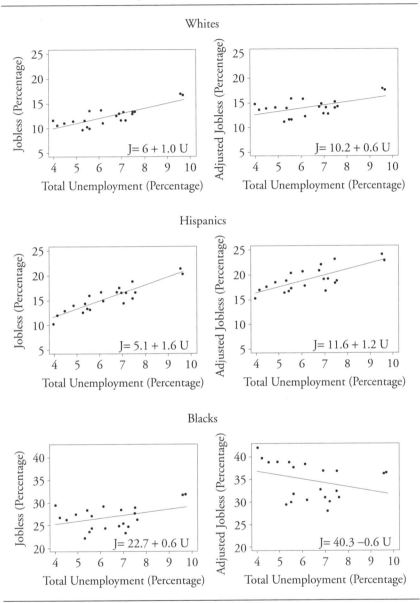

Source: Author's compilations.

Note: Regression lines indicate the trend. (All jobless rates count military personnel as employed.)

ment can be seen to be significantly overestimated among young, less-skilled black men. More than this, ignoring the penal population also causes us to underestimate the rise in racial inequality in employment. By 2000, young whites with just a high school education were about three times as likely to be holding a job as their black counterparts. Finally, linking trends in incarceration-adjusted joblessness to the national unemployment rate shows that the economic fortunes of men whose incarceration risks were highest became completely detached from trends in the labor market as a whole. As the unemployment rate sank to historically low postwar levels in the late 1990s, jobless rates among noncollege black men in their twenties rose to their highest levels ever. This increase in joblessness was propelled by historically high incarceration rates.

INCARCERATION AND THE RACIAL GAP IN WAGES

Employment figures provide just one indicator of economic status. We can also consider how wage trends are affected by the hidden disadvantage produced by high incarceration rates. All things being equal, wage and employment rates should move together. When the economy is expanding, demand for labor will be strong and employers will compete for workers, driving up wages and the level of employment. However, the risk of joblessness is not distributed evenly across the labor market. Employment among less-skilled men lagged behind the rest of the labor force. If those who are likely to earn low wages drop out of the workforce, the average level of wages may actually increase. That is, the average wage rises because the bottom end of the wage distribution is erased by joblessness. In this case, the rise in average wages is not due to any real improvement in the economic situation of wage earners; it is simply an artifact of less employment at the bottom. This is a type of sample selection effect. If those selected for employment are a nonrandom sample of all workers, the average wage will no longer reflect the typical economic status of all workers.

The sample selection analysis helps us understand the puzzle of declining employment among black men through the 1960s, a period when wages were growing strongly. Many researchers attributed the rapid growth in wages of black men relative to whites to the passage of the Civil Rights Act and other measures that reduced racial discrimination in the labor market. Richard Butler and James Heckman observed that income-transfer benefits increased at the same time as passage of the Civil Rights Act. Increased welfare benefits, they argued, drew low-wage men out of the labor force. Increased average earnings of blacks relative to whites was due to declining employment among low-pay black workers rather than an upward shift in the income distribution.[12]

Other researchers have wondered if earnings are a good measure of black economic progress given low employment rates among black workers. The economist Finis Welch asks if the "improvement in black/white wage ratios is an illusion." Gerald Jaynes observes that "the most important problem" for research on race relations "is to explain why, if the market's relative valuation of black labor has increased, black employment has been declining."[13] These comments reflect a suspicion that increased wages are an artifact of declining employment. If low earners are discouraged from seeking work or if they are in prison, average incomes will increase, not because pay is going up but because those at the bottom have dropped out of the workforce.[14] Under these conditions, deepening economic disadvantage may be misinterpreted as economic progress.

The sample selection analysis sheds light on invisible inequality in the context of the prison boom. Just as mass incarceration removes prison and jail inmates from official employment statistics, it also removes them from the wage distribution. The selection analysis puts wage trends of the 1980s and 1990s in a new light. From the mid-1980s to the late 1990s, the black-white gap in wages was shrinking among young men aged twenty-two to thirty (figure 4.5). In 1985, the average hourly wage of white men in their twenties exceeded that for young black men by about 30 percent. By the end of the 1990s, racial inequality in hourly wages had declined to 21 percent. However, joblessness among black men steadily increased during this period, mostly because of the increasing incarceration rate. Is the decline in wage inequality the product of a real improvement in the labor market situation of young black workers, or is it simply an artifact of escalating rates of imprisonment and other joblessness among those with little earnings power?

I assess the effect of imprisonment and joblessness on racial inequality in wages by predicting the wages of nonworkers and inmates. These predicted wages can be interpreted as the wage offers that nonworkers would have received had they been in the labor force. These predicted wages are then included with the wages of workers, to account for the effect of joblessness on the average wage. Adjusting average wages in this way can be understood to

Figure 4.5   Hourly Wages and Wage Ratio of Male Workers

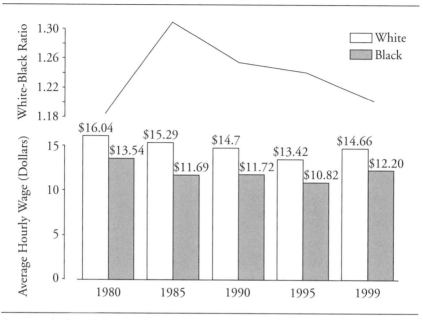

Source: Author's compilations.
Note: Wages are in 2003 dollars for men age 22 to 30.

monetize the economic status of marginal segments of the population who are typically ignored in studies of economic inequality.

Earlier research on selection and average wages focused on trends from the 1960s through the 1980s. I study wage inequality through the 1980s and 1990s by analyzing data from the Current Population Survey (CPS) and correctional surveys of inmates. Like previous research, wages of the jobless are predicted, given age and education that capture the main human capital differences in wages (see the appendix at the end of this chapter for more detail).[15] The analysis is restricted to non-Hispanic, nonfarm, civilian men aged twenty-two to thirty.

The analysis divides jobless men into two categories. First, there are the nonworkers, those who are unemployed and looking for work, and those not employed and not looking for work. To impute the wages of nonworkers, I match them to the wages of workers according to age and education. The wage offers that nonworkers are likely to receive will be lower than those we observe among workers. A more realistic estimate could simply take a frac-

Figure 4.6   Wages of Workers and Inmates at Incarceration

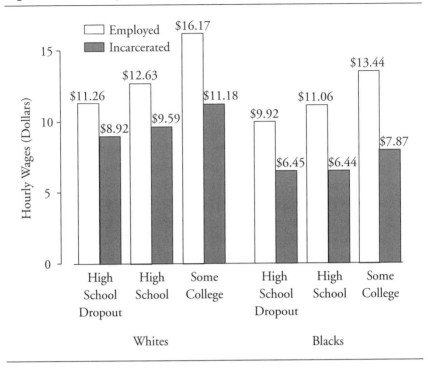

Source: Author's compilations.
Note: Wages are in 2003 dollars for men age 22 to 30.

tion of the observed wage among workers. I assume that nonworkers would receive only 80 percent of the wage offered to workers. This is a conservative assumption compared to other studies.[16] My estimates of the effects of labor inactivity on the black-white wage gap are probably a little conservative as a result. Second, there are prison and jail inmates. The hypothetical wage offers of incarcerated men are likely to be much lower than those for nonworkers. Fortunately, correctional surveys of inmates that ask respondents about their wages immediately before incarceration are available (see figure 4.6). About a third of inmates were not working when admitted to prison or jail. Pre-incarceration wages are reported by 30 to 50 percent of respondents in each of the nine correctional surveys fielded from 1979 to 1997. These data are used to estimate the hypothetical wage that inmates would receive if offered jobs on the open labor market.

Figure 4.7   Hourly and Adjusted Wage Ratios

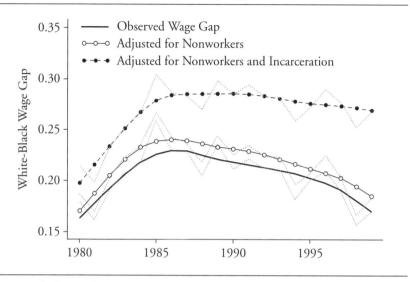

Source: Author's compilations.

Note: The wage gaps have been smoothed to highlight the trend. Estimates of the wage gap are indicated by the gray lines. (The wage gap is measured by the differences in mean log hourly wages.)

Underscoring their low of levels of ability and poor employment records, prison and jail inmates earn significantly less at the time of their incarceration than other young men aged twenty-two to thirty with the same level of education (see figure 4.6). Young white dropouts earned just over $11.00 an hour. By comparison, young white inmates averaged only $8.92 an hour at the time of their incarceration. The wage gap grows with education. Young whites with some college earned more than $16.00 an hour in 1999, compared to $11.18 for college-educated inmates. There is also a large wage gap between workers and inmates among African Americans. Despite the relatively low earnings of black workers, their wages exceed those of inmates by about 70 percent.

Figure 4.7 shows three measures of racial inequality in wages of young men aged twenty-two to thirty. The lower line shows the observed level of wage inequality calculated from the usual household survey. In 1980, the hourly wage of young white men exceeded that for black men by 17 percent. Racial inequality in hourly wages increased through the early 1980s and peaked in 1985, when whites earned about 26 percent more than blacks. Over the next fifteen years, however, wage inequality steadily declined. At the height of the 1990s economic expansion, in 1999, the black-white difference in hourly wages was 16 percent. Between 1985 and 1999, the ratio declined by 9 percentage points, or more than a third of the observed wage ratio. Was this gain in relative wages among young black men a real improvement relative to young whites, or did it result from declining employment fueled by the growth in imprisonment?

The upper time series in figure 4.7 begins to answer this question by showing estimates of the level of wage inequality we would observe if nonworkers and then prison and jail inmates were fully employed. If the unemployed and those who are not in the labor force are accounted for, the estimates indicate that in 1980 young white men would earn about 22 percent more than young blacks, 4 percent higher than the observed difference. Over the next five years, this adjusted level of wage inequality grew more quickly than the observed level. In 1985, whites are estimated to enjoy hourly wages 31 percent higher than those of blacks. Although the adjusted wage gap between blacks and whites is estimated to decline from the mid 1980s to the end of the 1990s, the inequality can be seen to be more enduring once race differences in joblessness are taken into account.

The top series in figure 4.7 reports the level of white-black wage inequality adjusting for nonworkers and prison and jail inmates. What would trends in wage inequality look like if nonworkers were fully employed and those incarcerated held jobs in the open labor market? Because of their low levels of education and earnings, prison and jail inmates add even more to the race gap in wages. Reflecting the large number of incarcerated poor men, wage inequality among young men would have been about 30 percent higher (34 compared to 26 percent) if the entire population were fully employed. Adjusting for nonworkers and prison and jail inmates also shows that the economic status of young black men has not improved relative to whites since the mid-1980s. After adjusting for nonworkers and prison and jail inmates, racial inequality in wages is estimated to fall just 9 percent (from .34 to .31 log points), instead of the observed decline of 35 percent (from .26 to .17 log points). By 1999, the observed ratio of white to black hourly wages understated the relative economic status of young black men by about 45 percent because such a large number of less-skilled black men were out of work or incarcerated.

In sum, the racial gap in wages provides a poor indicator of the relative economic status of young black men. Much of the economic disadvantage of black men, because of their high rates of unemployment and incarceration, is hidden from standard statistics on the wage gap. If we account for the large numbers of less-educated men out of work or in jail, racial inequality in 1999 would have been about twice as high as its observed level. Adjusting for racial disparities in joblessness and incarceration also suggests that young black men have experienced virtually no real economic gains on young whites in the fifteen years since 1999. Indeed, around three-quarters of the apparent gains in relative wages are attributable not to a real improvement in the economic situation of African Americans, but to escalating rates of joblessness and incarceration.

ECONOMIC PROGRESS AMONG BLACK YOUTH IN THE 1990S

There is strong evidence for large racial inequalities in employment and wages among young men through the 1980s and 1990s. These statistics, as gloomy as they are, overstate the economic status of young black men and underestimate inequality. Standard labor force statistics provide an optimistic picture of black economic progress because so many poor young black men are institutionalized, and thus outside the scope of labor market accounts. Poverty researchers have often argued that the poor are invisible, beyond the consciousness and social experience of the middle class. The invisibility of the penal population is even more profound, erased from economic reality altogether.

The effects of the prison boom on invisible inequality are especially important for interpreting economic trends through the 1990s. Incorporating prison and jail inmates in employment and wage figures suggests that the 1990s expansion did not improve the labor market situation of young non-college black men. Joblessness for young black men without college education increased through the late 1990s when job growth was strongest, and black employment rates fell significantly behind those of whites. Racial inequality in wages declined from 1985 to 1999, but about two-thirds of this drop appears due to attrition from the labor force, largely caused by rising incarceration rates.

The performance of the U.S. labor market at the end of the 1990s captivated policy makers and pundits in the United States and western Europe.

By standard accounts, the labor markets of western Europe were performing poorly compared to the American. France, Italy, and Germany had all experienced high levels of unemployment throughout the 1990s. High rates of official unemployment accompanied a high level of long-term unemployment, stagnant job growth, a high rate of disability, and significant youth unemployment. The booming labor market in the United States created large numbers of new jobs, drove unemployment to full employment levels. Although the U.S. labor market clearly performed better than those in Europe, the boldest claims were reserved for the poor. Young less-educated Europeans were mired in long-term unemployment, but the American labor market—it seemed—provided significant economic benefits to economically vulnerable groups.

Researchers pointed to institutional differences to explain why the United States was doing so well, and why Europe was doing so poorly. Institutional analysis of labor markets focused on the effects of social policy and industrial relations.[17] The United States provided a model of market deregulation. American unions were weak and the welfare state affected only those at the fringes of the job market. Contrast Europe, where employment relations are highly regulated. Unions set wages for entire economies and welfare states significantly influence the supply and demand for labor.

The U.S. economic expansion suggested that unregulated labor markets, those without strong unions or generous welfare states, could greatly reduce joblessness, especially for less-skilled workers. Without unions or welfare benefits, workers were forced to look for work, even at very low wages, to make ends meet. Market competition, unfettered by social protections, worked to the benefit of those with the least market power. In Europe, the analysts claimed, institutions introduced inefficiency: large welfare states and strong unions stifled labor demand, prevented wages from falling to market-clearing levels, and reduced work incentives.[18] In short, the unregulated labor market of the United States produced high rates of employment for the less-skilled, whose European counterparts remained idle because of the market-distorting inefficiencies of expansive welfare states and strong labor unions. Robust economic growth could apparently deliver the economic opportunity that welfare programs could not.

The invisible disadvantage produced by mass imprisonment challenges this account of how meager social protections benefit the least-skilled workers. At the end of the 1990s in the United States, these men were not forced on to the labor market in large numbers to look for low-wage work. Their economic marginality instead exposed them to the criminal justice system. Many were incarcerated. The government, rather than withdrawing from the lives of young disadvantaged blacks, significantly increased its role. Lawmakers who, in other contexts, would celebrate the value of limited government and free markets, adopted policies that massively and coercively regulated the poor. We have seen in this chapter that this led to a profound social exclusion in which the economic status of disadvantaged young men was significantly overestimated. This did not require any conspiracy on the part of policy makers. Invisible inequality was the unintended consequence of a mass imprisonment produced by a combustible mixture of elevated crime rates, a political upheaval in race relations, and a chronic shortage of jobs in poor inner-city communities. In the context of controversy about the merits of American and European models of labor market policy, we can see that chronic joblessness is as much a political as an economic fact. Missing, perhaps, some social supports of the European kind, violence, disorder and idleness flourished in America's ghettos, creating for government not just an economic problem, but a problem of social control.

CONCLUSION

Many sociologists like to remind economists that "institutions matter" and that not all social life is like a competitive market with rational buyers and sellers. Many economists are rightly indignant, because they know better than most the importance of institutions. Any economics text will discuss at length the effects of labor unions or unemployment benefits on wages and employment, for example. The message of this chapter is not just that institutions matter, but that noneconomic institutions matter. Economic reality is deeply embedded in social relations that determine who is in the economy, and who is out, who has an economic status, and who does not. From this perspective, the institutional landscape for low-wage work consists not of labor unions and government programs alone. In the era of mass imprisonment, we must also consider the significant labor-allocative effect of the American penal system.

We can think of the penal system's invisible inequality as the short-run effect of incarceration, the immediate consequence of institutionalizing large numbers of working-age men. Of course, nearly all those men are released from incarceration, and many negotiate the obstacles to job seeking they encounter as ex-offenders. This long-run effect of incarceration on the economic life of men released from prison and jail is the topic of the following chapter.

APPENDIX: ADJUSTING WAGES FOR SELECTIVITY

This analysis is based on that reported in Western and Pettit and further technical details are available there.[19] If log wages of white and black men are written y_w and y_b, then the difference in mean wages is given by $\bar{d} = \bar{y}_w - \bar{y}_b$. Because hypothetical offer wages of the jobless are not observed and the jobless are likely to come from the lower tail of the wage distribution, $\bar{d}$ is a biased estimate of the wage differential. To adjust for selective attrition from employment, calculate:

$$\hat{d} = \hat{y}_w - \hat{y}_b$$

where the adjusted means, $\hat{y}_i$ (i=b, w), are based on imputed mean wages for nonworkers. Omitting the race subscripts, the adjusted mean wage is the weighted average,

$$\hat{y} = (1 - p_N - p_I)\,\bar{y}_E + p_N\bar{y}_N + p_I\,\bar{y}_I,$$

where the subscript E denotes the mean calculated for workers from observed wages, $\bar{y}_N$ is the mean wage for nonworkers (the unemployed and those not in the labor force), $\bar{y}_I$ is the mean wage of the incarcerated, and the weights, p_N and p_I are proportions of the population not working or incarcerated. The proportions p are calculated from the age-race-education specific incarceration and jobless rates calculated by combining data from the Outgoing Rotation Group files of the Current Population Survey from 1980 to 1999, administrative counts of the correctional population (from the National Prisoner Statistics and the Survey of Jails series), and data from the *Survey of State and Federal Correctional Facilities* and the *Survey of Local Jails* (1978 through 1997).

Like previous research, wages of the jobless are predicted as a function of age and education.[20] Age is measured discretely in two categories: twenty-two to twenty-five, and twenty-six to thirty. Education is divided into three categories: less than a high school diploma or equivalent, high school diploma or GED, and at least some college. The predicted mean wage for workers and prison and jail inmates come from the regressions,

$$\bar{y}_j = \bar{X}'_j b_j, \quad j = E, \text{ or } I,$$

where age and education data are collected in the matrices, X_j, and $\bar{X}_j$ is a vector of covariate means. The imputed wage for nonworkers is given by $\bar{y}_N = k\bar{X}'_N b_E$, where the constant k is set to .8, where nonworkers' wage offers are assumed to be 80 percent of those obtained by workers. The 80-percent figure is indicated by estimates from the NLSY. (Judith Blau and Peter Beller make the stronger assumption of 60 percent, and other authors also make adjustments of this kind.)[21] The regression includes age by education interactions, yielding predicted wages for each age-education subgroup. Predicted wages for workers are obtained from the Outgoing Rotation Group files of the Current Population Survey (1980 through 1999). Predicted wages for prison and jail inmates are obtained from the *Surveys of State of Federal Correctional Facilities* and the *Survey of Local Jails* (1978 through 1997). If X_j consists of $2 \times 3 = 6$ columns of dummy variables indicating each cell in the age-by-education table, $\bar{X}_j$ is simply a vector of cell proportions for workers, nonworkers, and prison and jail inmates.

CHAPTER 5

The Labor Market After Prison

Through the end of the 1990s, the American labor market was celebrated for its dramatic job growth that contrasted with the stagnant employment figures coming out of western Europe. For young men at the bottom of the labor market, this triumphalism was premature. The mass incarceration of less-educated minority men concealed declining employment and produced phantom reductions in wage inequality. This invisible inequality defied buoyant assessments of American prosperity.

The economic expansion slowed, but did not reverse, a thirty-year rise in American economic inequality. Termed "the new inequality," the income distribution had spread more for men than women, and most clearly by levels of education.[1] The wage gap between rich and poor men (measured by the ratio of the 90th to 10th percentile) widened by about 20 percent from 1973 to 2001. The wage advantage of college graduates over men with high school diplomas grew by 65 percent.[2] Even though poverty and joblessness among disadvantaged men was hidden by the penal system, American economic inequality by the beginning of the new century was at its highest since World War II.

The economic losers of the last thirty years, young minority men with little schooling, were also captives of the prison boom. The relationship between prison growth and falling wages among disadvantaged young men can be interpreted several ways. Men with felony records have difficulty finding well-paid jobs. Some researchers have found that incarceration reduces earnings and employment.[3] Perhaps the prison boom has contributed to U.S. earnings inequality, at least among young men, by reducing the wages and employment of criminal offenders after they have been released from prison.

Of course, a different story could also be told. We saw in chapter 3 that falling wages and employment were closely associated with increasing imprisonment among young men with little schooling. Imprisonment increased largely because the criminal justice system had become more punishing. But these men were vulnerable to arrest in the first place because they were involved in violence and street crime more than most. If men with few legitimate job prospects resort to drug dealing or sticking up stores, unemployment and low pay may be due to a selection effect. Former prisoners may flounder on the labor market, not because they've been incarcerated, but because they lacked skills and work experience before they were first sent to prison.

Here I examine how incarceration affects ex-prisoners' employment, placing these effects in the context of the new inequality in the U.S. labor market. I treat incarceration as a key life event that triggers a cumulative spiral of disadvantage. Incarceration reduces not just the level of wages, it also slows wage growth over the life course and restricts the kinds of jobs that former inmates might find. Incarceration redirects the life path from the usual trajectory of steady jobs with career ladders that normally propels wage growth for young men. Men tangled in the justice system become permanent labor market outsiders, finding only temporary or unreliable jobs that offer little economic stability. Although this new class of stigmatized workers may swell the ranks of the severely disadvantaged, much of the analysis here also weighs the deficiencies of men involved in crime whose job prospects would be perilous even in the absence of incarceration.

THE LABOR MARKET AND CRIMINAL OFFENDERS

The young disadvantaged men who face the highest rates of incarceration are pulled in several directions as they try to make ends meet. The concentrated poverty of inner-city neighborhoods erodes the web of social connections that often restrains crime in urban areas. Lacking neighbors with their eyes on the street, and without much adult supervision for teenage males, poor neighborhoods are acutely exposed to the risks of crime and delinquency.[4]

Economic incentives also contribute to the correlation between crime and poverty. Thus many researchers have linked the rise of the illegal drug trade and other street crime to the collapse of urban labor markets for less-skilled men.[5] Crime provides an inviting alternative to a legitimate labor market where unemployment rates are desperately high. Drug dealing, robbery, thieving, and fencing stolen property can all help fill the economic gap in neighborhoods drained by deindustrialization of blue-collar jobs. This can be dangerous work, however, and as Levitt and Venkatesh showed in their research on Chicago gangs, low-level drug dealers see little of the ghetto fabulous lifestyle, earning little more than the minimum wage and regularly supplementing their incomes with legal earnings.[6] Freeman and Fagan probably best characterize the relationship of those involved in crime to the labor market: such men are fully engaged in neither crime nor legitimate employment. Instead, they drift back and forth as the possibilities for legal and illegal income ebb and flow.[7]

The association between crime and disadvantage is reflected in the skills and employment histories of the penal population. Table 5.1 compares young male prisoners to the general population along a variety of measures linked to labor market success. Prisoners have little education, with most having dropped out of high school.[8] The educational level of Hispanic prisoners, many of whom are immigrants, is particularly low. They average a full year less education than black and white inmates in state prison. Even given their poor education, prisoners also score low on cognitive tests. These skills have been measured prior to incarceration by the Armed Forces Qualification Test (AFQT), a standardized examination measuring math and verbal ability. Among young men who have dropped out of high school, prisoners score 20 to 50 percent lower on the AFQT than those who have never been incarcerated. Lacking education and cognitive skills, men going to prison fare poorly on the labor market. At the time of their incarceration, men in prison were less likely to have a job and, if they did, earned less than the rest of the population. Pre-incarceration employment rates are especially low for black prisoners. Over a third were not working when they were sent to prison. The income gap is also very large, with white prisoners at the time of their incarceration earning just half the monthly income of non-prisoners at the time of their incarceration. In short, these figures indicate that even be-

Table 5.1   Education, Cognitive Skill, and Employment

	Prisoners	Noninstitutional Men	Percentage Difference
Whites			
Average schooling (years)	10.6	13.4	21
Average cognitive score for dropouts	19.5	23.7	22
Percentage employed	76.4	87.5	13
Median monthly income (dollars)	1100	2000	45
Blacks			
Average schooling (years)	10.5	12.6	17
Average cognitive score for dropouts	7.6	11.4	50
Percentage employed	63.2	73.1	14
Median monthly income (dollars)	900	1520	41
Hispanics			
Average schooling (years)	9.4	10.8	13
Average cognitive score for dropouts	9.9	14.9	51
Percentage employed	73.5	85.3	14
Median monthly income (dollars)	900	1568	43

Source: Employment, earnings, and schooling figures for noninstitutional men are from the Current Population Survey (1997). Employment, earnings, and schooling for prisoners is given at time of prison admission and are from the Survey of Inmates of States and Federal Correctional Facilities (1997).

Note: Cognitive scores are the percentiles of the Armed Forces Qualification Test for male high school dropouts from the NLSY 1979 who were imprisoned some time between 1980 and 2000 and among those who have never been to prison.

fore incarceration, men at risk of going to prison have far less human capital, in the form of skill and labor market experience, than the rest of the population.

Men coming out of prison get low-paying, insecure jobs because they have few skills or work experience. An ex-offender is likely to get a bad job primarily because he is a poor worker. Although men involved in crime are at high risk of low pay and unemployment, can going to prison make things worse? Can incarceration damage a man's economic fortunes, even accounting for the poor opportunities for young men with very little skill or schooling?

THE ECONOMIC PENALTY OF INCARCERATION

Researchers have indeed found that men released from prison or jail do earn less, and are employed less, than those who have not been incarcerated. Estimates of the earnings loss associated with imprisonment range from 10 to 30 percent.[9] A few studies also report that youth detained in correctional facilities before age twenty have higher unemployment and receive lower wages a decade or more after incarceration.[10] Three explanations have been offered for the poor labor market experiences of formerly incarcerated men. The stigma of a criminal conviction, in the eyes of employers, makes ex-offenders undesirable job applicants. The experience of incarceration can reduce human capital, making ex-convicts less productive workers. Incarceration can also reduce social capital, eroding the social connections to legal employment.

A criminal conviction signals prospective employers that a man is untrustworthy and perhaps dangerous. Several early studies examined the effects of criminal stigma by sending employers fictitious job applications that contained the conviction status of job applicants.[11] Employers responded less positively to ex-convicts than to applicants who provided no such information. Surveys of employers also show that they would much prefer to hire a welfare recipient, high school dropout, or someone with little work experience than a former convict.[12] Perhaps the most compelling evidence is the audit study of Devah Pager. Pager randomly assigned resumes to pairs of specially trained black and white job applicants. The resumes showed identical work experience and education, but one of the two indicated recent employment in prison and listed a parole officer as a reference. The applicants interviewed for 350 jobs in Milwaukee in the summer of 2001. Pager recorded whether employers called back to offer a job or schedule a second-round interview. Among whites, applicants without a criminal record received callbacks from employers 34 percent of the time, compared to 17 percent for those who said they had been to prison. Among blacks, the figures were 14 percent and 5 percent.[13] That is, having a prison record reduced a job applicant's success by half to two-thirds.

In most jurisdictions, the stigma takes on a legal significance. A felony record can temporarily disqualify employment in licensed or professional occupations. Restrictions on employment often extend to jobs in health care, skilled trades, and sometimes the public sector.[14] In a few states, such as California and New York, antidiscrimination laws prevent employers from asking job applicants about arrests that did not result in a conviction. Most states, however, allow employers and occupational licensing agencies to obtain the full criminal records of job applicants and to use information about convictions in hiring. Take Florida, for example. Public agencies in Florida can deny employment for a felony conviction. Private employers and licensing agencies can refuse to hire or license anyone with a criminal conviction. These legal barriers extend beyond employment and include prohibitions on public assistance and food stamps for those convicted of drug trafficking.[15]

If the stigma of a criminal record reduces earnings, we might expect little difference in the effects of arrest, conviction, probation, or incarceration. From the employer's viewpoint, each run-in with the law carries similar information about the trustworthiness of a prospective worker. Different studies have distinguished the effects of juvenile delinquency, arrest, probation, and conviction from admission to prison. Prison admission and other incarceration are usually found to have larger and more persistent effects than other kinds of criminal justice contact or criminal behavior.[16] This suggests that criminal stigma may not be the only mechanism reducing the employment and wages of men coming out of prison.

Incarceration may also erode job skills. Where social stigma describes employer perceptions of those with criminal records, the erosion of job skills describes real deficiencies in the potential productivity of former inmates that result from the imprisonment. Incarceration may undermine job skills by removing men from the marketplace from which they might otherwise gain work experience. Evidence for this effect is given by research showing that the offenders serving long sentences suffer the largest loss in earnings.[17] Incarceration may also reduce an inmate's ability to stay in regular employment after release. Existing mental or physical illnesses can also be aggravated by prison time. Many behaviors that are adaptive for survival in prison—suspicion of strangers, aggressiveness, withdrawal from social interaction—are inconsistent with work routines outside.[18] These behavioral adaptations to prison life deplete an inmate's small supply of human capital and create obstacles to managing the routine of steady work.

Incarceration may affect social as well as human capital. Long terms of imprisonment, often in distant facilities, can thin the ranks of friends and acquaintances who might help former prisoners find work. Prisons and jails may attach men more closely to serious offenders. Indeed, the old reformers of the nineteenth century saw prison as a school for criminals, and introduced solitary confinement precisely to reduce the contagion of corrupting influence. In a contemporary context, ethnographers have described the diffusion of criminal contacts in prison through gang recruitment.[19] Because workers regularly find jobs through social contacts who can then vouch for job applicants to employers, job seekers without social ties to legitimate employment opportunities face significant disadvantages in the labor market.[20] Men returning home from prison—who are most closely tied to those involved in crime than to those who are not—are thus missing an important avenue to employment.

STUDYING INCARCERATION WITH SURVEY DATA

Research on the economic effects of incarceration often relies on official data on arrests, corrections, and earnings. Court or correctional records are commonly linked to earnings data from the unemployment insurance system because few surveys follow men in and out of correctional institutions.[21] Unemployment insurance records, however, are likely to understate much of the labor market activity of men involved in crime because such individuals often work in day labor and other casual jobs.[22] If earnings are observed only for those who find jobs in the formal economy, the analysis will suggest that former inmates are doing better on the labor market than they really are. On the other hand, the unemployment insurance data might significantly understate the earnings of ex-convicts who are able to make a good living with off-the-books incomes.[23] Administrative data also provide little information about offenders besides age and race. Many of the factors often used in labor market studies, such as schooling and work experience, are often simply not included in administrative data.

Survey data are rarely used because few surveys include institutionalized respondents or ask about imprisonment. One exception, the NLSY, reports on youth detention and adult incarceration and provides detailed data on employment and earnings.[24] Begun in 1979, the NLSY interviewed a national sample of young men and women aged fourteen to twenty at the end of 1978.[25] The respondents were interviewed each year until 1994, and every other year after that.

Although the survey respondents are not regularly asked if they have been to jail, the interviewer records the type of residence the respondent is living in. The most common is the respondent's own home, but dormitories, military bases, and other housing types are also registered. Every year, a number of respondents are listed as resident in "jail." Residence in a correctional facility, however, will not record everyone who has served time. Incarceration for less than twelve months (such as jail terms) may be missed in the yearly interviews. Sentences exceeding twelve months (as prison sentences typically are) are recorded. The NLSY incarceration rate closely matches national imprisonment rates for young men indicating accurate measurement in the survey of prison time among felony offenders.[26]

ESTIMATING THE LABOR MARKET EFFECTS OF INCARCERATION

The labor market experiences of former prisoners can be measured in several ways. Researchers often examine hourly wages because this gives a good indication of a worker's productivity. However, many ex-prisoners will have only a tenuous attachment to the labor market and this will be reflected more in their employment rates than their pay rates. I studied employment by examining the number of weeks worked in the year by the NLSY survey respondents. Finally, annual earnings provide an omnibus measure that reflects a worker's wage rate and his employment. More than hourly wages or annual employment, annual earnings also convey a sense of the living standards of working-age men.

Table 5.2 shows the average hourly wage, the annual number of weeks worked, and the annual earnings of the NLSY men at age twenty-seven. The hourly wages of men involved in crime are much lower than those of men who never go to prison. The wage gap is largest for whites. Those who will later go to prison earn only three-quarters of what their counterparts earn— $11.14 versus $14.70. For blacks and Hispanics, the wage gap grows after offenders have been incarcerated. The employment situation of all offenders deteriorates after incarceration. White, Hispanic, and black ex-prisoners all spend around six months a year or more out of work. The drop in earnings after getting out of prison is largest for black offenders, from $13,340 to $7,020. These raw figures suggest that incarceration damages the employment prospects of men with criminal records, but it is also clear that men bound for prison, even before they are incarcerated, do worse on the job market than the rest of the population.

Table 5.2   Wages, Employment, Earnings

	Incarceration Status		
	Never	Before	After
Hourly wages (dollars per hour)			
White	14.70	11.14	11.80
Hispanic	13.59	12.30	10.31
Black	12.34	10.25	9.25
Annual employment (weeks per year)			
White	44	37	23
Hispanic	43	35	24
Black	40	35	21
Annual earnings (thousands of dollars per year)			
White	26.44	13.70	9.76
Hispanic	23.90	13.29	9.14
Black	20.37	13.34	7.02

Source: Author's compilations.
Note: Figures are calculated from the NLSY. "Never" includes all those who have not been incarcerated by age forty. Hourly wages and annual earnings are in 2004 dollars. (N = 5010).

Because the penal system draws mostly from the lowest rungs of the socioeconomic ladder, simply measuring the wage gap between prisoners and nonprisoners overstates the penalty of incarceration. Low levels of education, cognitive deficits, and behavioral problems may explain why ex-offenders are out of work. Incarceration may add little to the problems of young men involved in crime. How can we tell if low wages and joblessness among former prisoners is caused by incarceration, or is simply a predictable result of skill deficiencies and a propensity to antisocial behavior?

Answering this question raises a challenge for casual analysis. In a capricious world in which people were imprisoned at random, men with prison records would share the same average levels of education, test scores and so on, as those without records. Selection for incarceration would resemble a randomized experiment, in which the treatment group (prisoners) was identical to the control group (nonprisoners) in all respects except incarceration status. If men with prison records differed only randomly from everyone else, we could calculate imprisonment's effect by comparing the wages of ex-prisoners to those of others. Because incarceration is assuredly not random, we must try to account for the distinguishing factors.

Social scientists have lately paid more attention to the challenge of causal analysis outside the laboratory, where treatments are not assigned randomly but instead closely associated with confounding factors. Where data are collected on both the treatment and confounding factors, we can narrow our comparison of treatment and control groups to those who share the same observed characteristics. Studies of training programs involving ex-offenders find that control groups drawn from the whole population yield inaccurate causal inferences about program effects. Choosing a control group that is similar to the treatment group—prison and jail inmates in our case—can greatly improve estimates of causal effects.[27] To narrow the comparison of the NLSY prisoners, I identified as a control a small group of men in the survey who were involved in crime but never interviewed in prison. They had got in trouble with the law as juveniles or reported that they had been unable to look for work because they were in jail. The control group helps ensure that we won't confuse the effects of incarceration with the preexisting problems of ex-offenders.

A similar approach involves regression analysis, which statistically controls for the effects of observed factors associated with imprisonment. We have seen that men in prison share low levels of education, low test scores, and little work experience. A regression analysis can control for factors like these to isolate the causal impact of imprisonment on employment. The focus on incarceration also leads us to account for things not usually included in labor market studies. For example, because prisoners are more likely to have problems with drug addiction, and addiction compromises regular work routines, the analysis controls for the drug use among NLSY respondents. In many cases, however, important factors confounded with a treatment are *not* observed. Prisoners are not unusual only for their poor schooling or drug use. Many also have behavioral and health problems not recorded by social surveys. These unmeasured idiosyncrasies—impulsive or aggressive personalities, say—can lead to overestimates of causal effects.

Data collected at several time points can be used to account for unobserved factors that might bias a causal analysis. With observations over time, we can compare individuals before and after they receive a treatment. Comparing a man's wages before and after imprisonment controls for all the enduring traits of personality and behavior. Statistical researchers call this a fixed-effect analysis. In this context, the fixed effects are the stable but unobserved characteristics of individuals that are removed from the analysis by examining variation within individuals over time. With time-series data, regression analysis can be augmented to control for both observed factors that change over time and fixed effects. This kind of analysis provides a significant advance over the usual regressions that control only for observed factors.

Two common findings about crime support the current approach. First, crime is strongly age graded; people tend to commit the most crime in late adolescence, that is, from ages sixteen to twenty.[28] Controlling for age and other time-varying factors such as school enrollment will thus capture a great deal of how an individual's propensity to crime changes over time. Second, though crime is age graded, people show stable differences in their tendency to commit crime.[29] Thus studies that track individuals over long periods find that most crime is committed by only a few offenders.[30] Fixed effects are well suited to such a population, capturing stable differences in an individual's criminal propensity.

What if confounding factors are not observed but do change over time? In this case, fixed effects may do little to reduce bias in a causal analysis. Some methods introduce new variables that try to mimic the randomized variation of the controlled experiment. For such methods to work here, we must observe conditions that are closely related to incarceration but little else. Unfortunately, as in many applications, such variables are hard to find. My approach then involves trying a variety of analyses, with several different outcomes, and examining the stability of the results across statistical models. Controlling for observed confounding factors with regression, introducing fixed effects, and restricting the analysis to men who are involved in crime, can go a long way to isolating the causal impact of incarceration on the labor market experiences of former prisoners.

INCARCERATION'S EFFECTS ON WAGES, EARNINGS, AND EMPLOYMENT

Estimates are based on NLSY data from 1983 to 2000. I begin by calculating the effects of incarceration on hourly wages, annual employment, and the annual earnings of crime-involved men in the NLSY survey. Wages and earnings were adjusted for inflation and reported in 2004 dollars.

Figure 5.1   Reduction in Employment, Wages, and Earnings Associated with Incarceration, 1983 to 2000

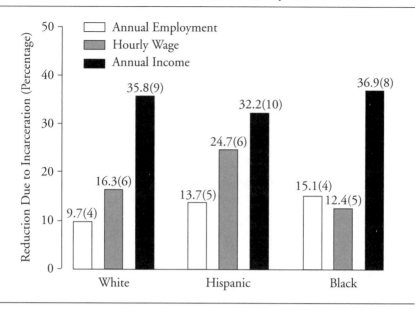

Source: Author's compilations.

Note: Wages and earnings are measured in 2004 dollars. Figures in parentheses indicates a 95-percent margin of statistical error. Estimates are from fixed-effect models that control for age, education, work experience, industry, region of the country, public sector employment, union status, marital status, drug use, school enrollment, urban residence, local unemployment, year, and an education-by-year interaction.

The results show that men who have been incarcerated have significantly lower wages, employment rates, and annual earnings than those who have never been incarcerated (see figure 5.1). Incarceration is generally estimated to reduce hourly wages by about 15 percent, but the effect is relatively large among Hispanics (24.7 percent). The average hourly wage of thirty-year-old Hispanic high school dropouts is about $7.45, and incarceration is estimated to reduce this by about $1.80. The effect is smallest for black ex-offenders, who are paid 12.4 percent less than blacks who have never been to prison. The large effect of incarceration on Hispanic men's wages is not replicated in data on employment. In this case, both black and Hispanic men work around 15 percent fewer weeks in the year (nearly eight weeks) than their counterparts. The effect of incarceration is slightly less for white men, reducing employment by 9.7 percent (about five weeks a year).

The negative effects on hourly wages and annual employment combine to substantially reduce annual earnings. Men with prison records are estimated to earn 30 to 40 percent less each year. A thirty-year-old black high school dropout, for example, earns on average nearly $9,000 annually, with incarceration resulting in a reduction of about $3,300. The parallel white earnings average $14,400, and the reduction about $5,200.

INCARCERATION AS A PATHWAY TO THE SECONDARY LABOR MARKET

So far we have seen strong evidence that former inmates earn lower hourly wages and annual incomes and are at greater risk of unemployment than their counterparts who have never been to prison. We can take the analysis further by considering how incarceration shapes the kinds of jobs ex-offenders might find.

Sociologists and economists have traced some inequalities in the labor market to a structural divide in which some workers hold stable career jobs and others are consigned to temporary or insecure work. Perhaps foreshadowing Richard Freeman's predictions of a two-tiered society produced by the new inequality, the economists Peter Doeringer and Michael Piore saw a sharp dividing line in the U.S. labor market of the late 1960s. On one side, well-paid career jobs clustered in what Doeringer and Piore called the primary labor market. On the other, low-income unsteady jobs characterized the secondary labor market. In the primary sector, large firms developed long-term employment relationships with workers who built skills and moved up well-defined career ladders, or acquired seniority in union jobs that protected against layoff. Union jobs, skilled trades, and public sector positions were all examples of primary sector jobs available to workers with only a high school education. In the secondary market, jobs were insecure and paid little.[31] Arne Kalleberg and his colleagues provide an updated picture of the secondary labor market with a catalogue of bad job characteristics from the 1995 Current Population Survey. Part-time or temporary work, paying low-wages, and offering no health or pension benefits accounted for one in seven of all U.S. jobs in 1995 and were staffed mostly by women and minorities.[32]

The long-term employment relationships of primary sector jobs are built on and foster trusting relations between worker and manager. To make investments in skills and training, managers must trust their workers to stay with the firm and repay the investment. Workers must trust managers to provide job security and a career ladder, particularly early on if primary sector wages are lower than those offered in the open labor market. George Akerlof has described this ethic of mutual obligation as a partial gift exchange, in which hard work and loyalty are exchanged for job security and the promise of high wages.[33] If primary sector jobs depend partly on the mutual obligation and trust between workers and managers, where does trust come from?

If a firm will commit its resources to a long-term employment relationship, it must find a match that will repay this commitment. Partly, it seems, this is narrowly an economic consideration. Highly skilled workers may be seen as the best bet for primary sector jobs. Employers may also rely on job referrals from friends and acquaintances. An acquaintance vouching for a job applicant may plant the seed of trust that might blossom into full-time employment. Indeed, referral networks have been found to be important for entering white-collar, skilled trade, and public sector jobs.[34] Contrast secondary labor markets, where employers pay only enough to attract job seekers and make no long-term promise of job security or a career. Successful job seekers in the market for low-wage work are less likely to be known to the employer.

A prison record prevents trust and the long-term employment relationships from developing. A prison record diverts ex-offenders from career jobs through its effects on skills, social connections, and criminal stigma. The stigma of incarceration does not prohibit employment entirely. It simply limits entry into high-status or career jobs. Researchers have found that men in trusted or high-income occupations before conviction are unable to return to those positions, and experience especially large earnings losses after release.[35] The civil disabilities that limit ex-felons' entry into licensed occupations and skilled trades further reduce their access to the primary sector of the labor market. The stigma of conviction, in its formal and informal forms, thus reduces ex-convicts' access to jobs requiring trust and offering reliable employment.

The low productivity of ex-offenders also harms their chances in the primary labor market. Primary sector employers invest in personnel training, expecting the investment to pay off as workers are promoted through the ranks. Without much schooling or cognitive ability, ex-inmates look like bad investments. Many ex-offenders are therefore restricted to the secondary sector, where employment is precarious and wages are stagnant.[36]

Finally, the social contacts that provide information about job opportunities may be eroded by incarceration. Social ties can provide the basis for trust that enables an employer to hire a job seeker. Long spells of incarceration erode prisoners' ties to their communities and the pivotal social contacts who might vouch for them in the labor market. Indeed, if prison strengthens a man's ties to those involved in crime, a former prisoner's social networks may actively inhibit the chances of finding a good job.

Although most research focuses on the average earning loss associated with incarceration, a few studies observe that the penal system channels ex-inmates into unsteady jobs with little wage growth. Thus Robert Sampson and John Laub found that time served in prison by youth aged seventeen to twenty-five was negatively related to continuity of employment and work commitment at ages twenty-five to thirty-two.[37] Urban ethnographers similarly report that the prison system provides a pathway to secondary labor markets and informal economies.[38] Mercer Sullivan's field work shows how trouble with the authorities sidetracked Hispanic youth in New York City from skilled employment. As teenagers, Sullivan writes, "participation in income-producing crime and the resulting involvement in the criminal justice system in turn kept them out of school and forced them to abandon their occupational goals. Gaspar Cruz and Mario Valdez gave up the vocational programs to which they had gained admission."[39] Appointments with probation officers, the lack of vocational skills, and the stigma of a criminal record all conspired against steady work as the boys got older.

> By the end of their teens most of these youths had found and lost several jobs and were definitely if insecurely participating in the labor market. Wages, though irregular, replaced theft as their major source of income. . . . They were still frequently unemployed and generally made low wages when they did work.[40]

Robert Evans, studying employment among parolees, makes a similar point: "Obtaining employment was not a real problem; instead it was the character and quality of the jobs that was the problem."[41] Although former inmates can often find work, they are short on the trust, skills, and social contacts that open doors to primary sector jobs.

If incarceration closes access to primary sector jobs, the effects of imprisonment are likely to extend beyond the wage and employment penalties I have estimated so far. In the secondary labor market, jobs don't just pay poorly; employment is also insecure. Besides low pay and insecure employment, secondary labor market jobs are missing the age-graded pay scales, union seniority provisions, and career ladders that drive wage growth for young men in the primary sector. In short, wage growth is slow for secondary-sector workers. If incarceration is a pathway to the secondary labor market, we should thus see high job turnover and slow wage growth among ex-offenders.[42]

I conducted two additional tests to study the involvement of former inmates in the secondary labor market. To examine job turnover, I calculated whether they had spent less time in their current jobs than those without prison records. The second test examined whether wages increased more slowly. Like the wage and employment analysis, I tried to improve estimates of the causal effects of incarceration by analyzing only data on men involved in crime, controlling for fixed effects and variables correlated with prison time and poor employment outcomes.

To describe incarceration's effect on job tenure, I calculated the time spent working in the current job for two hypothetical men. Except for their incarceration status, these men are observably identical, working in the same industry, having the same age, education, history of drug use, and so on. The incarceration gap in job tenure is not statistically significant for white men (figure 5.2, top panel). The difference is significant among minority men, however. A formerly incarcerated black man is estimated to have spent about fourteen weeks less in his current job than a man who has never been incarcerated (twenty-one versus thirty-five weeks job tenure). Hispanic workers in the NLSY averaged about twenty-eight weeks in their current job, but the job tenure of Hispanic ex-inmates is twelve weeks less. These results for blacks and Hispanics indicate that steady long-term employment is less common among men with prison records.

Slow-growing wages are related to rapid job turnover. The lower panel of figure 5.2 shows the inflation-adjusted wage for formerly incarcerated and never-incarcerated men at age twenty-five and thirty-five. White, black, and Hispanic former prisoners all experience significantly slower wage growth than their counterparts without prison records. Hourly wages for most whites grow by more than 20 percent from $11.18 to $13.81 in that decade. White ex-prisoners, on the other hand, experience virtually no growth from their starting wage of $10.61 an hour. Wages for blacks are lower than those for whites. A black man without a criminal record, at age twenty-five, earns

Figure 5.2   Job Tenure and Hourly Wage Growth

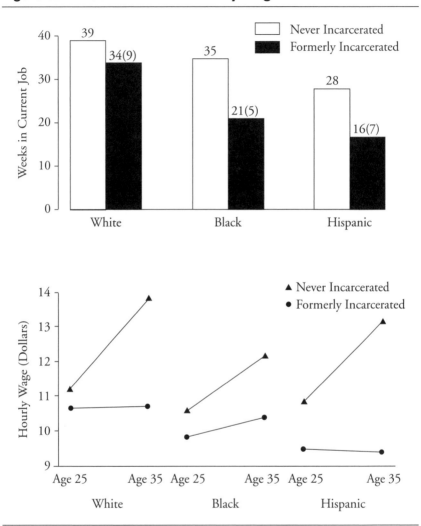

Source: Author's compilations.
Notes: Top panel depicts average weeks employed in current job at age twenty-five. (Statistical error in parentheses.) Bottom panel estimates of wage growth and job tenure are from fixed-effect models that control for age, education, work experience, industry, region of the country, public sector employment, union status, marital status, drug use, school enrollment, urban residence, local unemployment, year, and an education-by-year interaction.

about the same wage as a white man with a record—around $10.60 an hour. By age thirty-five, the black worker's wage had grown to around $12.15 an hour, an increase of 15 percent. Among black former inmates, wages grow only a third as fast—just 5 percent from $9.85 to $10.40. Hispanics show a similar pattern, with ex-prisoners experiencing no wage growth compared to those with clean records seeing 20-percent increases.

In sum, men without prison records experience strong growth in hourly wages through their late twenties and early thirties. Typical of men in the secondary labor market, ex-prisoners record no significant increase in pay as they age into their mid-thirties. These results for job tenure and wage growth of men with prison records offer strong evidence that incarceration carries not just an economic penalty on the labor market; it also confines ex-prisoners to bad jobs characterized by high turnover and little chance of moving up the income ladder. This economic cost of imprisonment underlines the economic immobility of men with prison records.

Normally as men age through their twenties and thirties, they enjoy the substantial wage growth of steady employment. This security of livelihood and prospect of economic improvement has sociological as well as economic significance. Secure employment and the expectation of economic mobility allow men to move along the life course and become integrated into a variety of social roles, as a breadwinner, head of a family, a spouse, and a father. A spotty employment record and low-wage jobs make men unattractive prospective marriage partners as well as making it difficult for them to support a household. Secondary labor market jobs thus inhibit ex-prisoners from completely fulfilling many other adult roles. Incarceration emerges as a decisive life event that largely forecloses upward mobility.

THE AGGREGATE EARNINGS PENALTY OF INCARCERATION

Earlier we saw that the life course of a generation of young black men born since the 1960s was transformed by the prison boom. Imprisonment became a normal stage in the development of those who left high school early, affecting over half of young black male dropouts by their mid-thirties. Analysis of the survey data suggests that the economic effects of imprisonment are substantial and long-lasting. Serving time behind bars reduces a man's wages, annual employment, and total annual earnings. It also redirects the life course by relegating ex-convicts to a secondary labor market that offers neither job security nor economic mobility. There is, then, strong evidence that the poor economic performance we see in ex-inmates is attributable to imprisonment.

The individual-level effects of imprisonment appear quite large—annual earnings are reduced by 30 to 40 percent, and a prison record extinguishes wage growth from age twenty-five to thirty-five. Do these individual-level effects combine with pervasive incarceration to yield large aggregate effects on the incomes of minority and less-educated men?

I extended the survey analysis by examining whether aggregate earnings would change much if none of the respondents had gone to prison. The first row of table 5.3 shows the prevalence of incarceration among the NLSY men. Over the course of the survey from 1979 to 2000, nearly one in five blacks and one in ten Hispanics had been incarcerated at some time, compared to one in twenty whites. Over the twenty-one years of the survey, incarceration is estimated to reduce a man's total earnings by between $85,000 and $114,000. The earnings loss of white ex-prisoners is large because whites in general earn more on average than blacks and Hispanics.

The total lost earnings resulting from incarceration is expressed as a fraction of the total earnings of incarcerated men, and as a fraction of the total earnings of all men (table 5.3, rows 3 and 4). Focusing first on those who go to prison, the total lifetime earnings would be about 40 percent higher if the men had not been incarcerated. The total dollar cost of lost earnings for the 556 male NLSY respondents who were incarcerated is estimated at $53.5 million. As a fraction of the total earnings of all men, the aggregate effect of incarceration is relatively small. Among white men, incarceration produces a loss of less than 1 percent of total lifetime earnings. The economic loss produced by imprisonment is more than twice as large for Hispanics, but even in this case, total lifetime earnings are estimated at only 2.1 percent higher than if the incarceration rate were zero. Among blacks, the earnings loss begins to acquire real importance. If incarceration were reduced to zero, the total lifetime earnings would be more than 4 percent higher.

Incarceration does not much reduce total earnings but does increase poverty. Poverty is usually measured by the share of the population who live on less than a given (very low) income. For this exercise, I define as poor those who fall in the lower tenth of the distribution of lifetime earnings. Row 5 of table 5.3 shows the percentage driven below this threshold because of incarceration. Among whites, incarceration has caused lifetime poverty among 1 percent. The effects are larger for minority men. If there were no

Table 5.3   Aggregate Levels of Imprisonment and the Aggregate Effects of Imprisonment on Lifetime Earnings, 1981 to 2000, NLSY Men

	White	Hispanic	Black
1. Men imprisoned by 2000 (percentage)	5.0	11.3	19.3
2. Average lifetime earnings loss ($1000s)	114.3	93.6	86.3
3. Lost lifetime earnings as percentage of total earnings of incarcerated	43.6	41.2	42.3
4. Lost lifetime earnings as percentage of total earnings of all men	.8	2.1	4.3
5. Percentage point increase in poverty rates among all men	1.0	2.7	4.0
6. Lost lifetime earnings as percentage of imprisonment cost	148.8	94.4	70.4

Source: Author's compilations, BJS (2004).
Note: Estimates of the lifetime earnings loss are based on inflation-adjusted 2004 dollars, calculated for the full male sample of the NLSY. Poor men (row 5) are defined as those in lower decile of the race-specific lifetime earnings distribution. Costs of imprisonment (row 6) are taken from a BJS (2004) report on state prison expenditures.

incarceration among Hispanics, the poverty rate would fall by 3 percentage points from 7 to 3 percent. The largest effect is found among poor blacks. With the current definition, 18.5 percent of black men are poor, falling into the bottom decile of the NLSY earnings distribution. Without incarceration, 4 percent of young blacks—one-fifth of all poor blacks— would be lifted out of poverty, and the poverty rate would fall to 14.5 percent.

Although incarceration contributes significantly to poverty among black men, it does not add much to racial inequality in lifetime earnings. For example, the difference in earnings between blacks and whites would be reduced only by about 3 percent if the incarceration rate were zero. The aggregate effects are small in part because those at risk of incarceration earn so little even if they do not go to prison. Although incarceration exacts a relatively large penalty at the individual level, a 40-percent earnings loss has little effect in the aggregate when those suffering the loss are already below the poverty line. These results show that mass imprisonment has contributed less to racial inequality than to inequality among blacks by raising the black poverty rate. More than driving a wedge between the incomes of blacks and whites, incarceration has increased the distance between poor blacks and the middle class.

Another calibration compares the earnings loss of incarceration to the cost of imprisonment. Usually, the cost of imprisonment is calculated only from correctional budgets and includes the salaries of prison staff, the costs of services provided to prisoners, and the other operating costs of running prisons. The earnings loss experienced by ex-prisoners is also an economic cost of the penal system, however. The lost earnings would otherwise pay taxes, support families, and generally contribute to the level of activity in the broader economy. How does the lifetime earnings loss compare to the cost of incarceration?

The Bureau of Justice Statistics reports that in 2001, the annual operating costs of the American state correctional systems totaled $28.4 billion, or $22,650 per inmate.[43] The cost of a prison bed is much higher in the Northeast, about $33,000 a year, and lower in the South, about $16,500. Using the average figure of $22,650, the total cost of imprisonment of the NLSY respondents from 1983 to 2000 equals $54 million. The lifetime earnings loss expressed as a fraction of this incarceration cost suggests that the real cost of incarceration is nearly 150 percent higher than its budgetary costs for whites (table 5.3, row 6). For Hispanics, the real cost is about 95 percent higher. Among blacks, because their earnings loss is relatively small, the cost is 70 percent higher In total, the lost earnings due to incarceration roughly doubles the prison budget.

Calculations like these recall similar figures produced by penologists to weigh the cost effectiveness of imprisonment. Estimates of the economic costs of crime are compared to correctional budgets to see whether "prison pays."[44] That research produced very little consensus about the economic cost of crime, with consequently little agreement about the cost-effectiveness of prison. My point here is not to muddy that water further, but simply to show that a variety of costs associated with imprisonment are typically not calculated in the usual assessments of criminal justice policy. If we think that prison pays, and the costs of incarceration offset the costs of crime prevented, a full accounting of the economic cost of incarceration should also consider the lifetime of lost earnings experienced by those released from prison.

CONCLUSION

Over the last thirty years, the emergence of a new inequality eroded the living standards of less educated minority men as economic opportunity accrued to those with college degrees in the expanding economies of the suburbs and the Sunbelt. Young minority men with just a high school education bore the brunt of deindustrialization in the inner cities and experienced the largest increases in incarceration. Earlier we saw that pervasive incarceration accompanied the eroding economic position of less-skilled blacks. Not only was economic disadvantage associated with an increased risk of incarceration, it was also deepened by serving time in prison. For those with a prison record, hourly wages were reduced by around 15 percent, and annual earnings fell by 30 to 40 percent.

Incarceration was more than a temporary setback that could be repaired with time in the labor force. Instead, spending time behind bars was a turning point that punctuated the working lives of many less-skilled men involved in crime. A prison record—with its stigma and effects on human capital and social networks—hampered former inmates from entering that cadre of labor market insiders. For the insiders, steady employment and career jobs laid the foundation for progress through the life course—getting married, establishing a household, and having children. Former prisoners, on the other hand, experienced little wage growth and none of the modest affluence that comes with age. These individual-level effects of incarceration were large. The aggregate consequences of imprisonment (at least for the NLSY survey respondents) were smaller, however. At the aggregate level, incarceration has had its largest effect within the black community, increasing the distance between poor men and the middle class. The diminished earning potential, on the other hand, is not a major source of the income gap between black and white men. Still, the economic cost of incarceration is significant when compared to the cost of prison beds. The lifetime of lost earnings that results from a prison record doubles the cost of incarceration measured by correctional budgets.

The lost earnings and employment also threaten penal policy's goal of crime control. Criminologists regularly report evidence of rehabilitation rooted in steady employment. A stable, supervised job eliminates the idleness that provides men with an opportunity to commit crime. The routine of daily work reinforces an ethic of mutual obligation between the worker and employer, and between the worker and those that depend on that paycheck.

These obligations provide those who are involved in crime with a stake in conformity that reduces offending. By reducing earnings and consigning ex-prisoners to the secondary labor market, incarceration produces the economic conditions for continued crime. If a stable job offers a route to criminal desistance, limited employment opportunities raise serious obstacles to fully joining society after an offender has served his time.

The costs of a high incarceration rate for the poor urban communities that supply most of the nation's prison inmates do not stop with the labor market. The strong urban labor markets of the 1950s held the fabric of social life together, supporting families and preventing crime. The collapse of urban labor markets for less-skilled men in the 1960s and 1970s swelled the ranks of the ghetto poor. Rising urban poverty in turn contributed to increases in the number of children born outside marriage and in the growing number of female-headed households. The diminished working lives of former inmates are also likely to have these follow-on effects on family life and children. We now turn our attention to families and children caught in the web of the penal system.

APPENDIX: ANALYZING THE NLSY

The results here are based on regression analyses of log hourly wages, log annual earnings, and weeks worked per year.[45] All these analyses are confined to subsamples of crime-prone men who are either incarcerated, report criminal justice contact in the 1980 crime module, or who report jail incarceration in the employment supplements of 1989 to 1993. For respondent i at time t, the regression is written:

$$y_{it} = a_1 C_{it} + a_2 P_{it} + x'_{it}b + u_{it},$$

where C_{it} is dummy variable that indicates those currently in prison, P_{it} scores 1 in all years after the first incarceration, and zero otherwise, and x_{it} is a vector of covariates. The error term, u_{it}, consists of a fixed effect for each respondent and random error. The coefficient a_1 just measures the incapacitation effect—the earnings lost while in prison. The coefficient, a_2, measures the post-release effect of incarceration. The effects of incarceration reported in this chapter are based on the post-release coefficient, a_2. To estimate the effect of incarceration on wage growth, I fit an interaction between age and incarceration, P_{it}.

CHAPTER 6

Incarceration, Marriage, and Family Life

As imprisonment became common for less-educated black men by the end of the 1990s, the penal system became familiar to their families. By 1999, 30 percent of noncollege black men in their mid-thirties had been to prison and through incarceration many were separated from their wives, girlfriends, and children. Women and children in low-income urban communities now routinely cope with husbands and fathers lost to incarceration and adjust to their return after release. Poor single men are also affected, burdened by the stigma of a prison record in the marriage markets of disadvantaged urban neighborhoods.

Discussions of the family life of criminal offenders typically focus on the crime-suppressing effects of marriage rather than on incarceration. Researchers find that marriage offers a pathway out of crime for men with histories of delinquency. Not a wedding itself, of course, but marriage in the context of a warm, stable, and constructive relationship offers the antidote to crime.[1] Wives and family members in such relationships provide the web of obligations and responsibilities that restrain young men and reduce their contact with the male friends whose recreations veer into antisocial behavior.[2] The prison boom places the link between crime and marriage in a new light. If a good marriage is important for criminal desistance, what effect does incarceration have on marriage?

The connections between incarceration, marriage, and the family are also implicated in the larger story of rising urban inequality. Over the last three decades, American family life was transformed by declining marriage rates and growth in the number of single-parent households. Between 1970 and 2000, the share of white women aged twenty-five to thirty-four who were married declined from over 80 percent to just over 60. Marriage rates for African American women dropped from 60 to around 30 percent. The decline in marriage propelled growth in the number of single-parent households, although this effect was confined to those with little education.[3] The share of college-educated single mothers remained constant at around 5 percent but that of their less-educated counterparts increased from 8 to 18 percent. Trends were most dramatic among less-educated black women, with the share of single mothers increasing from about 30 to over 50 percent. By 2000, stable two-parent households had become relatively rare, especially among blacks with less education.

Poverty researchers closely followed the changing shape of American families. Growing numbers of female-headed families increased the risks of enduring poverty for women and children. Growing up poor also raised a child's risk of school failure, poor health, and delinquency. Writing in the mid-1980s, William Julius Wilson traced the growth in the number of female-headed black families to the shrinking number of "marriageable men" in poor urban neighborhoods.[4] The shortage was driven by two processes. High rates of male incarceration and mortality tilted the gender ratio, making it harder for poor urban women to find partners. These effects were small, however, compared to the high rate of joblessness that left few black men in inner cities able to support a family. Many studies later examined the impact of men's employment on marriage rates and found that the unemployed are less likely to be married and that joblessness can increase chances of divorce or separation.[5] Studies of the effects of employment dominated research on marriage among the disadvantaged, and the idea that incarceration destabilized family life was not developed.

Here I study the effects of the prison boom on marriage and the family. Given its prevalence among young less-educated black men, imprisonment may have devastated family life in poor urban neighborhoods. Before accepting this hypothesis, though, we should consider that criminal offenders are unlikely to marry or develop strong family bonds, even if they do not go to prison. I try to untangle the links between the penal system, marriage, and the family with three pieces of empirical evidence. First, to better understand the familial bonds of prisoners, I calculated marriage rates in the penal population, and estimated the number of children with incarcerated fathers. Next, data from two social surveys—the National Longitudinal Survey of Youth 1979 (NLSY), and the Fragile Families Survey of Child Wellbeing—were used to estimate the effects of incarceration on a single man's chances of marriage and a married man's risk of divorce. Although marriage is generally associated with criminal desistance and a reduced risk of poverty, marriages with former inmates may be different from others. Serious offenders have histories of antisocial behavior, lower cognitive ability, and a tendency to impulsive behavior. Whatever the salutary effect of marriage in general, women may be better off without husbands with prison records, particularly if they are violent or abusive. Finally, then, to assess the welfare of women married to formerly incarcerated men, I return to the Fragile Families data to examine the links between incarceration, marriage, and domestic violence.

THE EFFECTS OF INCARCERATION: SELECTION OR INCAPACITATION?

The effects of imprisonment on marriage and families depend on the strength of an incarcerated man's attachments to his kin and community. An outcast without friends or other social ties will be less missed than a pillar of the community who is closely involved with family and neighbors.

Studies of the effects of crime and the economy on marriage support a skeptical view of imprisonment's corrosive effect on family life. Criminal offenders are often found to have weak family attachments. For example, the young delinquents Robert Sampson and John Laub studied were two to four times more likely to get divorced than their nondelinquent counterparts. While married, men with criminal backgrounds were two to three times more likely to be only weakly attached to their wives.[6] Fathers with criminal records are also less likely to be closely involved with their children, and their families are more unstable.[7] Consequently, low rates of family attachment among ex-prisoners may be due to a selection effect and not imprisonment. Criminal offenders are less likely to develop strong ties to wives and children regardless of whether they are incarcerated.

We needn't even appeal to prisoners' criminality to doubt their attachments to wives and children. Weak marital and family connections long predated the prison boom in poor black neighborhoods. Wilson's work re-ignited interest in the family structure of disadvantaged African Americans, but black men's tenuous attachment to women and children in the inner cities had been observed at least since W. E. B. DuBois's nineteenth-century study of Philadelphia's Seventh Ward. In that ghetto, low marriage rates were thought to echo the "lax moral habits of the slave regime" and reflect the strains of supporting a household without a living wage.[8] A line of sociological analysis from DuBois through E. Franklin Frazier and Gunnar Myrdal to Daniel Patrick Moynihan's report on *The Negro Family* also traced family instability among poor urban blacks to the legacy of slavery and the deprivations of irregular employment and low wages.[9] Urban ethnographers took up this analysis, often emphasizing the economic roots of men's detachment from their families. For Elliot Liebow's idle black men on *Tally's Corner*, "the plain fact of supporting one's wife and children defines the principal obligation of a husband," but "money is chronically in short supply and chronically a source of dissension in the home."[10] Liebow concludes that

> marriage is an occasion of failure. To stay married is to live with your failure, to be confronted by it day in and day out. It is to live in a world whose standards of manliness are forever beyond one's reach, where one is continuously tested and challenged and continually found wanting.[11]

This is the historical and social context of the selection effect. In poor inner-city neighborhoods where gender relations are contentious and marital bonds are vexed by poverty, how could the prison boom make things worse? In these communities, jobless men involved in crime, without steady partners or ties to their children, leave few footprints. They have few bonds to be broken by imprisonment. In short, the hypothesis of selection warns that men at risk of imprisonment have traits and live in situations that frustrate the development of stable two-parent families.

Against this skepticism about the effects of imprisonment, some ethnographers have described the rich network of kinship relations of men with criminal records. In these accounts, the penal system cuts deep into family life. If we think that men who go to prison are embedded in families and communities, sending a man to prison produces an "incapacitation effect." The term incapacitation usually describes how incarceration reduces crime by restraining prisoners from committing crime in society.[12] Just as the penal system restrains prisoners from crime, it may also restrain them from performing the prosocial roles of suitor, spouse, and parent. While incarcerated, prisoners of course have little opportunity to meet partners and get married. Married men are prevented from contributing emotionally and financially to their primary relationships.

The attachment of incarcerated men to their families is reflected in the commitment they profess to their roles as fathers. For example, Kathryn Edin and her colleagues found that fatherhood was a turning point which provided new meaning to lives of men involved in crime. Many of the fathers Edin spoke with described their children as "saving them" from the streets.[13] Field researchers also find little evidence that formerly incarcerated men adhere to a deviant subculture that rejects parenting as a value. Instead, ex-prisoners commonly express the desire to be close to their children, despite the obstacles of unemployment, limited education, and a criminal record.[14] Field observation echoes other urban ethnographies in which men and women in poor ghetto neighborhoods place a high value on close-knit two-parent families, but face significant barriers to maintaining them.

For incarceration to negatively affect family life, however, more is needed from prisoners than affirmations of family values. Prisoners must have family and friends to be affected. Edin and her colleagues interviewed a large number of incarcerated fathers and their children in Charleston, South Carolina, and argued that the effects of a father's absence are far-reaching:

> Incarceration often means that fathers miss out on those key events that serve to build parental bonds and to signal to the community that they intend to support their children both financially and emotionally. These key events include attending the child's birth or observing developmental milestones such as walking and talking. The father's absence at these crucial moments, we argue, can weaken his commitment to the child and, years later, the child's own commitment to his or her father.[15]

Reporting on his fieldwork in the poor neighborhoods of southeast Washington, D.C., Donald Braman relates the story of Kenny, in jail and awaiting trial for murder: "Kenny had been one of the primary caretakers of his children, had helped his mother with mortgage payments and contributed to his niece's college education at Howard."[16] Kenny himself observes

> They're trying to fix the house up and . . . it's slower now because I'm not there to do the work. . . . I fix the car, and I fix all the plumbing and, you know, and when nobody's there and nobody has finances to pay a person to

come in and do that, it becomes a strain when you have to find money to fix things.[17]

For Edin and Braman, even poor families provide a net of social supports and mutual aid. Indeed, poor women and children depend particularly on family networks because they cannot afford to buy help in the marketplace. The loss of fathers to incarceration thus imposes a heavy burden.

For those who claim the disruptive effects of imprisonment, families are also seen to pay a price for their ties to incarcerated relatives. Family members must overcome the obstacles to communicating with relatives in prisons—taking the bus to far-flung facilities, accepting expensive collect calls, exchanging mail screened by correctional authorities.[18] Like the inmates, those who visit are exposed to the many small routines and humiliations of institutional life: waiting to be called, passing through metal detectors, surrendering identification, submitting to searches, and so on. They too are in some degree institutionalized.

The hypotheses of selection and incapacitation offer two contrasting accounts of the strength of an incarcerated man's family ties. The hypothesis of selection says that men who go to prison would be weakly attached to wives and children even if they weren't incarcerated. The incapacitation hypothesis says that imprisoned men are committed to their parental role, have ties to kin and community, and their removal inflicts hardships on family members left behind. These are the basic terms of debate. Let's now turn to some empirical evidence to unravel these rival claims.

FATHERHOOD AND MARRIAGE IN THE PENAL POPULATION

To study the family ties of prisoners, I begin by simply describing the levels of marriage and fatherhood in the penal population. Figure 6.1 compares rates of marriage and fatherhood in the penal population to those for men who are not incarcerated. Levels of marriage are measured for noninstitutional men and male prison and jail inmates, aged twenty-two to thirty, in 2000. Rates of fatherhood are the percentage of noninstitutional men and male state prisoners, aged thirty-three to forty, who have ever had children by 1997 or 1998.

Marriage rates among prison and jail inmates are very low compared to those on the outside. White male inmates in their twenties are less than half as likely to be married as their noninstitutional counterparts. The incarcera-

Figure 6.1   Marriage and Fatherhood Among Inmates and Free Men

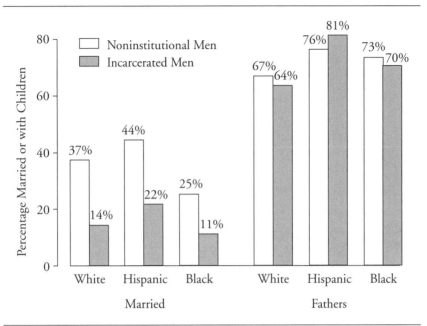

Source: Author's compilations.
Note: The marriage rate is calculated for men age 22 to 30 in 2000. The prevalence of fatherhood is calculated for men age 33 to 40 in 1997 to 1998. See appendix for data sources.

tion gap in marriage is also large for blacks and Hispanics. The general level of marriage is highest for Hispanics, but in this case inmates are only half as likely to be married as their counterparts in free society. Marriage rates are lowest for blacks. Only 11 percent of young black inmates are married, compared to 25 percent of those who are not incarcerated. In short, marriage rates among male prisoners in their twenties are only around half as high as in the free population.

Although marriage is uncommon among prisoners, fatherhood is not. Figure 6.1 shows the percentage of men who by their late thirties have ever had children. The prevalence of fatherhood among prisoners is almost identical to that on the outside. Among blacks, for example, these shares are 70 percent to 73 percent. The percentages are also very similar among whites and Hispanics.

The combination of high incarceration rates with a large proportion of fa-

Figure 6.2   Children with Fathers in Prison or Jail

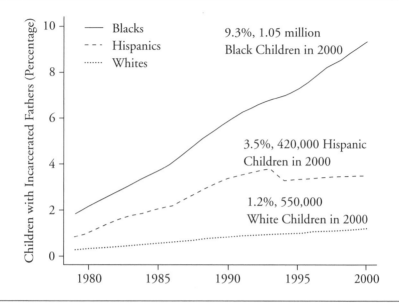

Source: Author's calculations based on data from Surveys of Inmates of State and Federal Correctional Facilities and Surveys of Inmates of Local Jails, and data from the March Current Population Survey (1979–2000).

thers among inmates means many children now have incarcerated fathers. Data from surveys of prison and jail inmates can be used to calculate the numbers of children with fathers in prison or jail. A time series for 1980 to 2000 shows that the total number of children with incarcerated fathers increased sixfold from about 350,000 to 2.1 million, nearly 3 percent of all children nationwide in 2000 (figure 6.2). Among whites, the fraction of children with a father in prison or jail is relatively small, about 1.2 percent in 2000. The figure is about three times higher (3.5 percent) for Hispanics. Among blacks, more than a million, or one in eleven children, had a father in prison or jail in 2000. The numbers are higher for younger children: by 2000, 10.4 percent of black children under age ten had a father in prison or jail. Just as incarceration has become a normal life event for disadvantaged young black men, parental incarceration has become commonplace for their children.

High rates of parental incarceration translate into high rates of family disruption. A Bureau of Justice Statistics report finds that about 45 percent of prisoners in 1997 were living with their children at the time they were incarcerated.[19] Prisoners often stay in contact with their children. Over 60 percent of state prisoners have at least monthly contact mostly by mail or telephone calls. Visits are relatively rare. More than half of the U.S. prison population is housed more than a hundred miles from home and only one in five is visited at least monthly by his children. Mothers are frequently the gatekeepers in these relationships. If male prisoners remain on good terms with the mothers, the children are more likely to visit and write.[20] Despite low marriage rates among African Americans, however, children are more likely to retain some contact with their incarcerated fathers than whites or Hispanics.

Prisoners may be unlikely to be married, but they do have extensive kinship ties, reflected in the many children with incarcerated fathers. About half of these children have some ties with their fathers, living with them at the time of and maintaining contact during the incarceration.

THE EFFECTS OF INCARCERATION ON MARRIAGE AND DIVORCE

The prevalence of marriage and fatherhood among prison and jail inmates tells us something about the incapacitation effect of incarceration. Men behind bars cannot fully play the role of father and husband. Single men are unlikely to get married while they're incarcerated. On the outside, the incapacitation effect takes the form of lopsided gender ratios in poor communities. For example, there are only sixty-two men for every one hundred women in the high incarceration neighborhoods of Washington, D.C.[21] Studying U.S. counties, William Sabol and James Lynch quantify the effects of the removal of men to prison. After accounting for educational attainment, welfare receipt, poverty, employment, and crime, Sabol and Lynch find that the doubling of the number of black men admitted to prison between 1980 and 1990 is associated with a 19-percent increase in the number of families headed by black women.[22]

The incapacitation effect captures only part of the impact of the prison boom on marriage. In Wilson's terms, incarceration also damages men's marriageability. Wilson traced declining marriage rates among the ghetto poor to the increasing inability of young disadvantaged black men to support families.[23] Incarceration erodes men's economic desirability even more. We saw earlier that incarceration reduces men's wages, slows the rate of wage growth, increases unemployment, and shortens job tenure. If a poor employment record damages the marriage prospects of single men and contributes to the risk of divorce among those who are married, the economic effects of incarceration will decrease the likelihood of marriage among men who have been to prison and jail.

Wilson measured marriageability mostly by employment, but a man's criminal record also signals his ability to care and provide for his family. While poor women care about men's economic status, they also worry about men's honesty and respectability. Edin's ethnographic interviews showed that these noneconomic concerns weighed heavily on low-income women in metropolitan Philadelphia.[24] The women Edin interviewed were deeply distrustful of men. The respondents were often reluctant to marry or develop romantic relationships because they viewed men's marital infidelity as inevitable. Some women's trust in men was shaken by boyfriends who spent household savings on drugs or drink, and then neglected children in their care. This wariness was compounded by the men's low social status. For the women in Edin's sample, marriage offered a route to respectability, but "marriage to an economically unproductive male means. . . permanently taking on his very low status."[25] Elijah Anderson makes a similar point in the opposite way, describing the dreams of teenage girls in ghetto neighborhoods, a "dream of living happily ever after with one's children in a nice house in a good neighborhood—essentially the dream of the middle-class American lifestyle."[26] In these cases, it is the social status of jobless men and their lack of esteem as much as their material resources that limits their appeal as husbands.

If reliability and reputation measure the noneconomic aspects of marriageability, incarceration has likely eroded the pool of marriageable men. Just as the stigma of incarceration confers disadvantage in the labor market, it also undermines a man's prospects in the marriage market. Men in trouble with the authorities cannot offer the respectability that many poor women seek from their partners. A prison record—the official stamp of criminality—can convey trouble to mothers looking for a stable home. For example, Edin's interviews described women's aversion to drug dealing, even when it provided a couple with income: "Mothers fear that if their man gets involved in drug dealing, he might stash weapons, drugs, or drug proceeds in the household, that the violence of street life might follow him into the household."[27] Because marriage offers a way of enhancing status, the trouble foreshadowed by a prison record may be even more repellent than chronic unemployment.

The stigma of incarceration also strains existing relationships. Erving Goffman describes stigma's contagious quality, suffusing personal relationships: "In general the tendency for a stigma to spread from the stigmatized individual to his close connections provides a reason why such relations tend either to be avoided or to be terminated where existing."[28] Braman's fieldwork in Washington, D.C., provides empirical support. The high prevalence of incarceration, he finds, does little to reduce its stigmatic effect. Braman describes the experience of Louisa, whose husband Robert was arrested on an old armed robbery charge after a lengthy period out of prison and while in recovery from drug addiction. The couple

> had come to think and present themselves as morally upstanding citizens and churchgoers. Because of this, Louisa felt the stigma of her husband's most recent incarceration all the more intensely. She began to avoid friends and family, not wanting to talk about Robert's incarceration and lying to them when she did.[29]

Louisa came to withdraw from her extended family as well and grappled with depression during Robert's incarceration. Braman argues that the stigma of incarceration is even more severe for family members than the offender, because wives and children live and work outside the prison, exposed to the condemnation of neighbors and other community members.

The separation imposed by incarceration also weighs heavily on relationships. Interviews with former offenders suggest that the friendships that underlie romantic relationships are diluted by time apart. Often women become more independent and self-sufficient while their partners are incarcerated.[30] Just as Edin's female respondents distrusted men's commitment, Anne Nurse reports that her California sample of juvenile offenders was constantly suspicious of the fidelity of their wives and girlfriends. Often these fears were well-founded and many romantic relationships failed when men were still incarcerated.[31]

The burdens of incarceration may further weaken the fragile relations between men and women in poor urban neighborhoods. The incapacitation effect of imprisonment —the removal of men from the marriage market—reduces the opportunities for marriage. The economic penalty of incarceration and its costs in social status may have deepened the declining marriageability of men with conviction records. The effects of incapacitation, economic disadvantage, and stigma should be seen in low rates of marriage and high risks of divorce or separation among men with prison records. Any empirical test, however, must allow that low marriage rates among ex-prisoners may be due to selection rather than incarceration. I weigh these competing claims by analyzing survey data from the NLSY.

INCARCERATION EFFECTS IN THE NLSY

I illustrate how the chances of marriage evolve over time by calculating the fraction of the population getting married for the first time at a given age. Calculating the marriage rate at regular age intervals shows how the prevalence of marriage rises as a population gets older. The NLSY can be used to construct rates of first marriage, both for men who are never incarcerated and for those who are incarcerated before they are forty. Like the earlier analysis of wages, incarceration is indicated by respondents who are interviewed in prison or jail. I also use data from a special set of questions asked in 1980 that record respondents who have spent time in a correctional facility. Throughout the marriage analysis, NLSY respondents are tracked from age eighteen to marriage or age forty, whichever comes sooner. (A handful of male respondents married before age eighteen are discarded from the analysis.)

Rates of first marriage for those who were never incarcerated and those who were are shown in figure 6.3. The solid line indicates marriage rates for men who are never incarcerated. At age eighteen, the entire sample of NLSY men is unmarried, but the share of never-married plunges between ages twenty and twenty-five. By age twenty-six, over half of all men who have never been incarcerated have gotten married. The rate of marriage slows from this point, but only one in eight of those never incarcerated remain unmarried by the time they're forty. Compare marriage rates among men who go to prison or jail. By age twenty-six, about 25 percent of men involved with the penal system have married compared to 46 percent of those without incarceration records. By age forty, two of five incarcerated men remained unmarried.

Of course, the low marriage rate among incarcerated men is not due entirely to the effect of imprisonment. The selection into prison also explains a large share of the incarceration gap in marriage. Men spending time behind bars are more likely to be African American, have little education, and be in-

Figure 6.3   Rate of First Marriage for Men

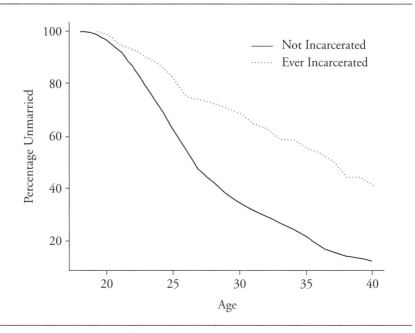

Source: Author's compilations from the NLSY.

volved in crime. These factors are also associated with a low likelihood of marriage regardless of involvement in the criminal justice system. To isolate the impact of incarceration, we need to account for the many factors associated with incarceration that also affect a man's chances of marriage. In effect, we must find a comparison group that resembles our incarcerated men in all respects but their history of imprisonment.

To do so, I adjust for the effects of factors that influence the likelihood of marriage and incarceration. Statistical adjustments for things like race and education that are correlated with marriage and incarceration help allow for the nonrandom selection of men into the penal system. Race and education controls allow us to calculate the difference in marriage rates for an ex-inmate and a non-inmate of the same race and level of schooling. Many variables can be introduced to minimize the differences between those who have been incarcerated and the comparison group who have not. Previous research on marriage suggests we should control for where a man lives, whether he is Catholic or very religious, and whether he has fathered children before marriage. (Premarital births increase the likelihood of marriage.) Selection can also be controlled by allowing that criminal behavior rather than incarceration may make men less likely to get married. To help separate these two effects, I also control for the respondent's recent use of drugs and his self-reported history of violent delinquency. Accounting for demographics, religion, and criminal behavior provides a comparison group that is relatively similar but differs mostly in incarceration status. As we will see, most of the incarceration gap in marriage rates is due to the effects of these control variables.

Control variables can also be used to study the causal mechanisms that explain how incarceration reduces the likelihood of marriage. The three mechanisms—incapacitation, stigma, and economic disadvantage—are all observable in varying degrees. Incapacitation is the most transparent, captured by the low likelihood of marriage among men in either jail or prison. The stigma of incarceration is difficult to measure with survey data, but if stigma reduces marriageability, the effect of incarceration will persist after release as the reputation for criminality follows the offender through his reentry into society. Economic disadvantage is directly observed in men's employment rates, measured here by the number of weeks worked by a man in the previous year. Imprisonment reduces marriage rates through economic disadvantage, where reduced employment due to incarceration makes men less attractive marriage partners. If controlling for employment significantly reduces the estimated effect of incarceration, we can say that differences in employment between non-inmates and ex-inmates help explain the incarceration gap in marriage.

INCARCERATION AND FIRST MARRIAGE

The analysis of first marriage estimates two incarceration effects. First, incapacitation is captured by calculating the reduction in marriage rates in the year a man is in prison or jail. Second, to gauge the effects of stigma and economic disadvantage, I also examine whether men with incarceration records marry at lower rates after they have served their time.

Not surprisingly, the data clearly show that men in prison are unlikely to get married. Under a variety of statistical models with different control variables, men behind bars are about 70 percent less likely to get married in the year they are incarcerated than their counterparts. Although the incapacitative effect of incarceration is large, its implications are less far-reaching than the possible effects of social stigma and economic disadvantage which may reduce marriage rates among men coming out of prison. How strong is the evidence for the postrelease effect of incarceration on marriage?

The effect of incarceration is shown by comparing the probability of first marriage by age forty for two men who are similar in many ways except incarceration status. The probability of marriage is calculated for a never-married man with a twelfth-grade education, living in the Northeast, who uses drugs but has no history of violent delinquency, who is not religious, and who has a child. We compare this man's chances of marriage to another with identical characteristics but who was incarcerated for one year at age twenty-five. Figure 6.4 shows the effects of incarceration on marriage under two assumptions. First, we assume that men's employment has no direct impact on marriage. If men with high rates of employment are more likely to get married, low rates of marriage among ex-inmates will be due partly to their high unemployment. Next, we assume that employment directly affects marriage. After adjusting for employment, the estimated incarceration gap in marriage will get smaller if economic disadvantage explains the low marriage rate of former inmates.

The effects of incarceration are different for white, Hispanic, and black men. Just over 95 percent of white former inmates get married by age forty, virtually the same rate among their counterparts who have never been to prison. There is stronger evidence of an incarceration gap in marriage rates among Hispanics. Just over 84 percent of former inmates get married, compared to just over 87 percent of observably identical counterparts. Although statistically significant, this gap is in fact quite small. It is larger among blacks. A black man without a prison record has about a 54-percent chance of marriage by his late thirties, compared to his counterpart's 43-percent chance.

If ex-inmates don't marry because they don't have jobs, the incarceration gap in marriage should shrink when correcting for differences in employment. Controlling for employment fully explains the incarceration gap in marriage among Hispanic men. This adjustment only partly explains the gap among blacks, however, reducing it from 11.4 to 5.7 percentage points. Of course, the employment deficit of former inmates is not due entirely to incarceration. Estimates from chapter 5 showed that incarceration reduces the

Figure 6.4   **Effects of Incarceration on Man's Probability of Marriage**

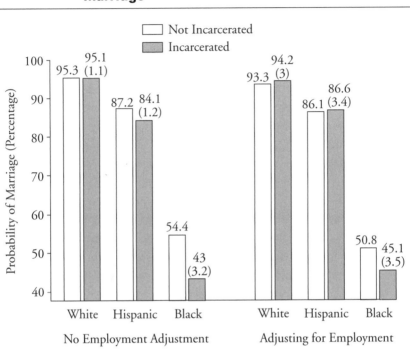

Source: Author's compilations from NLSY.
Note: Figures in parentheses show the statistical error of prediction, approximately equal to 1.65 times the predictive standard error.

employment of black men by around 15 percent. Still, the results suggest that improving employment among men released from prison will help their marriage prospects.

INCARCERATION AND DIVORCE

So far, we have seen evidence that incarceration suppresses marriage, at least among African American men. Moving forward in the life course, we can also ask about the effects of incarceration on married couples. Figure 6.5 shows the risk of divorce or separation for men in their first marriage who have never been incarcerated and those that have been. Because marriage rates are so low among incarcerated men, there are few cases of men with prison records in long-lasting marriages. Nevertheless, the divorce rate inside

Figure 6.5   Risk of Marital Dissolution Among First Marriages

Source: Author's compilations from NLSY.

prison is also 50 percent, but is reached in about a third of the time as it is outside.

Marriages are thus particularly at risk when men are in prison or jail. During incarceration, shame and anger of men's families is most severe,[32] just as the chance that wives will develop other romantic attachments is also greatest.[33] After release from prison, the stigma of incarceration may endure and ex-inmates may be less able to contribute financially to their families. The statistical analysis tries to capture these processes by estimating the chances of marital dissolution while a husband is incarcerated and after he has been released.

Here, too, I estimate the effect of incarceration on divorce or separation, accounting for a variety of other factors. In this case, I control for incarceration prior to marriage. When specifying a comparison group to measure the effect of incarceration, those imprisoned before marriage share much of the propensity to crime that we see in men who are incarcerated during marriage. Controlling for prior incarceration thus provides strong test of the disruptive effects of incarceration during marriage. Figure 6.6 reports rates of

Figure 6.6   The Effects of Incarceration on Man's Probability of Divorce

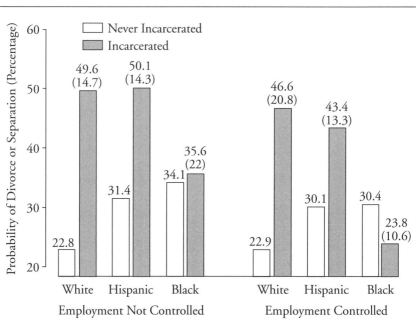

Source: Author's compilations from NLSY.
Note: Figures in parentheses show the statistical error of the prediction, approximately equal to 1.65 times the predictive standard error.

divorce or separation six years after marriage. The benchmark divorce rate is calculated for a man aged twenty-three at first marriage, living in the Northeast, with a twelfth-grade education, using drugs, not religious, with a child from the marriage, but with no history of violence or prison incarceration.

The divorce rate among such men varies by race and ethnicity. A white man with these characteristics is 22.8 percent likely to separate after six years of marriage and a white ex-inmate is more than twice as likely. Similarly, incarceration is estimated to raise the failure rate among Hispanics from just over 31 to 50 percent. The effect among blacks, however, is negligible. This result is due to limitations of the data: very few married black men were incarcerated. It does not appear that high divorce rates among incarcerated and formerly incarcerated men are attributable to their low employment rates.

AGGREGATE EFFECTS ON MARRIAGE AND DIVORCE

A prison record substantially reduces the chances that a black man will get married. However, it does not follow that high imprisonment rates have greatly reduced black marriage rates. Because men with less education who are involved in crime are unlikely to marry, the prison boom may be affecting only those whose marriage rates are very low to begin with. To examine the aggregate effect of incarceration in the NLSY sample, I predicted the level of marriage and divorce under two scenarios. I first calculated marriage and divorce rates at the observed level of incarceration, and then predicted these rates assuming that none of the men in the NLSY sample were sent to prison (see figure 6.7).

Aggregate marriage rates in the NLSY would only be slightly changed if none of the respondents were incarcerated (figure 6.7). The largest effect of incarceration is on marriage rates of African American men. About one-quarter of black men remain unmarried by age forty. Although the black marriage rate (75 percent) is much lower than the whites (93 percent), it would be increased by only 3 percentage points if the black incarceration rate were zero.

The effects of incarceration on aggregate divorce rates are even smaller. In this case I predict the percentage of men who are still married after eighteen years. For whites, Hispanics, and blacks, the divorce rate would be changed by less than a percentage point if the incarceration rate in the NLSY were zero. Although the individual-level effects of incarceration on divorce are much larger than those on marriage, the aggregate rate of divorce would barely change if the NLSY men were never incarcerated. The aggregate effect is small because marriage rates are so low among men who go to prison. The NLSY does tend to underestimate imprisonment among those with low levels of schooling.[34] Even allowing for this undersampling of less-educated prison inmates, the same pattern of results would obtain. The destabilizing effects of incarceration, in the aggregate, are largest among those who are not yet married and even in this case the effects are small.

Incarceration may not greatly reduce overall marriage rates, but it does significantly reduce marriage among those with little schooling. For example, 32.4 percent of black male dropouts in the NLSY remain unmarried by age thirty-nine but, by the current estimates, this number would fall to 26.1 per-

Figure 6.7   Predictions on Men Remaining Unmarried and Married

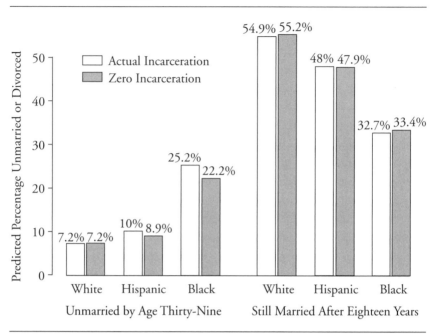

Source: Author's compilations from the NLSY.

cent were there no incarceration. Black and Hispanic men who dropped out of high school are 10 to 30 percent less likely to get married than college educated men (table 6.1). Educational inequality in marriage rates would be eliminated among Hispanics and significantly reduced among blacks if the incarceration rate were reduced to zero. As in the analysis of earnings, incarceration does not greatly increase inequality between whites and minorities, but does between well-educated and less-educated minorities.

MARRIAGE AND SEPARATION IN FRAGILE FAMILIES

The NLSY analysis suggests that incarceration reduced marriages rates, either by reducing the chances of marriage among single men or by increasing rates of divorce and separation among those who were married. Although the NLSY draws from a national sample observed over a long period, the sam-

Table 6.1   Men Unmarried by Age Thirty-Nine

	All Men	White	Hispanic	Black
Observed incarceration				
High school dropout	14.5%	6.3%	10.6%	32.4%
College	10.9	7.9	9.5	23.1
College-dropout ratio	.76	1.25	.90	.71
Zero incarceration				
High school dropout	12.6	6.4	9.0	26.1
College	10.8	8.0	9.4	22.0
College-dropout ratio	.86	1.26	1.04	.84

Source: Author's compilations from the NLSY.
Note: Nonmarriage rates are calculated given the observed level of incarceration in the NLSY and assuming no incarceration.

pling frame captures only a small number of incarcerated men and offers little information on men's partners.

Another survey, the Fragile Families and Child Wellbeing Study, remedies some of the limitations of the NLSY. Fragile Families is a longitudinal survey of new (mostly unmarried) parents and their children in urban areas. Data were collected in twenty U.S. cities, stratified by different labor market conditions and welfare and child support regimes. New mothers were first interviewed at the hospital within forty-eight hours of having given birth. About 60 percent of the fathers were also interviewed in the hospital, and another 15 percent were soon after the child left the hospital. Mothers and fathers were first interviewed between 1998 and 2000, and then again twelve months later. The Fragile Families data are unique, because information about men's incarceration status is obtained from the men in the survey and their partners. This provides a more complete accounting than the NLSY, yielding data on incarceration even for men who are unable to be located for a survey interview. Even more than the NLSY, the Fragile Families survey provides detailed information on the living arrangements of poor urban couples. Unlike the NLSY, however, Fragile Families data are available only at several points in time. Still, the data offer valuable new information on a segment of the population that is difficult to study with traditional survey methods.

The short time series of the Fragile Families allows us to examine the liv-

Table 6.2   Men Living with the Mother of Their One-Year-Old Child

	Living Together	Married	Sample Size
Father white			
Not incarcerated	18%	68%	715
Incarcerated	35	23	157
Father black			
Not incarcerated	31	25	1100
Incarcerated	34	8	558
Father Hispanic			
Not incarcerated	42	35	678
Incarcerated	40	19	228

Source: Author's compilations from the Fragile Families Survey.

ing situation of a formerly incarcerated man, a year after his child is born (table 6.2). In this sample of mostly poor, minority urban couples, incarceration is much more common than in the NLSY. Whereas only 7.8 percent of the NLSY men were ever interviewed in prison, 27 percent of the Fragile Families men were known to have been incarcerated, either by their own report or by their partners'. As in the NLSY, men who have never been incarcerated are much more likely to be married (40 percent) than their previously incarcerated counterparts (13 percent). Marriage rates were extremely low among black men. Only 25 percent of those who were never incarcerated and 8 percent of those who were married a year after the birth of their child. Incarceration is not systematically related to cohabitation. However, adding those married and those living together shows that former inmates are much more likely to be separated from the mother of their children. For whites, 42 percent of former inmates are separated from the child's mother, compared to 14 percent of those never incarcerated. Separation rates are highest for blacks who were incarcerated, at 58 percent.

The Fragile Families data lacks the long time series of the NLSY, but a similar analysis can be conducted using data from the two available time points. First, I looked at fathers who were unmarried when their child was born to see if they were married a year later. There are likely to be many differences between unmarried couples living together and those living apart. In trying to provide a demanding test of the effect of incarceration, I examine only couples whose likelihood of marriage is low—those living apart at the time of their child's birth. Second, I studied couples living together at the birth of their child and calculated the chances that they had separated by the following year. Because marriage rates are so low in the Fragile Families data, I looked at separation among those who were initially married or living together. In studying the effect of incarceration on the chances that a couple has married or separated, I accounted for the mother's and father's age, race, ethnicity, education, and whether the mother has any older children. Father's economic status is measured by whether he worked in the previous week. The analysis also includes measures of the quality of the relationship, including mother's reports of whether her partner shows affection or tends to compromise with her in disagreements. Finally, to capture the father's propensity to be involved in crime, that is distinct from the effect of incarceration, I accounted for whether the father has hit the mother or uses drugs or alcohol heavily.

The effects of incarceration are measured against the probability of marriage for a couple, both with high school educations, aged twenty-six, with their first child (see figure 6.8). The probabilities of marriage, estimated for just one year, are much smaller than the NLSY estimates, which added marriage rates over a twenty-year period. If we take no account of father's employment, 4.9 percent of couples with white fathers will marry within a year of the child's birth, provided the father has not been incarcerated. If the father has been to prison or jail, the likelihood of marriage is only 1 percent, although a large statistical error accompanies this estimate. Like the NLSY analysis, the only statistically significant effect of incarceration on marriage is found among blacks. Couples with black fathers are more than twice as likely to get married if the father has a clean record (2.6 percent compared to 1.1 percent for ex-inmates). Accounting for the men's employment makes little difference to the effects of incarceration in the Fragile Families data. Only the effect of incarceration among blacks is estimated precisely enough to confidently infer an incarceration gap in marriage rates.

As with the NLSY, the Fragile Families data offer stronger support for the effects of incarceration on separation than marriage (see figure 6.9). For black, white, and Hispanic men, ex-inmates are more likely to be in failing relationships than those who have not been incarcerated. Similarly, the destabilizing effects of incarceration are largest among whites. A white male high

Figure 6.8   Probability of Couple Marrying After Birth of Child

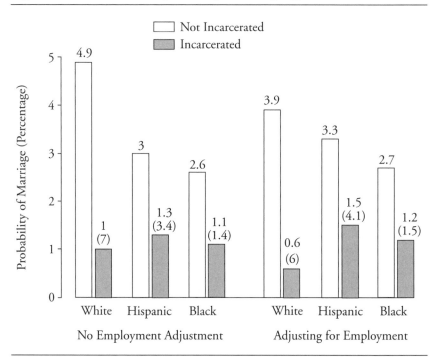

Source: Author's compilations from the Fragile Families Survey.
Note: Figures in parentheses show the statistical error of prediction, approximately equal to 1.65 times the predictive standard error.

school graduate, aged twenty-six is 12.7 percent likely to have separated from the mother of his twelve-month-old child. A man with those identical characteristics is nearly three times (34.5 percent) more likely to be separated if he has a prison record. Among Hispanics, men with prison records are twice as likely to separate as those who haven't been incarcerated. Although the effects of incarceration are small for African Americans, they are statistically significant in the Fragile Families data, indicating that incarceration raises the risk of separation by about half, from 30 to 45 percent.

Because the effects of incarceration are large and because there are many more men with prison and jail records in the Fragile Families sample than in the NLSY, the aggregate effects of incarceration are also much larger. That effect compares predicted rates of marriage and separation assuming the actual level of incarceration observed among the Fragile Families men, and assuming no incarceration. Table 6.3 shows that 5 percent of single men are pre-

Figure 6.9   Estimated Probability of Couple Separating After Birth of Child

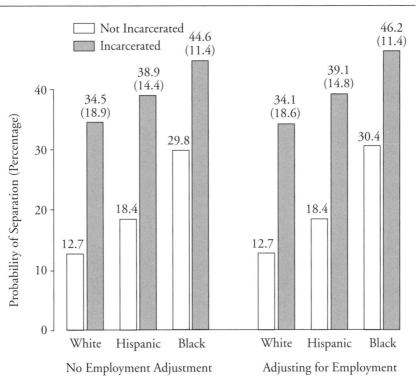

Source: Author's compilations from the Fragile Families Survey.
Note: Figures in parentheses show the statistical error of prediction, approximately 1.65 times the predictive standard error.

dicted to marry after one year, but that the marriage rate would be about 6 percent if none of the fathers in the study were incarcerated. The effect is largest for whites and blacks. The estimates indicate that marriage rates would be 20 to 30 percent higher at zero incarceration. The effect on rates of separation is also larger than we saw with the NLSY. Whereas 18 percent of Fragile Families fathers are estimated to separate from their partners after one year, the rate would be 15 percent if none of the fathers had been to prison or jail. The effects are largest for whites. With no incarceration, the separation rate among whites is estimated to fall by one-quarter, from 13 to 9.6 percent. The aggregate effects of incarceration on marriage and divorce are small in the NLSY, but the Fragile Families Survey uses a more permissive

Table 6.3 **The Percentage of Fathers Getting Married or Separating, One Year After the Birth of Their Child, at the Observed Level of Incarceration and Assuming Zero Incarceration, by Race and Ethnicity, Fragile Families Survey**

| | Assumed Incarceration | | Percentage Difference |
	Actual	Zero	
Percentage marrying			
All	5.0%	6.0%	20
White	4.9	6.4	31
Hispanic	10.6	11.7	10
Black	3.7	4.5	21
Percentage separating			
All	18.0	15.0	−17
White	13.0	9.6	−26
Hispanic	13.6	11.0	−19
Black	27.4	24.4	−11

Source: Author's compilations from the Fragile Families Survey.

measure of incarceration and draws from a poor urban sample. With these data, incarceration is estimated to reduce marriage rates and raise separation rates by 10 to 25 percent.

Statistical analysis of the NLSY and the Fragile Families data provide similar results. Black single men, but not white or Hispanic, are especially likely to remain unmarried if they have prison records, with the gap in marriage rates estimated to be anywhere between 20 and 200 percent. The data point more strongly to the destabilizing effects of incarceration on couples, whether they are married, as in the NLSY, or living together, as in the Fragile Families data.

Why are marriage rates low among black ex-inmates, but not others? NLSY results suggest that low employment rates are part of the reason. The remainder is harder to explain, but we can speculate that it relates to the social context to which black ex-inmates return. Marriage rates for black men, accounting for age, education, and employment, are a third lower than those for whites. Where marriage is more selective, women may attach more weight to negative characteristics like a prison record. Edin's respondents who emphasize the importance of a man's respectability convey this outlook in inner-city Philadelphia.[35] Black women, living amid concentrated poverty, may judge formerly incarcerated black men to be less respectable and have worse prospects than their white counterparts. Other researchers suggest that communities receiving white and Hispanic former prisoners offer a richer web of family and neighborhood social supports.[36] Because such communities better foster criminal desistance, white and Hispanic ex-offenders may be better reintegrated into their local marriage markets.

This analysis began by warning that the low rates might be due not to imprisonment, but to a selection effect in which criminal offenders are unlikely to marry, even if not incarcerated. Are my claims for the effect of incarceration on marriage and divorce contaminated by selection? I accounted for selection by controlling for men's drug use and history of violence, in addition to the demographic factors usually associated with marriage. The NLSY results for divorce, which adjusted for incarceration before marriage, offer the strongest control over criminal offenders' antipathy to marriage. The Fragile Families results, which rely on two time points with incarceration occurring some time before the first, should be viewed more cautiously. Because marriage and separation are discrete events, I cannot use the fixed-effect methods that provided stronger causal claims in the earlier analysis of wages and employment.[37] Still, analyzing two surveys is better than one. We can draw additional confidence from the consistency in the results across two very different samples produced by two different research designs. We can also look at the problem of selection in a different way, by shifting the focus from marriage and divorce to the quality of relationships reflected in patterns of domestic violence.

THE QUALITY OF MARRIED LIFE: DOMESTIC VIOLENCE IN FRAGILE FAMILIES

The evidence so far suggests that the prison boom separated many fathers from their children and contributed to low marriage rates and high risks of divorce among poor urban residents. By disrupting families and reducing marriage rates, growth in the penal population rate has incurred a large and uncounted social cost. Absent fathers in prison and jail and low marriage rates among ex-convicts ultimately increase the number of female-headed households. The risks accompanying these households are well-known. About half of all female-headed families live below the poverty line, their children face high risks of school failure, teen pregnancy, poor health and delinquency. The follow-on costs of incarceration for American families would thus seem to be substantial.

In estimating the effects of incarceration, I have tried to account for how the men who go to prison and jail are different from the rest of the population. By adjusting for demographic characteristics, criminal behavior, and other factors, the analysis acknowledges that criminal offenders are unlikely to marry even if they haven't been incarcerated. The implications of the argument can be extended to marriage itself. Marriages with men involved in crime may not have the positive effects of poverty reduction, good health, and school success. Indeed, a woman may be well-served by a man's incarceration if he is violent. From this point of view, the social costs associated with low marriage rates may be balanced by gains in public safety obtained by distancing dangerous men.

The balance sheet is often acknowledged, but we rarely see a close accounting of costs and benefits. For example, Joan Petersilia observes that "a solid marriage can give a prisoner emotional support upon release. . . . On the other hand, marriage can also produce dynamics that contribute to family violence, substance abuse, and economic pressure."[38] Jeremy Travis offers a similar formulation: "For some families, the arrest of a parent may be a blessing: removing a violent or emotionally oppressive mother or father may improve the well-being of the family unit. . . . For other families, the arrest of mother or father may signify the removal of a breadwinner and force the family into poverty."[39] Although close-knit families can help deflect crime and poverty, Petersilia and Travis recognize that the household's intimacy can expose family members to violence and abuse.

Does the negative effect of incarceration on marriage at least serve public safety by separating women from dangerous men with prison records? Answers to this question should distinguish different categories of criminal offenders. In particular, men convicted of violence may be more dangerous than drug offenders. This argument is often made in relation to the war on drugs which, critics claim, introduced sentencing and policing policies that incarcerated many drug users and small-time drug dealers who posed little risk to public safety.[40] This view is consistent with evidence that releasing drug offenders would save money on corrections because the economic cost of their offending is so low.[41]

I investigated this issue by returning to the twelve-month Fragile Families

Figure 6.10   Men Assaulting Partners, by Incarceration Status

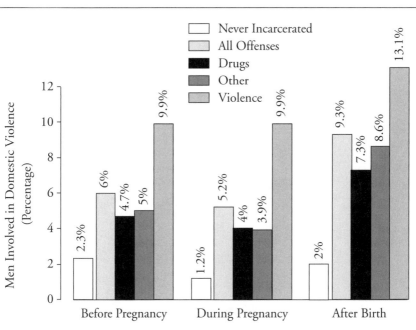

Source: Author's compilations from the Fragile Families Survey.

survey, which asked mothers whether the father of her child "ever cut, bruised or seriously hurt [her] in a fight."[42] The interviewer then recorded if injuries were sustained before, during, or after pregnancy. To probe differences between crime types, the data also categorize former inmates by their most recent offense, distinguishing drug offenders from those convicted of violence or other offenses (mostly property and public order offenses). Violence against mothers was relatively rare, with 3.3 percent reporting injuries before pregnancy, 2.3 percent reporting injuries during pregnancy, and 4.0 percent reporting injuries in the year after the child was born (figure 6.10). Domestic violence was much more common among men who had been incarcerated, with 6 percent having assaulted the mothers of their children before pregnancy, 5.2 percent having done so during pregnancy, and 9 percent doing so after birth of the child. Violent offenders were also more likely than drug offenders to assault their partners. After the birth of the child, for example, 13.1 percent did so, compared to 7.3 percent of drug offenders. In

Figure 6.11   Men Assaulting Partners, by Relationship Status

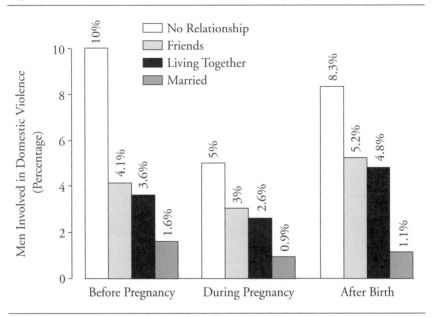

Source: Author's compilations from the Fragile Families Survey.

short, formerly incarcerated men were involved in domestic violence at a rate about four times higher than the rest of the population.

Perhaps low marriage rates among formerly incarcerated men at least make women safer by reducing their exposure to violence. Complicating this picture, however, women with the weakest connections to their partners face highest risk of violence (figure 6.11). A woman is eight to ten times more likely to have been assaulted by a partner with whom she has no ongoing relationship than by her husband. The direction of causality here is ambiguous. Violence may afflict separated couples because women have left abusive men. However, women who are permanently separated, whether at the time of the child's birth or one year later, are at higher risk of violence after birth (6.7 percent) than those who separate after the child is born (3.2 percent). Here, the data's message seems clear. Women remain at high risk of violence even if they have left a violent partner.

The effects of incarceration on domestic violence can be compared to the effects of marriage. With data from several points in time, I estimated the effects of marriage and cohabitation on domestic violence after a child's birth,

Table 6.4 Probability of Domestic Violence by New Fathers, Year After Birth of Child

	No Controls	Adding Controls for	
		Prior Violence	Relationship Quality
Chance of domestic violence for never-incarcerated twenty-five-year-old black man with a history of violence	2.6%	9.3%	7.8%
Effect on probability of domestic violence			
Incarceration for violence	9.3	10.7	9.6
	(3.5)	(5.5)	(6.5)
Incarceration for drugs	4.6	7.5	6.5
	(3.4)	(6.9)	(7.3)
Incarceration for other offenses	5.7	10.1	9.2
	(2.1)	(4.9)	(5.8)
Cohabiting in prior year	−.2	−.8	.1
	(.8)	(4.0)	(4.0)
Married in prior year	−1.6	−5.0	−3.1
	(.6)	(3.2)	(3.6)

Source: Author's compilations from the Fragile Families Survey.
Note: All models control for father's race, ethnicity, and age. Figures in parentheses indicate 90-percent confidence intervals.

controlling for a man's history of violence before and during pregnancy. Controlling for this helps us specify the effect of marriage on preventing violence. It also guards against the possibility that low levels of spousal abuse in married couples are attributable to the high risk of dissolution in couples with violent men.

Table 6.4 shows the baseline probability of domestic violence for a twenty-five-year-old black man with a history of spousal abuse. The effects on domestic violence are expressed as the changes in the baseline associated with incarceration, marriage, and cohabitation. With no control variables, violent offenders are estimated to be more likely than drug offenders to assault new mothers. Violent offending is associated with an additional 9.3 percentage point chance of violence, while drug offending adds 4.6 percentage points. The rate of violence is 1.6 points lower in married couples, offsetting high rates of spousal abuse among former inmates. Accounting for whether a man assaulted his partner before and during pregnancy helps explain the high risk of separation in marriages with abusive men. With this adjustment, the probability of domestic violence is 7.5 to 10.7 percentage points higher among ex-inmates, whereas marriage is associated with a reduced probability of 5 percentage points. These figures suggest that marriage can reduce the high levels of violence among drug offenders by about two-thirds, and the high level of violence among violent offenders by about one-half.

What is it about marriage that appears to reduce the risk of domestic violence? Robert Sampson and John Laub suggest that it is not marriage itself but a strong "spousal attachment" that restrains men from crime.[43] The Fragile Families survey offers several measures of the quality of an intimate relationship reflecting spousal attachment. Mothers were asked whether their partners often showed affection[44] and how long a couple has been together. When controlling for husband's affection and the length of the relationship, married women's risk of violence shrinks substantially, and there is no longer a statistically significant difference in the risk of violence between married and unmarried couples. The results suggest that relationships which are long-lasting, in which men show affection, are unlikely to be marked by violence. High-quality relationships, rather than marriage itself, deflects the chances of domestic violence.

How can we interpret these results? The risk of intimate partner violence is much higher among separated women than married women. Marriage, it seems, is a marker for high-quality relationships in which both partners are strongly committed to each other. These measures of relationship quality explain a significant fraction of the effect of marriage on domestic violence. Because incarceration appears to undermine such relationships, low marriage rates among ex-offenders offer little support for the idea that women who have separated from men with criminal records are necessarily at less risk of violence. Indeed, by undermining the development of high-quality relationships, imprisonment may increase women's exposure to violence in the long run.

CONCLUSION

The penal system's influence seeps through the kinship networks of incarcerated men and women. When men are only weakly attached to families and communities, their imprisonment affects few but themselves. We have seen evidence, however, that incarcerated men have extensive family connections. Although their marriage rates are only half as high as those outside the penal system, incarcerated men are just as likely as others to have children. As a result, more than two million children, and one in ten black children under age ten, had a father in prison or jail by the end of the 1990s. The prison boom also magnified the effects of incapacitation and joblessness that drives the shortage of marriageable men in poor urban neighborhoods. Survey data show that imprisonment further reduces the marriage prospects of poor and minority single men. Marriages interrupted by incarceration are unlikely to survive. In national samples, the aggregate effect of incarceration on overall marriage rates is small. In the mostly minority urban sample of the Fragile Families survey, the aggregate effect of incarceration is larger, underlining the concentrated effect of the prison boom on the poor in inner cities. Have reduced marriage rates among former inmates necessarily made their partners and children worse off? Ex-inmates are more likely to assault their partners than other men, but this likelihood is reduced if they develop strong and long-lasting relationships. Unfortunately then, the effects of imprisonment may be self-defeating to some degree. By eroding the familial bonds that curb violence, imprisonment undermines the conditions for desistance.

There is also a larger context to this story. Over the last two decades, poverty researchers have linked growth in the numbers of female-headed families among blacks to the failure of urban labor markets. Persistent joblessness among less-skilled blacks decreased the supply of men with the means to support families in inner-city neighborhoods. In the era of mass imprisonment, the penal system has joined the labor market as a significant influence on the life chances of young less-educated blacks. The evidence in this chapter suggests that the influence of the penal system ranges beyond the negative effects of imprisonment on men's wages and employment. Imprisonment has also inhibited the formation of stable two-parent families in the low-income urban communities from which most of the penal population is drawn. Stable families provide the poor with a valuable means of improving welfare. Families pool resources, socialize and supervise children, and provide networks of mutual aid. From this perspective, the prison boom has diminished a valuable social resource already in short supply in America's inner cities.

APPENDIX: MARRIAGE RATES AND CHILDREN OF INCARCERATED FATHERS

The number of children of incarcerated fathers was calculated using the *Surveys of Inmates of State and Federal Correctional Facilities* and *Surveys of Inmates of Local Jails.*[45] Intersurvey years were interpolated. Estimates are slightly low because the surveys only count an inmate's first six children. Data from the March Supplement of the Current Population survey were used to estimate the total number of minor children in the population.[46] Marriage rates for the prison and jail population were estimated with the *Survey of Inmates of State and Federal Correctional Facilities* and the *Surveys of Inmates of Local Jails.*[47]

APPENDIX: ANALYSIS OF THE NLSY

Estimates of the effects of incarceration on first marriage and divorce in the NLSY are calculated from a discrete-time event history model. Using life table methods, predicted probabilities of marriage and divorce in each year are used to calculate the prevalence of marriage and divorce by age forty (for marriage) or after eighteen years (for divorce). Estimates of statistical error are generated from normally distributed predictions of the annual risk of marriage or divorce. Simulation methods yield confidence intervals for the overall marriage and divorce and rates. To obtain the marriage and divorce rates reported in this chapter, models were fit separately for blacks, whites, and Hispanics.

Quasi-likelihood logistic regression results for the full NLSY sample event history models are given in table 6A.1 All predictors are dummy variables unless indicated.

APPENDIX: ANALYSIS OF THE FRAGILE FAMILIES SURVEY

Data from the Fragile Families study came from the baseline and twelve-month follow-up interviews (see Western, Lopoo, and McLanahan for details

Table 6A.1 Discrete Time Event History Model of Divorce and First Marriage, 1979 to 2000

	First Marriage				Divorce			
	(1)		(2)		(3)		(4)	
Intercept	-3.936	(.207)	-4.274	(.213)	-1.842	(.313)	-1.714	(.312)
Now incarcerated	-1.773	(.367)	-1.502	(.370)	1.246	(.275)	1.059	(.278)
Was incarcerated	-.158	(.132)	.013	(.135)	.423	(.342)	.238	(.343)
Education (years)	-.003	(.013)	-.007	(.014)	-.117	(.014)	-.114	(.014)
Midwest	.099	(.090)	.098	(.091)	-.222	(.110)	-.219	(.110)
South	.538	(.084)	.522	(.084)	.024	(.099)	.035	(.099)
West	.258	(.092)	.258	(.093)	-.012	(.110)	-.023	(.110)
Black	-1.009	(.078)	-.948	(.079)	.450	(.085)	.414	(.085)
Hispanic	-.162	(.088)	-.140	(.089)	.080	(.103)	.083	(.102)
Drug user	-.378	(.062)	-.384	(.062)	.614	(.072)	.625	(.072)
Delinquency	.059	(.104)	.102	(.105)	.344	(.108)	.335	(.108)
Catholic	-.177	(.071)	-.186	(.071)	-.157	(.085)	-.159	(.085)
Very religious	.029	(.058)	.019	(.058)	-.011	(.067)	-.002	(.067)
Pre-marital birth	.583	(.075)	.583	(.075)	—		—	
Employment (weeks)	—		.014	(.002)	—		-.009	(.002)
Incarcerated pre-marriage	—		—		-.025	(.195)	-.075	(.196)
Age at first marriage	—		—		-.026	(.011)	-.019	(.011)
Nonmarital birth	—		—		.153	(.078)	.152	(.078)
Marital birth	—		—		-.557	(.072)	-.560	(.072)
Person-years	20401		20401		21681		21681	
Persons	2041		2041		2762		2762	

Source: Author's compilations from the NLSY.

Note: Logistic regression coefficients (quasi-likelihood standard errors).

Table 6A.2   Analysis of Marriage and Separation

	Marriage (1)		Separation (2)	
Intercept	−3.687	(.935)	−.524	(.418)
Father's characteristics				
Incarcerated	−.805	(.347)	.801	(.125)
Age (years)	−.029	(.027)	−.046	(.013)
Less than high school	.295	(.347)	−.046	(.144)
Some college	.771	(.358)	−.043	(.152)
College degree	.598	(.677)	−.469	(.311)
Affectionate	.750	(.356)	−.196	(.151)
Critical	.607	(.632)	.574	(.334)
Compromises	.411	(.279)	−.507	(.119)
Heavy drug or alcohol use	−.758	(.463)	.276	(.142)
Hit mother	−.016	(.743)	−.298	(.381)
Worked last week	.590	(.403)	.197	(.161)
Mother's characteristics				
Age (years)	.033	(.034)	.002	(.016)
Less than high school	−.388	(.344)	.346	(.144)
Some college	−.123	(.349)	−.183	(.155)
College degree	−.446	(.771)	−.976	(.314)
Couple's characteristics				
Black	−.444	(.362)	.739	(.142)
Hispanic	.665	(.406)	−.321	(.172)
Mixed	−1.133	(.005)	1.277	(.300)
First birth	−.584	(.307)	.104	(.131)
Sample size	1125		2303	

Source: Author's compilations from the Fragile Families Survey.
Note: Logistic regression coefficients (quasi-likelihood standard errors).

Table 6A.3 Model of Domestic Violence in Year After Child's Birth

	(1)		(2)	
Intercept	−3.363	(.466)	−3.274	(.580)
Incarceration for violence	1.801	(.264)	1.235	(.332)
Incarceration for drugs	1.165	(.352)	.910	(.425)
Incarceration for other offense	1.330	(.215)	1.191	(.244)
Cohabiting at child's birth	−.066	(.197)	.114	(.236)
Married at child's birth	−1.008	(.380)	−.481	(.434)
Father's age (years)	−.013	(.014)	−.017	(.017)
Father black	.045	(.266)	.235	(.317)
Father Hispanic	.221	(.282)	.394	(.332)
Assault during pregnancy	−		3.090	(.332)
Assault before pregnancy	−		1.802	(.323)
Father is affectionate	−		−.438	(.238)
Length of relationship (years)	−		−.092	(.035)
Sample size	3344		3344	

Source: Author's compilations from the Fragile Families Survey.
Note: Quasi-likelihood logistic regression coefficients (standard errors).

on measurement of incarceration combining mothers and father's reports).[48] Quasi-likelihood logistic regression estimates of the odds of marriage at the follow-up interview among couples unmarried at baseline, and the odds of separation at follow-up among couples married or cohabiting at baseline are reported in table 6A.2. Results for a logistic regression on domestic violence are reported in table 6A.3.

CHAPTER 7

Did the Prison Boom Cause the Crime Drop?

Prisons conceal and deepen social inequality. Hundreds of thousands of disadvantaged jobless men are excluded from the usual measures of poverty and unemployment. Men who have been incarcerated make less money, see more unemployment, and are more likely to split up with their partners. The poor are made poorer and have fewer prospects for a stable family life. For much of the policy debate about prisons, these findings are beside the point. Prisons are not social welfare agencies; they are instruments for crime control. In policy debates, the utility of incarceration is usually judged by its effect on crime, not on social inequality. The conventional focus on crime is too short-sighted, however. Crime and inequality are closely connected. If crime stems from poor economic opportunities and broken homes, and incarceration reduces pay and family stability, mass imprisonment may be a self-defeating strategy for public safety. Imprisonment may sow the seeds for more crime, rather than less.

My findings of unemployment and marital strife among ex-prisoners should make us skeptical about the effects of prison on crime, but this skepticism seems to defy the facts. Through the 1990s, record levels of imprisonment preceded a massive decline in serious violence that returned crime rates to levels not seen since the 1960s. Whatever the negative effects of incarceration, they may be overshadowed by the public safety gained by keeping dangerous criminals off the street.

To fully understand the social impact of mass imprisonment, we must finally return to the topic of crime and assess the effects of the prison boom on the crime drop of the 1990s. I begin the analysis by charting the extent and social patterning of the crime drop. We will see that the fall in crime rates through the 1990s improved the quality of life of low-income and minority men and women. Research on the effects of imprisonment gives us three main hypotheses linking incarceration to the fall in crime. Prison programs might have rehabilitated the many offenders entering the penal system through the 1990s. Crime rates might also have fallen simply because large numbers of offenders were locked up. This incapacitation effect of the prison boom has been a popular focus among students of declining crime rates.[1] Finally, high incarceration rates and tough new penalties might have deterred would-be offenders from committing crime.

CHARTING THE CRIME DROP

The 1990s crime drop provided a remarkable improvement in public safety and quality of life, particularly for the disadvantaged Americans at highest risk of crime. The scope of the crime drop is seen most clearly in the homicide rate, which is measured more accurately than other type of crime (figure 7.1). From 1975 to 1991, the homicide rate fluctuated between eight to ten deaths per hundred thousand of the U.S. population. In 1991, murder and nonnegligent manslaughter left about twenty-four thousand dead. Levels of serious violence declined steadily through the 1990s and by 2001, the homicide rate had fallen to 5.6 per hundred thousand, its lowest level since 1965.

Figure 7.1 also shows time series of homicide rates for young black and white men. As in the general population, the rate for those aged eighteen to twenty-four increased quickly at the end of the 1990s. But, like trends in the general population, these levels fell steadily through the 1990s. The trend for young black men is particularly striking: they are about twenty times more likely to die by violence than the general population, and about ten times more likely than their white counterparts. The increase in homicides through the late 1980s and early 1990s is often traced to an epidemic of violence surrounding the crack trade. Murderous violence—indexed by deaths and arrests, often involving handguns—increased sharply among young black men in big cities.[2] Even in this high-risk group, however, the homicide rate declined by more 40 percent from 1993 to 2001.

Detailed crime statistics show that improvements in public safety were

Figure 7.1   Homicide Rates

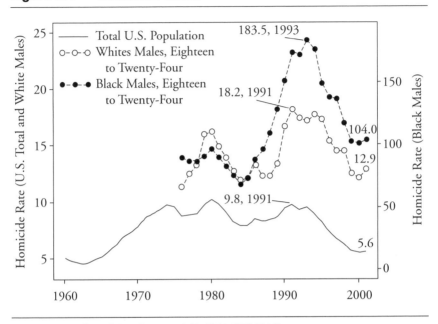

Source: FBI Uniform Crime Reports 1960–2001 (BJS 2005).

not confined to young men and their declining risk of homicide. Table 7.1 reports violent and property crime rates for different groups in 1993 and 2001. Violent crime rates were halved among men and blacks. Although the poor are more likely to be victims than the rich, the decline in violence was fairly evenly distributed across income levels. Property crime, mostly burglaries and car theft, also declined substantially. The fall in property crime was as deep in cities as in the suburbs and rural areas. Property crime rates also declined substantially for minorities and those in the bottom third of the income distribution. Finally, serious violence in large cities fell precipitously in the 1990s. In New York, for example, the homicide rate fell by nearly 70 percent. Improvements in public safety were not always as spectacular, but significant declines were registered in nearly all major urban centers.

The crime drop improved the quality of life of the most disadvantaged. Homicide rates among young black men and violent and property crime rates among minorities, low-income households, and urban residents all fell dramatically. Explanations of the crime drop have thus focused on changes

Table 7.1   Changes in Crime Rates

	1993	2001	Percentage Change
Violent crimes per 1,000			
Total aged twelve and over	49.9	25.1	−49.7
Gender			
Males	59.8	27.3	−54.3
Females	40.7	23.0	−43.5
Race and ethnicity			
Whites	47.9	24.5	−48.9
Hispanics[a]	55.2	29.5	−46.6
Blacks	67.4	31.2	−53.7
Income			
Bottom third	62.6	34.9	−47.4
Middle third	49.1	25.8	−48.0
Top third	43.7	19.3	−56.1
Property crimes per 1,000			
Total households	318.9	166.9	−47.7
Urbanization			
Urban	404.8	212.8	−47.4
Suburban	305.1	156.7	−48.6
Rural	246.4	131.9	−46.5
Race and ethnicity			
Whites	309.7	165.1	−48.9
Hispanics[a]	429.7	224.1	−47.8
Blacks	349.6	179.7	−52.3
Income			
Bottom third	295.1	180.9	−38.7
Middle third	314.8	174.2	−44.7
Top third	349.9	179.5	−48.7
Homicides per 100,000, five largest cities			
New York	26.5	8.7	−67.2
Los Angeles	30.5	15.6	−48.9
Chicago	30.3	22.9	−24.4
Houston	25.9	13.4	−48.3
Philadelphia	28.1	20.4	−27.4

Source: Author's compilations.

Note: Violent and property crime figures are from the National Crime Victimization Survey, reported in *Criminal Victimization, 2001* (Rennison 2002). Homicide rates are from the Uniform Crime Reports as reported in the *Sourcebook of Criminal Justice Statistics* (1994, 2002).
[a]May be of any race.

in poor urban communities. Big-city police forces grew significantly during the 1990s. Some observers add that the aggressive prosecution of misdemeanor offending reduced more serious crime, though many cities experienced large falls in crime even without zero-tolerance policing. Urban drug markets also became more tranquil following the spate of extreme violence associated with the crack trade in the late 1980s. Some have argued that falling unemployment rates through the economic expansion also helped lower crime, though the employment opportunities of young blacks showed little improvement. The legalization of abortion in the early 1970s may also have been important for reducing crime rates twenty years later.[3]

The growth in imprisonment is often added to this list of causes of the decline in crime. Although mass imprisonment sharply increased incarceration among the poor, minorities, and city-dwellers, growth in the American penal system may have at least reduced crime and violence in those communities that supplied the most prison inmates. Prisons can reduce crime three ways. Inmates who participate in prison education or treatment programs might be rehabilitated, and turn away from crime after they are released. Prisons might simply incapacitate offenders, locking them away to prevent crime in society. Finally, prisons might deter those who would commit crime were it not for the threat of incarceration. Let's consider each of these arguments in turn.

REHABILITATION AND THE PRISON BOOM

The main studies of the effects of the prison boom on the fall in U.S. crime rates through the late 1990s focused overwhelmingly on incapacitation and deterrence.[4] Few took seriously the possibility that the growth of imprisonment has expanded the population of former inmates reformed by rehabilitative programs. Critics of criminal justice policy point to statistics showing that spending on prison programs has declined and the demand for drug treatment, education, and vocational training exceeds supply.[5] Supporters of tough-on-crime policy echo the policy analysis of the 1970s reporting that rehabilitation did not work.[6] Indeed, we saw in chapter 3 that many of the policies and politics that drove the prison boom were premised on the failure of rehabilitation programs.

Is it true that prisons failed at rehabilitation and any reduction in crime related to the prison boom is attributable to incapacitation or deterrence? The broadly held view that rehabilitation is an impossible task is relatively recent among correctional professionals. The rehabilitative mission inspired the earliest institutions in Pennsylvania and New York in the 1830s and 1840s. It was not until the mid-1970s that confidence in rehabilitation began to disintegrate among policy experts.

The watershed event was the publication in 1974 of Robert Martinson's article in the *Public Interest*, "What Works? Questions and Answers about Prison Reform." The article summarized a massive volume published the following year that described studies in eleven treatment categories, with seven program effects.[7] Martinson's article focused on one question pulled from that larger review: can prison programs reduce recidivism? Across a variety of programs—education, training, counseling, psychotherapy, milieu therapy, probation, parole, and others—Martinson concluded that there was no clear evidence of reduced crime among program participants. Where researchers reported successful rehabilitation, those studies often suffered from selection biases, other inadequacies of research design, or simply claimed more than was delivered.[8] In a bold summary of more than two hundred evaluations of correctional programs conducted from 1945 to 1967, Martinson concluded, "with few and isolated exceptions, the rehabilitative efforts that have been reported so far have had no appreciable effect on recidivism."[9] This conclusion hardened into policy orthodoxy when a National Research Council panel and others offered similar assessments.[10]

Although Martinson modeled a pessimistic style of policy analysis that took hold among researchers, his main findings were challenged at the outset and a sophisticated defense of rehabilitation evolved over the next twenty years. A year after the article was published, Ted Palmer replied that Martinson was tendentiously gloomy, overlooking many partially positive results.[11] This critique was formalized by the statistical methods of meta-analysis that pooled together results from many studies. If two studies suggest that a literacy program, say, reduces recidivism, combining the results will provide stronger evidence than either of the studies on their own. When applied to hundreds of programs, meta-analysis also provided positive evidence for the possibility of rehabilitation.[12] Twenty-five years after Martinson, a modern review of correctional programs could state without much controversy: "Most correctional treatments for adult prisoners probably have modest positive effects."[13] The programs that worked best were tailored to the behavioral problems that led people into crime. Programs that helped offenders think through the consequences of their actions, reduce impulsivity, and resolve conflicts were all found to reduce offending. These programs seem to work better for juveniles than adults, and perhaps work better in community settings than in custody. For juveniles, these programs reduce recidivism by around twenty percentage points, from 60 to 40 percent. For adults, the program effects are only one-fifth as large.[14]

The new round of correctional evaluations also provides some support for the effects of the old staples of prison programming—work and education programs. The evaluation of the federal Post Release Employment Project is impressive for its long follow-up, measuring recidivism twelve years after release from prison.[15] Prisoners in the program, young men with less than a twelfth-grade education, took vocational training and worked in prison industries. They were matched to a comparison group who had similar demographic characteristics and criminal histories but did not participate in work or education programs. Ten years after release, the recidivism rate for those in vocational training was about 30 percent lower than in the comparison group. The largest reductions in crime were recorded by minority offenders.[16] There is also evidence that education programs can help ex-prisoners return to society. Tyler and Kling provide a careful analysis of the effects of high school GED programs in Florida prisons. They also find that benefits of prison programs are largest for black and Hispanic offenders. Analyzing quarterly earnings, they show that minorities who obtain a GED in prison earn about $200 more than similar offenders who do not enroll in education programs. The positive effects, however, are transitory and by the third year after release the earnings gap between those with prison GED and dropouts is close to zero.[17]

These temporary effects of prison programs are common and may be explained by the social setting in which prisoners are released. In the first few years, parole officers, friends and family may help ex-offenders keep their jobs, stay off drugs, and steer clear of their crime-involved peers. After release from parole and while spending time in high-crime neighborhoods, old routines of drug use and crime may recur. Although this pattern helps explain why programs only modestly reduce recidivism, it also suggests the importance of social supports in the community after release.

If modern evaluations of correctional treatment are indeed correct and prisons can have some rehabilitative effect, perhaps crime rates fell in the 1990s because offenders were reformed by imprisonment. Although there is now good evidence that prison programming modestly reduces recidivism, rehabilitation is an unlikely source of the crime drop because the resources

Table 7.2   Correctional Resources in Educational Programming

	1979	1995
State prisoners	274,563	941,642
Correctional staff	94,336	321,941
Educational staff	9,877	9,856
Educational staff (percentage of all staff)	10	3
Prisoners in educational programs (percentage)	41	22
Inmate to educational staff ratio	11	21

Source: Figures for 1979 were tabulated from the 1979 Census of State Correctional Facilities (1979). Figures for 1995 were taken from Stephan (1997), *Census of State and Federal Correctional Facilities*.

devoted to programming were shrinking through the 1980s and 1990s. Systematic data over long periods are hard to come by, but the Census of State Correctional Facilities in several years recorded the number of correctional staff employed in educational programs, and the number of prisoners enrolled in those programs.[18] The prison census shows that in 1979, fewer than ten thousand of the 94,336 correctional staff in state prisons were employed in educational programs. By 1995, the number of people teaching in prison education programs had fallen slightly, despite a threefold rise in the state prison population and the numbers of prison staff (table 7.2). Whereas 10 percent of correctional staff taught in education programs in 1979, only 3 percent did so by 1995. Participation in education programs had also fallen significantly. Two in five prisoners were enrolled in education programs in 1979 compared to just one in five in 1995. Because enrollments in education programs fell more slowly than the share of correctional staff in educational programming, class sizes also got larger. The ratio of inmates to educational staff roughly doubled from 1979 to 1995.

Other observers also report on the declining provision of rehabilitative programming, the scarcity of drug treatment, and gainful work in prisons.[19] Despite evidence for the positive effects of rehabilitative programs, declining programming effort suggests rehabilitation is an unlikely cause of the crime drop. I now turn to the incapacitation and deterrent effects of prison that have occupied most of the attention of those studying the effects of mass imprisonment on the fall in U.S. crime rates through the 1990s.

THE EFFECTS OF INCAPACITATION AND DETERRENCE

The paradigm of rehabilitation was eclipsed in the 1970s by the twin objectives of incapacitation and deterrence. Incapacitation describes how criminals are prevented from offending by the physical restraint of incarceration. Deterrence describes how would-be offenders refrain from crime in fear of the penalties. Although these theories of crime control sound simple, there are some significant complications, and empirical tests produce a wide range of results

Incapacitation

As rehabilitation was discredited through the 1970s, the rationale of incapacitation became increasingly popular among academics, commentators, and policymakers. James Q. Wilson speculated that "the gains from merely incapacitating convicted criminals might be very large."[20] Two decades later, William Spelman likened incapacitation to a catfish—an ugly looking creature that can be surprisingly tasty, nevertheless.[21] Part of the appeal of incapacitation was its simplicity. The columnist Ben Wattenberg captures the argument, observing that a "thug in prison can't shoot your sister."[22] On the other hand, rehabilitation was, at best, a complicated business that was possibly beyond the competence of government. Controlling crime through incapacitation required only that prisons do their job, and keep the inmates locked up and removed from society.

Like most theories, the details are more involved than they first appear. Assessing the effect of incapacitation involves the deceptively difficult task of calculating how much crime an offender would commit if not behind bars. Information about offending rates has been collected from official records and survey interviews.[23] This research finds that involvement in crime varies enormously. The findings of Paul Tracy, Marvin Wolfgang, and Robert Figlio are typical. Tracy and his colleagues tracked two cohorts of boys in Philadelphia from age ten to eighteen. About one-third were involved in delinquency at some time, but 60 percent of the crime was committed by a small group of chronic recidivists who made up just 7 percent of the population.[24] Surveys of adult offenders paint a similar picture. A Rand Corporation survey of prison and jail inmates found that half of all burglars committed no more than six crimes a year, but the top 10 percent committed more than two hundred.[25] The penal system will most effectively reduce crime through incapacitation if it can pick out the most active criminals.

The story is complicated further by the effects of age and the social context in which crime is committed. A central fact of criminological research is that men and women are most involved in crime in late adolescence. Criminal activity declines, even among serious offenders, as people age through their late twenties and thirties.[26] Prisoners serving very long sentences may ultimately pose little risk to society if released, simply as a result of aging. Age influences an individual's offending, whereas the social context of crime shapes the impact of incapacitation in the community. If crimes are committed in groups, the reduction in crime in a community will be less than the reduction in crime for the individual locked up. A burglary ring, for example, may continue its work even though a confederate has been arrested.[27] With drug dealing in particular, several researchers have claimed that the community impact of incapacitation is small. John DiIulio and Anne Piehl surveyed prison inmates to measure criminal activity among severe offenders. Like the Philadelphia delinquency study, Piehl and DiIulio also found great variation in criminal activity. Although most offenders were involved in violence and property crime, 27 percent were involved in drug crime only. For these 27 percent, Piehl and DiIulio argue that incarceration has no incapacitation effect.[28] Street corner drug dealers sent to prison will be immediately replaced. Similar reasoning led James Q. Wilson to revise his earlier faith in incarceration by observing that "very large increases in the prison population can produce only modest reductions in crime rates."[29]

Deterrence

Ideas about the deterrent effect of punishment can be traced to the earliest philosophers of punishment, Jeremy Bentham and Cesare Beccaria. For them, criminal penalties were evils, made necessary by the larger evils of crime. Punishment should be used sparingly with the purpose of deterring crime. Bentham, the philosophical utilitarian, foreshadowed the rationalistic theory of crime. Offenders weigh the costs of punishment against the benefits of crime. They will be deterred if the costs of crime—that is, punishment—exceed the benefits. The costs of punishment depend partly on the likelihood of being caught and the severity of the penalty. If penalties are very severe, but the chances of arrest are remote, the penalties will have little deterrent effect.

The distinction between the certainty and severity of punishment has spawned two kinds of studies of deterrence. One strand of research examines the effects of policing. Another studies incarceration. Policing studies have examined drunk driving, drug dealing, gun possession, and a variety of other offenses.[30] Police crackdowns on drug markets or drunk driving have been found to have some deterrent effect, but the reductions in offending are usually temporary. The deterrent effect declines as would-be offenders learn that they have overestimated the risk of being caught. Scenario studies have shed more light on these effects. Scenario studies ask respondents how they would behave if they were at risk of being arrested for, say, date rape or tax evasion. These studies consistently find that certainty of punishment, and to a lesser extent severity, can deter offending.

In trying to understand the deterrent effect of punishment, Daniel Nagin distinguished between its private and public consequences.[31] His scenario studies of tax evasion indicate that the public event of a criminal conviction has a much larger deterrent effect than the private event of civil penalty. This result suggests that the stigma of punishment, the public shame that accompanies detection, is an important source of deterrence, perhaps even more than the pain of the penalty. The stigma is largest, Nagin argues, when punishment is rare.

Nagin's literature review suggests that the risks of detection, and the stigma that follows, are at least as important sources of deterrence as the severity of punishment. This view is reinforced by Paul Robinson and John Darley, who argue that tougher laws are an ineffective way to deter crime.[32] They begin by arguing that potential offenders must know the penalties to be deterred and neither the general public nor criminal offenders are well informed about the penal code. David Anderson's survey of convicted felons found that only 22 percent thought they knew "exactly what the punishment would be" for the crime they committed. Another 18 percent had no idea or "thought they knew but were wrong." More than a third reported that they "didn't even think about" their punishment at the time they committed their crime.[33]

Even if potential offenders know the law, will they be able to effectively control their behavior? Robinson and Darley summarize the research:

> Available evidence suggests that potential offenders as a group are people who are less inclined to think at all about the consequences of their conduct or to guide their conduct accordingly. They are often risk-seekers rather than risk-avoiders, and as a group are more impulsive than average.[34]

They go on to observe that desires for revenge, retaliation, suddenly induced rages, feelings of threat and paranoia, and self-perceptions of brilliance in the grandiose phase of manic depression all limit a potential offender's ability to exercise self-control. Add to these personality traits the pervasive influence of addiction, drugs, and alcohol: 31 percent of state prison inmates report being on drugs at the time of their crime and 17 percent committed their crime to get money to buy drugs.[35] Add the influence of peers also involved in crime who likewise downplay the long-term consequences of punishment. Taken together, these factors suggest that, even if they knew the law, a significant fraction of offenders would not even be able to make the calculation to avoid crime.

Finally, even if the potential offender knows the law and is able to be influenced by it, the cost of offending is influenced not just by the amount of punishment but also by the probability of being caught. Psychological experiments show that deterrence declines quickly with the likelihood of punishment. In an experiment in which subjects were punished half the time following every transgression, subsequent responses were reduced by 30 percent. If subjects were punished just one time in ten, the deterrent effect dropped close to zero.[36] These findings are consistent with studies of policing which indicate that deterrence depends more on the risk of being caught than the severity of punishment, particularly for those low-rate offenders for whom punishment is most stigmatizing.

Robinson and Darley, much like Nagin, do not doubt that deterrence is possible; the key lever, however, is not the severity of punishment, but the visibility of police and the risk of detection.[37] These writers also point to the diminishing returns of punishment. Chronic offenders who already bear the stigma of a criminal conviction and who have learned they can do the time are very difficult to deter.

ESTIMATING DETERRENCE AND INCAPACITATION EFFECTS

The theories of deterrence and incapacitation resonate with commonsense. If you lock up criminals, they can't commit crime. If penalties are severe, potential criminals will be unwilling to take the risk. The reality is more complicated. Some offenders commit many crimes, and their incarceration will prevent many more. Other offenders commit few crimes, and it's often difficult to tell the two apart. Moreover, few criminologists now believe that incarcerating low-level drug dealers can significantly reduce the drug trade in local communities. Theories of deterrence are also less compelling when scrutinized closely. The idea of deterrence assumes that potential criminals can act rationally, understand risks of being caught, and the punishment that will follow. Much crime, however, is not rationally motivated. The personalities of criminals and the context in which crime is committed subvert rationality. For those who can weigh the costs and benefits of offending, the risk of arrest has greater deterrent power than the severity of punishment. Indeed, the private pain of punishment may be a less effective deterrent than the public shame of a criminal conviction. None of this suggests that prison cannot reduce crime through incapacitation or deterrence. Rather, the effects are difficult to calculate and may be smaller than we might initially expect.

The two major efforts to explain the effect of the rise in imprisonment on the fall in crime were provided by Steven Levitt and William Spelman.[38] The two men take similar approaches, using data on index crime rates from the Uniform Crime Reports and state prison populations from the fifty states from the 1970s through the 1990s. Both report that increasing imprisonment significantly reduces crime. Using similar data and methods, they calculate what I'll call an "imprisonment effect" of −.4: a 1 percent increase in the incarceration rate reduces the index crime rate by about four-tenths of 1 percent. Although Spelman's language is cautious, he finds that the prison expansion from 1971 to 1997 reduced violent crime by about 35 percent, and accounts for about 25 percent of the decline in serious violence through the 1990s.[39] Levitt's analysis is similar, but his claims are bolder. Levitt finds that the effects of prison are larger on violent crime than property crime. His cost-benefit analysis indicates that the incarceration of violent offenders yields an annual social benefit of over $40,000, well in excess of the $25,000 annual cost of a prison bed.[40] These figures suggest that more than a third of the 34-percent decline in violence in America from 1991 to 2001 results from the increase in state imprisonment.[41] After reporting large effects of incarceration on crime, Levitt concludes his analysis:

> In the absence of strong alternatives to imprisonment at the present time. . . increased reliance on incarceration appears to have been and continues to be, an effective approach to reducing crime.[42]

These estimates of the imprisonment effect on crime offer a careful and sophisticated effort to calculate the effects incarceration has on reducing crime.

Levitt and Spelman find that their estimates are robust under a variety of statistical assumptions. The results are also consistent with survey data showing that prisoners had committed, on average, fifteen crimes in the year before incarceration. Their two studies are also the first to adjust for the effects of crime rates on imprisonment. The estimates appear to show in a compelling way that the prison boom has made a major contribution to declining crime in America.

Despite the sophistication of the analysis, an imprisonment effect of −.4 that both Levitt and Spelman report is almost certainly too large. Other research estimates the imprisonment effect to be around −.1, only a quarter the size of their estimates.[43] The large imprisonment effects they calculated result from adjusting for the reverse causation of crime on the incarceration rate. In theory, imprisonment reduces crime through incapacitation and deterrence. Crime however influences the scale of imprisonment through its effects of the number of arrests and the flow of offenders through the courts. If we don't consider the positive impact of crime rates on imprisonment, the negative causal effect of prison on crime will be underestimated. In the language of econometric analysis, the imprisonment rate is endogenous to the crime rate.

In an ingenious approach Levitt developed, prison overcrowding litigation in twelve states through the 1980s is used to identify shifts in imprisonment mandated by the courts and unrelated to trends in crime.[44] By relating the decline in incarceration through federal court orders to changes in crime rates, Levitt could calculate an imprisonment effect that was apparently uncontaminated by the effect of crime on incarceration. Before adjusting for the effect of crime on imprisonment, he calculated an imprisonment effect of −.1, an estimate consistent with earlier research that indicated that the crime rate fell by .1 of 1 percent following a 1-percent rise in the imprisonment rate. After using data on overcrowding litigation to adjust for the dependence of imprisonment on crime, the imprisonment effect grows from −.1 to −.4.

The size of the adjustment tips us off that something may be wrong. The imprisonment effect increases fourfold, when adjustments are made for the influence of crime on the scale of imprisonment. If the unadjusted imprisonment effect that takes no account of the impact of crime on incarceration is wrong by a factor of four, this implies that the crime rate has a large effect on the imprisonment rate. How large is the implied effect of crime on incarceration? It is impossible to know precisely with the information we have, but if we assume that shifts in crime explain 5 to 10 percent of the variance in imprisonment, I calculate that the implied effect of crime on the incarceration rate is between about .2 and .4. That is, a 1-percent rise in crime produces a .2 to .4 rise in the incarceration rate (later in the chapter I detail these calculations). The adjustments for endogeneity suggest that the effect of crime on imprisonment is roughly equal to the imprisonment effect on crime.

Does crime really influence incarceration enough to justify the large imprisonment effects that Levitt and Spelman report? Those studies are missing an explanation of how the scale of imprisonment depends on crime and other causes. Chapters 2 and 3 provided an extended analysis of the causes of the growth imprisonment through the 1980s and 1990s and showed that crime trends were weakly related to trends in imprisonment. Growth in the penal system after 1980 was due, not to crime, but to changes in criminal processing—an increased chance of prison among those who were arrested, increased time served among those who were convicted, and an increased chance of parole revocation among those who were released. Further diluting the crime-incarceration correlation was a sharp increase in the prosecution of drug crime not reflected in the usual crime statistics. Crime among young men and youth also registered large declines unrelated to incarceration. The crime decline could be seen among poor male juveniles, whose incarceration rates did not increase dramatically, and among less-educated young men, whose incarceration rates rose sharply. These findings were consistent with a sociology of punishment in which trends in crime are only loosely and indirectly related to the scale of imprisonment. Now, if crime rates exercise little influence on the level of imprisonment, as the evidence strongly indicates, the large adjusted imprisonment effect is almost certainly a significant overestimate.

Overestimating the imprisonment effect has been traced to the use of information on overcrowding litigation to adjust for the dependence of imprisonment on crime. Nagin observes that the deterrent effects of prison are found by focusing on one change in the scale of imprisonment—court orders to reduce prison overcrowding.[45] Because court orders forced the discharge of prisoners, the adjusted imprisonment effects should be interpreted narrowly to indicate the effects of early release schemes such as parole abolition. Delaying release among those in prison may have very different effects from sending to prison those who would not have otherwise gone. Other measures that affect prison admissions rather than release—tougher drug laws or three-strikes provisions, for example—will not be tapped. Bert Useem and his colleagues worry that the states involved in overcrowding litigation are not representative of the rest of the country. Seven of the twelve are southern states, and southern penal systems, particularly those subject to federal court intervention, are unlikely to be typical. Deterrent effects may also not generalize to other parts of the country, or to other historical periods.[46] Finally, overcrowding litigation is assumed by the statistical analysis to depend neither on the crime rate nor on the imprisonment rate. Yet it is difficult to imagine how lawsuits challenging prison crowding would not be prompted in some way by changes in the size of the penal population.

If these adjusted imprisonment effects overstate the impact of the prison boom on falling crime in the 1990s, how much did rising incarceration really reduce crime? The answer, as Levitt and Spelman each persuasively show, depends on how much one thinks crime affects the incarceration rate. A number of studies estimate the effect of prison on crime, assuming the effect of crime on imprisonment to be zero. Using data on state crime rates from the early 1970s through the mid-1990s, these studies report imprisonment effects between 0 and −.2 (table 7.3). Those estimated by both Zsolt Besci and Bert Useem, Anne Piehl, and Raymond Liedka were often less than −.1, indicating that a 1-percent rise in the imprisonment reduced crime by less than one-tenth of a percent.

I also calculated imprisonment effects using the Uniform Crime Report's index crime rates from the forty-eight contiguous states for the 1971 to 2001 period. My estimates were also in the range of recent studies, but much smaller than those that both Spelman and Levitt obtain (table 7.4). My estimates indicate that a 1-percent rise in the state imprisonment rate reduced the rate of serious crime by .07 of 1 percent.[47] The estimated effects are somewhat larger for the murder rate, but lower for all violent crimes. Of course, my analysis understates the effect of the prison boom on the crime drop because it does not account for the reverse effect of crime on the scale of imprisonment. Columns 2 and 3 of table 7.4, adjust the imprisonment effect under two scenarios. The first assumes that a 1-percent rise in the crime rate raises imprisonment by .05 of a percent, a modest effect in line with theories of punishment claiming that the scale of incarceration is not closely related to the level of crime in society. The second scenario assumes that the effect of crime on imprisonment is equal to the larger estimates of

Table 7.3 **Effects of Imprisonment on Index Crime Rates in Four Studies**

Levitt (1996)		
Violent crimes	−.38 ± .36	Fifty states and D.C., 1971 to 1993
Property crimes	−.26 ± .24	
All index crimes	−.31	
Marvell and Moody (1994)		
Violent crimes	−.06 ± .11	Forty-nine states, 1971 to 1989
Property crimes	−.17 ± .06	
All index crimes	−.16	
Becsi (1999)		
Violent crimes	−.05 ± .04	Fifty states and D.C., 1971 to 1993
Property crimes	−.09 ± .03	
All index crimes	−.09 ± .03	
Useem, Piehl, and Liedka (2001)		
All index crimes	−.06 ± .05	Fifty states and D.C., 1972 to 1997
All index crimes (lagged effect)	−.04 ± .04	

Source: Author's compilations.
Note: Imprisonment effects describe the percentage change in the crime rate resulting from a 1-percent increase in the state imprisonment rate. Table is adapted from Spelman (2000, 102). Spelman's analysis replicates Levitt's results using the same data and several additional years of observation. The margin of error represents a 95-percent confidence interval.

the effects of imprisonment on crime: a 1-percent rise in crime raises imprisonment by .15 percent.[48] Assuming that crime greatly affects the level of incarceration produces larger imprisonment effects, but the margin of error of the estimates also increases. Indeed, the margin of error is so large as to prevent a confident conclusion that increased imprisonment reduces crime. In sum, my estimates indicated that the imprisonment effect on crime is between −.07 and −.18.

If the true imprisonment effect is in the range of −.07 to −.18, how much has the prison boom contributed to the drop in crime rates through the 1990s? Figure 7.2 compares two scenarios to the actual trend in the rate of index crimes between 1971 and 2001. Both scenarios assume that the rate of state imprisonment has not increased since 1971. The first assumes that the imprisonment effect is −.07, a low but relatively common estimate in the re-

Table 7.4   Effects of Imprisonment on Index Crime Rates, 1971 to 2001

	Feedback Effect of Crime on Imprisonment		
	.00 (1)	.05 (2)	.15 (3)
All crime	−.07 ± .02	−.08 ± .10	−.18 ± .29
Murder	−.11 ± .09	−.11 ± .11	−.21 ± .30
Violent crime	−.03 ± .04	−.07 ± .10	−.17 ± .30
Property crime	−.07 ± .03	−.08 ± .10	−.18 ± .29

Source: Author's compilations.

Note: Dependent variables and predictors are differences of logs, controlling for spending on police, percent black, unemployment, and state and year fixed effects. Observations are weighted in proportion to population. Adjustments for endogeneity are based on a Bayesian sensitivity analysis proposed by Leamer (1993). Margin of error indicates a 95-percent confidence interval.

search literature. The second assumes that the imprisonment effect is −.18, a larger estimate but consistent with a large effect of crime on imprisonment. Under both, crime rates would still have fallen significantly between 1991 and 2001. If the imprisonment effect is just −.07, crime rates would have fallen from fifty-eight to forty-three per thousand, a 26-percent decline. If the effect is −.18, they would have dropped from sixty-six to fifty-one per thousand, a 23-percent drop. In reality, crime fell by 28 percent, from fifty-three to thirty-eight per thousand. These figures suggest that the growth in imprisonment through the 1990s reduced crime by between 2 and 5 percent of a total decline of 28 percent. Roughly nine-tenths of the decline in serious crime through the 1990s would have happened even without the prison boom.

CONCLUSION

The evidence reviewed in this chapter suggests that mass imprisonment helped reduce crime and violence in the United States in the late 1990s, but the contribution was not large. Incarceration is usually thought to reduce crime through rehabilitation, incapacitation, and deterrence. Although pol-

Figure 7.2   Observed and Hypothetical Index Crime Rates

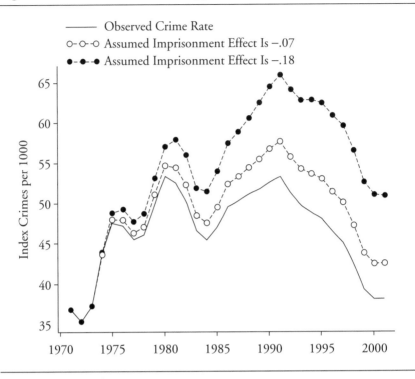

Source: Author's compilations.
Note: Hypothetical rates of crime assuming no increase in incarceration rates since 1970, and assuming the imprisonment effect is –.07 and –.18.

icy scholars of the 1970s and 1980s were widely skeptical of rehabilitative programs, there is now reasonable evidence that programs can reduce offending, but the effects are largest for juveniles, not adults. In any case, rehabilitation is not the likely cause of the 1990s crime drop because the growth in imprisonment accompanied declining support for programming. The proportion of prisoners enrolled in education programs, for example, was halved from 1979 to 1995.

Studies of the impact of the prison boom on the crime drop have focused on the deterrent and incapacitative effects of incarceration. Leading studies suggested that the growth in state imprisonment rates through the 1990s can explain about one-third of the drop in serious crime. My best estimate suggests that the 66-percent increase in the state prison population, from

725,000 to more than 1.2 million prisoners reduced the rate of serious crime by 2 to 5 percent—one-tenth of the fall in crime between 1993 and 2001. Fully 90 percent would have happened without the 480,000 new inmates in the system. In 2001, the annual cost of incarcerating a state prisoner was $22,000. This suggests that the 2- to 5-percent decline in serious crime over the eight years from 1993 to 2001 was purchased for $53 billion. Why were the crime-control effects of mass imprisonment so modest?

Three main arguments have been offered. First, locking up drug offenders does not avert serious crime.[49] As drug offenders have become an increasing share of the state prison population, incapacitation and deterrence have declined. More generally, as the legal threshold for imprisonment fell through the 1980s and 1990s, incarceration may have increased among less dangerous offenders, perhaps with fewer prior convictions, or more involved in public order offenses than violence. The incapacitative effect of imprisonment would generally decline as lower-risk prisoners are admitted. Second, as rates of incarceration become very high, the stigma of incarceration is diluted and the power of incarceration to deter crime is weakened.[50] Indeed, we saw in chapter 1 that imprisonment has become a normal part of young adulthood among less-educated African American men, suggesting that the stigma of incarceration in high-incarceration communities may be very weak indeed.

Finally, incarceration may not dramatically reduce crime because some of those released from prison may be more likely to be involved in crime, *because they were incarcerated.* In one version of this account, prison is a school for criminals, surrounding first-timers with those who have spent many years in the criminal justice system. In another version, criminal desistance—that is, finding a pathway out of a life of crime—depends on forming social bonds that provide offenders with routines, social supports, and a sense of a promising future. The importance of these social bonds has been studied most closely perhaps by Robert Sampson and John Laub. They constructed life histories of a cohort of serious delinquents born in the Boston area in the mid-1920s. They show that delinquent boys who grew up to find stable jobs and who developed mutually supportive and long-lasting marriages also found a pathway out of a life of crime. Other boys, who never settled down and never found a steady job, remained involved in crime at least into middle age, and sometimes beyond.[51] Although a good marriage and a steady job helps pave the way to normal life for a young man with a criminal record, incarceration precisely undermines economic opportunity and family stability. We have seen that ex-prisoners can find jobs after incarceration, but these jobs usually offer no earnings growth and little employment security. We have also seen that few relationships survive incarceration, and ex-prisoners are more likely than others to be involved in domestic violence. The life course builds a web of social ties and obligations that prevents young men from straying into crime and other antisocial behavior, but incarceration prevents the life course from unfolding. The large negative effects of incarceration on employment and family life help us understand why the prison boom has done so little to reduce crime in America.

APPENDIX: ANALYZING ENDOGENEITY

If the crime rate, C, and the imprisonment rate, P, are jointly normal and determined by the equations, $C = \beta P + \gamma x + e$, and $P = \theta C + \delta z + u$, where x and z are exogenous covariates, then the least squares regression of C on P and x yields a biased estimate of β, where the bias is given by, $\beta^* = \tau^2(1 - \beta\theta)/\theta$.

The bias in the estimated effect of prison on crime depends on the true effect, β, the feedback effect of crime on prison, θ and τ^2 which is a complicated function the residual variances and the cross-equation correlation: $\tau^2 = (\theta^2\sigma_e^2 + \theta\sigma_{eu})/(\theta^2\sigma_e^2 + 2\theta\sigma_{eu} + \sigma_u^2)$ (Leamer 1993). If the cross-equation correlation, σ_{eu}, is 0, the variance ratio, τ^2, describes the percentage of variance in P explained by the exogenous variation in C. If Levitt's instrumental variables estimate[52] of β and the least squares estimate measure the true effect and the bias, we can obtain estimates of θ given assumed levels of τ^2.

We can also adjust least squares estimates β for the feedback effect of prison on crime, using a Bayesian prior distribution. In the Bayesian regression on C, P is included among the regressors twice, once to estimate β and once to estimate the bias term, β^*. The effect of β^* is not identified in a classical analysis, but can be identified by a proper prior distribution on β^*. This Bayesian analysis with prior means $\theta = .05$ and $\theta = .15$ is reported in table 7.4. For this analysis, the prior variances were set equal to the prior means.

Conclusion

In the last decades of the twentieth century, mass imprisonment became a fact of American life. The deep involvement of poor black men in the criminal justice system became normal. Those drawn into the net of the penal system live differently from the rest of us. Employment is more insecure, wages are lower. Families are disrupted as incarceration separates children from their fathers and breaks up couples. Pervasive incarceration and its effects on economic opportunity and family life have given the penal system a central role in the lives of the urban poor.

The evidence to support this picture was pieced together from many sources. I began by calculating rates of incarceration for recent cohorts of young black and white men. Black men born in the late 1960s are more likely to go to prison than to finish a four-year degree or serve in the military. One-third of black men with only a high school education have prison records. Crime did not create the prison boom but it provided part of the context. Although crime rates increased significantly in the 1960s and 1970s and street violence became a serious problem for poor communities, policy makers could have responded in many different ways. By building more prisons, severely criminalizing drug-related activity, mandating prison time, and lengthening sentences, lawmakers chose a punitive course that abandoned the long-standing ideal of rehabilitation. The newly punitive regime of criminal justice was pushed hardest by a resurgent Republican Party that was making significant inroads among traditional Democrats in the South, the suburbs, and among working-class whites.

Mass imprisonment was not built by punitive criminal justice alone. Chronic joblessness among less-educated minority men in urban neighborhoods led some into the drug trade and other street hustles. Idleness in public space left others exposed to the close scrutiny of the police. Partly through crime, but more through policing and prosecution, falling wages and employment among young unskilled blacks became closely tied to mounting incarceration rates in the 1980s and 1990s. Carceral inequality was magnified as less-educated men bore the brunt of increased imprisonment.

Mass imprisonment had far-reaching effects on labor and marriage markets. By taking vast numbers of poorly educated young men out of the labor market, economic statistics on wages and employment were artificially improved. After counting prison and jail inmates among the jobless, I found that employment among less-educated black men actually declined through the economic expansion of the 1990s. The wages of young black men also appeared to grow faster than those of whites through the 1990s, but this trend was an artifact of falling labor force participation and rising imprisonment among black men. Mass imprisonment not only concealed economic inequality, it deepened inequality by reducing the pay and employment of ex-prisoners. Men with prison records were largely relegated to secondary labor market jobs that paid little, offered less security, and provided no earnings growth. The prisonized low-wage labor market contrasts with the usual picture of America's free market in low-skill work. The criminal justice system tightly grips the low-wage labor market, hiding inequality behind prison walls and deepening the disadvantage of ex-prisoners after release.

Family life in poor communities was also disrupted by mass imprisonment. One in ten young black children had a father in prison or jail by the end of 1990s. Married couples with a man in prison were at severe risk of divorce or separation. Women may be better off separated, given my findings that the partners of men with prison records were more likely to be victims of domestic violence. Domestic violence was less common in long-lasting and affectionate relationships, but prison time undermines the formation of these kinds of relationships. After this analysis, we are left with a picture of family life made difficult by difficult men, but also degraded by the forced confinement of incarceration.

Incarceration may have weakened families and economic opportunity in poor communities, but several influential studies credited mass imprisonment with reducing violent crime in the 1990s. The 1990s crime drop was a real and significant social trend that improved the quality of life among the rich and poor alike. Some analysts attributed a third or more of the 1990s crime drop to growth in the penal system. These estimates are greatly inflated in my view. My analysis of state crime rates indicated that the 66-percent increase in the state imprisonment rate between 1993 and 2001 reduced the rate of serious crime by 2 to 5 percent, about one-tenth of the 1990s crime drop. The remaining nine-tenths would likely have happened anyway, as a result of other factors like the growth in urban police forces and the pacification of the drug trade following the crack-related violence of the early 1990s.

The poor marriage and job prospects of former inmates helps explain why mass imprisonment reduced crime only slightly. A good job and a stable home life can be important stepping stones to a life out of crime. Incarceration precisely upsets the passage through these life stages. Instead of helping to draw criminal offenders into normal adult life, incarceration is a diversion from the mainstream. Although originally conceived to control the crime and disorder of the inner cities, mass imprisonment has become part of the problem, preventing the full integration of poor urban communities into the American social fabric.

Although I found that mass imprisonment had only slightly reduced serious violence, my analysis has tried to weigh the effects of incarceration not chiefly on crime but instead on social inequality. Here I draw two conclusions. First, that mass imprisonment has significantly sealed the social immobility of poor blacks. Second, if we view the effects of the prison boom in the context of its causes, mass imprisonment has significantly subtracted from the gains to African American citizenship hard won by the civil rights movement.

REPUDIATING REHABILITATION AND SOCIAL MOBILITY

I began this story by arguing that America's earliest prisons, charged with the task of moral correction, expressed a democratic ambition. In the mission of the nineteenth-century penitentiary, even those who had fallen into crime could be reformed and returned to society. The rehabilitative ideal, and the institutions it spawned, were instruments for repairing citizenship. The progressive movement of the early twentieth century articulated this democratic rationale for rehabilitative institutions. In the progressive view, crime bred in the slums and ghettos of an urbanizing America blocked the development of an equal citizenry. David Rothman links the rehabilitative ideal to the progressive project in the following way:

> The model was clear: all Americans were to become middle-class Americans. Everyone was to become hardworking, to abandon Old World vices, to respect and accumulate private property. "It is fatal for democracy," argued that leading Progressive, John Dewey, "to permit the formation of fixed classes," and a host of Progressive organizations, from the settlement houses and the playgrounds to new-style public schools and health clinics, set out to bridge the gap between the classes.[1]

The expanded democracy of the progressive vision itself rested on a democratic presumption. The project of class abatement assumed a formal equality of America's citizens in which all could be assimilated to a more perfect society. Poverty and criminality were not permanent traits in this view. These deficits could be erased by the good works of rehabilitative institutions. Public policy would serve the cause of American democracy by promoting social mobility.

The punitive criminal justice policy that flourished in the 1980s and 1990s repudiated the rehabilitative ideal in two ways. A scientific skepticism questioned whether rehabilitation was indeed possible. For social scientists who saw few positive effects in the evaluation studies of the 1950s and 1960s, criminality was a stubborn trait, impervious to work programs, education, and other treatments. The new conventional wisdom among policy experts was fully captured by the two-word summary of Robert Martinson's evaluation of correctional programming: "Nothing works." In politics, the social problem of crime was linked to another permanent trait, to race. The specter of black criminality was first raised in national politics by the Goldwater campaign in 1964, as much in response to civil rights activism as a real increase in crime. But later, as crime rates rose through the late 1960s and 1970s, drugs and violence were framed as problems of the ghetto poor. In political campaigns and media portrayals, criminal offenders were regularly personified by poor young black men. The racial stain, unlike poverty or school failure, was an unfading deficiency beyond the reach of government reform. Scientific evidence for intractable criminality and the political association of race with crime undercut the basic assumption of the rehabilitative outlook—that criminal offenders could change their behavior and be like the rest of us. The formal equality of citizens that justified the rehabilitative ideal was replaced by polarized picture of society that pitted law-abiding citizens against a persistently criminal class.

We have seen that incarceration interrupts the normal life course. Former inmates cycle in and out of low-wage jobs, unable to obtain the steady earnings growth that might provide economic security for a household. Home life is also disrupted. Men with prison records have unstable and volatile family relationships. Through its effects on work and families, incarceration redirects the life course onto a road of lasting disadvantage. Inspired by beliefs about its permanent inferiority, mass imprisonment cemented the distress of the black underclass.

THE RETRENCHMENT OF AFRICAN AMERICAN CITIZENSHIP

Writing in 1950, the British sociologist T. H. Marshall described citizenship as a "basic human equality associated with… full membership of a community."[2] Marshall tells how British citizenship, produced by the state in different forms over hundreds of years, became broader and deeper. Broader, by widening the circle of community members. Deeper, by extending citizenship rights to political freedoms of association in the nineteenth century, to claims on social welfare by the twentieth.

We can read the story of mass imprisonment as part of the evolution of African American citizenship. Each piece of this story—pervasive incarceration, unemployment, family instability—shows how mass imprisonment has created a novel social experience for disadvantaged blacks that is wholly outside of the mainstream of social life. The mass-imprisonment generation of poorly educated black men born after 1965 suffer the civil disabilities that restrict their social rights to welfare and certain occupations and political rights to the franchise. More than this legal exclusion, these men also contend with the effects of incarceration on the labor market long after prison release. The children and wives of former prisoners are also drawn into the orbit of the penal system, through the disruption of family life and the contagious stigma of incarceration. These individuals and their families are excepted from the "basic human equality" that Marshall associated with full membership in a community.

African American history is often written as a political contest over citizenship, over full membership in American society. The last chapter of this history, the civil rights movement, offered the promise of full citizenship. By 1968, a thirty-year campaign to secure the legal equality of blacks had abolished segregation and discrimination in public accommodations and employment, and eliminated the impediments to black suffrage. Lawmakers and civil rights activists were hopeful that the main barriers to blacks' full participation in American social life had finally been removed. Equal citizenship, by itself, did not amount to racial equality. But as Charles and Barbara Whalen wrote, "without this fundamental right, the pursuit of happiness… could not begin."[3] This cautious optimism was misplaced, however, and, because of the prison boom, the basic human equality hoped for from full citizenship began to recede immediately after civil rights were proclaimed.

The contraction of citizenship produced by mass imprisonment did not affect blacks as a whole. Instead, the effects were concentrated among those with little schooling. College-educated blacks, though more likely to go to prison than whites, escaped the rising incarceration rates of the 1980s and 1990s. Imprisonment became common only among poorly educated black men. The penal system thus added unemployment and family instability to those with the least economic power and family support. Because the negative effects of imprisonment were concentrated at the bottom of the social ladder, I found little evidence that mass imprisonment greatly increased family and economic inequality between blacks and whites. Instead, the largest inequalities were produced within the black population. The income gap and that in marriage rates between middle class and poor blacks would be significantly smaller, but for the effects of incarceration. In this way, mass imprisonment has institutionalized the marginality of poor blacks, setting them apart from white society and crystallizing social inequality within the African American community.

The social inequality produced by mass imprisonment is a creature of the post–civil rights era. Although racial animus certainly plays some part, discrimination is not the main driver. Economic marginality and family disruption rooted in imprisonment is largely associated with the high rate of crime among young black men. Indeed, if the analysis stopped there, the injuries of mass imprisonment would seem largely self-inflicted. For supporters of puni-tive criminal justice, the inequalities of mass imprisonment probably appear legitimate for this reason. But, beyond the social patterning of crime, mass imprisonment was produced by a historic collision between the political forces of racial conservatism and the collapse of urban labor markets. It was this collision that massively increased the scale of criminal punishment. Al-though civil rights laws established a legal equality between blacks and whites, they could not protect against the powers of economic dislocation and political reaction.

THE FUTURE OF MASS IMPRISONMENT

The uneven progress of African American citizenship finally leads us to ask whether mass imprisonment can be sustained. Will it now recede, leaving that birth cohort of black men born between, say, 1965 and 1975, stranded on an island of inter-generational disadvantage? My analysis suggests it will remain a feature of the regulation of urban poverty in America. Although in-creasingly expensive and perhaps a little obsolete in a time of low crime rates, mass imprisonment is likely to be preserved by the political and economic forces that created it.

Policy makers and voters appear to retain a keen appetite for punishment. Despite some softening of public opinion in recent years, for example, a solid majority continues to support the death penalty. Illustrating the pub-lic's zeal for harsh punishment, Larry Bobo and Devon Johnson's analysis of a 2001 survey found that support for capital punishment barely diminished even after evidence of wrongful convictions.[4] Recent electoral politics also indicate the public's willingness to stay tough on crime. In the 2004 election, Californian voters mobilized against Proposition 66, which would have elim-inated life sentences for nonviolent offenders on their third felony convic-tion. Campaign advertisements, funded by victims' advocates and the correc-tional officers' union, warned that it would free tens of thousands of predatory criminals. Despite early popular support, Proposition 66 was de-feated 53 to 47 percent.[5] More generally, I have found that large racial dis-parities in incarceration accompanied increasing class disparities through the 1980s and 1990s. As a result, the criminality of poor blacks may loom even larger in the public mind in the early 2000s than at the outset of the prison boom in the 1970s. Under these conditions, it seems likely that policy makers and voters will continue to support the incapacitative and retributive objectives of imprisonment. Appearing soft on crime will still carry significant political costs.

Just as political support for mass imprisonment remains strong, its economic preconditions also seem favorable. The 1990s economic expansion showed that less-skilled men in poor urban neighborhoods are unlikely to find work in large numbers, even in the best economic times. The political salience of inequality, if it exists at all, is minimized because the full extent of black joblessness and wage stagnation is omitted from the official statistics that shape public understanding of social problems. The inequalities on which mass imprisonment is built are deepened by it. Imprisonment undermines economic opportunity and, by weakening family bonds, strips poor communities of social capital. Mass imprisonment is thus a key component in a system of inequality—a social structure in which social inequalities are self-sustaining and those at the bottom have few prospects for upward mobility. Because they are more likely to be involved in a crime, and because they are a political lightning rod for punitive sentiment, it has become difficult to imagine how chronically idle young men would *not* be under some form of official supervision. In short, mass imprisonment is profoundly disempowering, reducing the capacity of poor communities to escape from the policies of penal discipline.

Although my analysis forecasts continuing mass imprisonment, some commentators see a thaw in criminal justice policy. A great contradiction of the prison boom was its strong support among economic conservatives who, in other spheres, would favor limited government. Even through good economic times, a growing correctional population can confront state government with the problem of either cutting other spending areas or raising state taxes. Recession in 2001 challenged state governments to pay for burgeoning correctional budgets with shrinking state tax revenues. State budget shortfalls in the early 2000s created pressures to reduce the size of the penal system. Facing budget crises in 2002, twenty-five states reduced their correctional spending. Half cut their capacity by closing prisons or otherwise eliminating prison beds.[6] Indeed conservative governors and state legislators, facing tight budgets and declining revenues, may be more eager to close prisons than to raise taxes.

In addition to the fiscal constraints, there are also signs of a more rehabilitative approach to corrections. Having passed through the prison boom, a return to the rules and philosophy of penal welfarism is no longer possible. However, new forms of rehabilitative policy have emerged in the movement for prisoner reentry programs. These provide discharge planning for prisoners, who on release receive transitional employment, housing, drug treatment, and other services.[7] Model programs in Texas, Chicago, and New York report reduced recidivism among parolees receiving these services. In their details, prisoner reentry programs often resemble the individualized case management of traditional parole supervision. Political support for reentry programs may be gathering at the national level. The 2004 State of the Union Address showed signs of softening the usual law-and-order message common in presidential politics since the late 1960s. Proposing a new spending initiative to provide job training and housing to released prisoners, the president observed that "America is the land of second chances, and when the gates of the prison open, the path ahead should lead to a better life."[8] This redemptive rhetoric would have been hard to imagine in presidential addresses of the 1980s and 1990s.

But the prisoner reentry movement is, in many ways, rehabilitation for the mass imprisonment era. The proponents of the programs assume that large-scale early release in the United States is now unlikely and policy makers must accept the inevitability of large cohorts of former prisoners returning to society. The primary goal of reentry programs is not so much to reform offenders, but the public safety and the social well-being of the poor communities to which prisoners return. Unlike the traditional rehabilitative outlook, reincarceration looms in the background for ex-prisoners who do not commit to sobriety, work, and a measure of personal responsibility. Prisoner reentry policies have been shown to benefit former inmates but are much more an adaptation to mass imprisonment than a step to decarceration.

Even if prisoner reentry programs are widely adopted, unemployment among low-skill men remains a formidable problem in the poor communities that lack a healthy local economy. Building work routines and treating addiction cannot mend the life path of men who have long been involved in crime unless a steady job that can support a household lies at the end of the program. Ultimately, reversing mass imprisonment may depend less on embracing a rehabilitative philosophy of criminal punishment and more on promoting a viable legitimate economy in ghetto neighborhoods.

The prudent forecast should probably predict a mass imprisonment moderated by fiscal constraint and a renewed, if faint, commitment to rehabilitation. Still, the small budgetary and policy retreats from mass imprisonment must contend with a powerful systemic logic in which race and class inequality are becoming greater rather than less. The self-sustaining character of mass imprisonment as an engine of social inequality makes it likely that the penal system will remain as it has become, a significant feature on the new landscape of American poverty and race relations.

NOTES

PREFACE
1. Western and Beckett (1999).
2. Western and Pettit (2000).
3. Pettit and Western (2004).

INTRODUCTION
1. Beaumont and Tocqueville (1833/1964, 34).
2. Beaumont and Tocqueville (1833/1964, 35, 117–18).
3. Pastore and Maguire (2005), tables 6.1 and 6.2.
4. Oshinsky (1996), Meyers (1998).
5. Harrison and Beck (2005, 11).
6. Pettit and Western (2004).

CHAPTER 1
1. Irwin (1985, 1–17).
2. Maguire and Pastore (2001, 519).
3. Blumstein and Beck (1999, 36, 49).
4. Mauer (2003).
5. Census estimates of black and white men's unemployment rates are calculated by Robert Fairlie and William Sundstrom (1999). Gopal Singh and Stella Yu (1995) reports race differences in infant mortality. John Scholz and Kara Levine (2002) review research on racial differences in wealth. Herbert Smith, Philip Morgan, and Tanya Koropeckyj-Cox (1996) report on nonmarital fertility from 1960 to 1992.
6. Christopher Uggen and Sara Wakefield (2005) review the literature.

7. Robert Sampson and John Laub (1993; Laub and Sampson 2003) and Mark Warr (1998) have studied the effects of marriage on desistance from crime. John Hagan (1993) and Christopher Uggen (2000) have studied the role of employment.

8. Elder (1987, 543). The effects of military service on status attainment over the life course have also been studied by Dennis Hogan (1981), Glen Elder (1986), and Yu Xie (1992).

9. Sampson and Laub (1993, 223) and Katherine Edin and her colleagues (2004) both report on qualitative interviews in which ex-inmates see incarceration as a transforming event that led away from crime.

10. Harry Holzer (1996) and Devah Pager (2003) have used audit studies and surveys to study employers' aversion to hiring men with criminal records. The Office of the Pardon Attorney (1996) and Amy Hirsch and colleagues (2002) list the civil disabilities limiting the access of ex-felons to occupations and welfare benefits. Christopher Uggen and Jeff Manza (2002) study felon disenfranchisement.

11. Elder's (1974/1999) classic study describes the collective experience of a cohort of Californian boys, growing up through the Depression.

12. Sampson and Laub (1996) and Elder (1999, 153–73; Dechter and Elder 2004) have studied the positive life course consequences of military service for World War II veterans.

13. Modell, Furstenberg, and Hershberg (1976), Hogan (1981).

14. Allen and Jewel (1996).

15. Sutton (2000).

16. Freeman (1996, 25).

17. Irwin and Austin (1997, 156).

18. Garland (2001a, 1–2).

19. I focus on prison, rather than jail, because millions of people cycle through America's jail system each year and there are no national data sources that record the entry and exit of jail inmates.

20. Dropouts of the late 1990s, just 14 percent of the 1965 to 1969 cohort, may be less able and more crime-prone than the dropouts of the late 1970s who represented more than 25 percent of the 1945 to 1949 cohort. If the selectivity of education were influencing imprisonment, we should also see increased imprisonment among college-educated blacks, as college education became more common. However, risks of imprisonment among college-educated black men slightly declined, not increased. We can also guard against the effects of selectivity by considering all noncollege men, whose share of the black and white male populations remained roughly constant from 1980 to 2000. The risks of

imprisonment for all noncollege men, black and white, grew significantly from 1980 to 2000.

21. Garland (2001a, 1).
22. Garland (2001a, 2).
23. Wacquant (2001, 103).
24. BJS (1990, 1993, 1994, 1997a, 2001).
25. BJS (1997b, 1997c, 1997d, 1999a).
26. Pettit and Western (2004).
27. Bonczar and Beck (1997).

CHAPTER 2

1. Alfred Blumstein (2000) discusses homicide and robbery rates among young black men in the 1990s. The association of race and economic disadvantage with high rates of homicide offending has been analyzed by Judith and Peter Blau (1982), Gary LaFree and Kriss Drass (1996), and Steven Messner, Lawrence Raffalovich, and Richard McMillan (2001).
2. Merton (1968, 223).
3. Becker (1968).
4. The links between marriage and crime are analyzed by Mark Warr (1998) and John Laub, Daniel Nagin, and Robert Sampson (1998). Sampson and William Wilson (1995) argued that the socially isolated, poor, urban neighborhoods lacked the social supports and role models to prevent violent crime among youth. Sampson, Jeffrey Morenoff, and Thomas Gannon-Rowley (2002) review recent empirical studies of the effects of neighborhood characteristics on crime.
5. In addition to the study by Kenneth Land, Patricia McCall, and Lawrence Cohen (1990), both Bruce Western, Meredith Kleykamp, and Jake Rosenfeld (2004) and Richard Freeman (1995) review research on the effects of labor market conditions on crime.
6. Sampson (1987).
7. Sampson and Wilson (1995), Sampson and Raudenbush (1999).
8. Bourgois (1989, 10).
9. Bourgois (1989, 10).
10. Venkatesh and Levitt (2000, 447). John Hagan (1993) reviews more of the ethnographic research.
11. Anderson (1999, 134). William Julius Wilson (1996, 59–61) provides a similar analysis.
12. Sullivan (1989, 161).

13. Braman (2004, 21–22).

14. See, for example, Donziger (1996, 42–43), Mauer (1999, 30–32), and Christie (2000, 105–8).

15. Christie (2000, 107).

16. Levitt (2004).

17. *Sourcebook of Criminal Justice Statistics 1984*, 635, Maguire and Pastore (2001, 485).

18. Maguire and Pastore (2001, 494).

19. Garland (2001b, 152–53), Ruth and Reitz (2003, 16–17).

20. Ruth and Reitz (2003, 40–45).

21. Pastore and Maguire (2005, table 3.106).

22. Blumstein (1982, 1993).

23. Blumstein and Beck (1999).

CHAPTER 3

1. Rusche (1933/1978, 4). Rusche's 1933 essay "Labor Market and Penal Sanction" (originally a research proposal to the Frankfurt Institute for Social Research), digests the main theoretical intuitions of *Punishment and Social Structure*, Rusche's historical account of the transformation of criminal punishment, ultimately published with the contributions and editorial work of Otto Kirchheimer (Rusche and Kirchheimer 1939/2003).

2. Quinney (1974), Spitzer (1975).

3. Spitzer (1975, 645).

4. Steven Box and Chris Hale (1982) studied the relationship between unemployment and imprisonment rates in Britain. Harsh treatment by court officials of minority youth has been studied in Britain by Stuart Hall (1978) and in the United States by Charles Tittle and Debra Curran (1988).

5. Dubber (2001).

6. See, for example, Duneier (1999, 304–7) and Anderson (1990, 193–98).

7. Wilson (1968, chap. 2), Chambliss (2000, chap. 3).

8. Arguments about judges' perceptions of the culpability and rehabilitation of low-status defendants have been made by James Kluegel (1990), Darrell Steffensmeier, Jeffery Ulmer, and John Kramer (1998, 770), David Greenberg (1977b), Celesta Albonetti (1991).

9. Spohn and Holleran (2000), D'Alessio and Stolzenberg (2002).

10. See also Tonry (1995, 104–16). One of the few studies that systematically observes how policing produces racial disparities in drug arrests is provided by

Beckett and her colleagues (2004) in their analysis of open-air drug markets in Seattle.

11. Wacquant (2000, 2001).

12. Wacquant (2000, 284).

13. Wacquant (2001, 103–4).

14. David Garland (2001b, 65–68) discusses the growing skepticism of policy experts with incarceration. The American Friends Service Committee (1971), Robert Somer (1976), and Calvert Dodge (1975) offer influential criticisms of incarceration.

15. Rothman (1980/2002), Blomberg and Lucken (2000, 99–116).

16. David Rothman (1980/2002, 165–74) provides a historical discussion of parole. Joan Petersilia (1999) discusses parole's rehabilitative aspirations.

17. Garland (1990).

18. Edgardo Rotman (1995) and Rothman (1980/2002) both discuss the historical failure of the rehabilitative ideal.

19. DiIulio (1987, 49–95).

20. Myers (1998), Oshinsky (1996), Ayers (1986).

21. Beckett (1997), Guetzkow (2004, 151–58).

22. Mauer (1999, 146–47), Blumstein (2002, 466–67). See also chapter 2.

23. Blumstein (2002, 468).

24. Beckett (1997), Gest (2001).

25. Niemi, Muller, and Smith (1989).

26. Thomas and Mary Edsall (1991) discuss the importance of ethnicity, region, and class for Republican support from the 1960s. Jeff Manza and Clem Brooks (1999, 66–67) describe the shift in the working class vote to the Republican Party (but compare, 80).

27. Button (1978, 121–55).

28. Zimring and Hawkins (1992, 147).

29. George Bush quoted by Edsall and Edsall (1991, 225).

30. The high-incarceration governors included Judd Gregg (New Hampshire), John Ashcroft (Missouri), Carroll Campbell (South Carolina), Michael Castle (Delaware), Wallace Wilkinson (Kentucky), and Evan Mecham (Arizona). Wilkinson was the lone Democrat. The low-incarceration governors in the comparison states included John McKernan (Maine, Republican), Joan Finney (Kansas, Democrat), James Martin (North Carolina, Republican), William Schaefer (Maryland, Democrat). Joseph Davey (1998) contrasts Arizona with California, Nevada, New Mexico, and Utah, whose governors were evenly di-

vided between Democrats and Republicans in 1987. California may be a poor point of comparison because state incarceration rates grew strongly there through the 1980s under Republican Governor George Deukmejian.

31. Davey (1998, 56–57).
32. Murakawa (2004, chap. 3).
33. Windelsham (1998, 104–7).
34. Greenberg and West (2001, 625).
35. Jacobs and Helms (1996).
36. Jacobs and Carmichael (2001).
37. Greenberg and West (2001).
38. Somer (1976).
39. American Friends Service Committee (1971, 124).
40. Wilson (1975, 172).
41. Garland (2001b), Tonry (1996), Griset (1991, 31–35).
42. Marvell (1995). See also Crotty-Nicholson (2004).
43. Christie (1993), Tonry (1996, 200–23).
44. Tonry (1996, 49–59).
45. Petersilia (2003, 65), Marvell and Moody (1996, 110–11).
46. Petersilia (2003, 66), Hughes, Wilson, and Beck (2001).
47. Blumstein (1988, 238), Rothman (1980/2002, 188–89).
48. Marvell and Moody (1996).
49. Hughes, Wilson, and Beck (2001, table 7).
50. Tonry (1996, 145–46).
51. Griset (1991).
52. Gonnerman (2003).
53. Bureau of Justice Assistance (1996, 6–7).
54. Abramsky (2002).
55. Zimring, Hawkins, and Kamin (2001, 64).
56. Ditton and Wilson (1999, 3).
57. Ditton and Wilson (1999, 2).
58. David Jacobs and Ronald Helms (2001) report evidence of the effects of economic inequality imprisonment, but inequality effects were rejected by Sean Nicholson-Crotty (2004), Jacobs and Jason Carmichael (2001), and David Greenberg and Valerie West (2001). Jacobs and Carmichael (2001) and Kevin Smith (2004) both report the positive effects of Republican political strength on incarceration, in contrast to Greenberg and West (2001).

59. Theodore Chiricos and Miriam Delone (1992) and Bruce Western, Len Lopoo, and Sara McLanahan (2004) review the literature.

60. Greenberg and West (2001), Beckett and Western (2001).

61. Frey (2004).

62. Other analyses, not reported, also studied the effects of Republicans in the state legislatures. These analyses yielded results similar to those reported below.

63. Because some researchers found that sentencing guidelines slowed the growth of incarceration, I also estimated their effects in isolation. The results were similar to those found for determinate sentencing, in general.

64. Ayers (1984).

65. See, for example, Jacobs and Carmichael (2001), Jacobs and Helms (2001), Greenberg and West (2001), Smith (2004).

66. Hispanics are not included in the analysis because they are not recorded in a consistent way across states in the NCRP data.

67. I also experimented with data on UCR crimes, as in the state analysis, and obtained results substantively identical to those below.

68. Similar to the state analysis, the estimated effects of earnings and employment may be biased by the impact of imprisonment on the labor market. In particular, imprisonment may create the appearance of improved earnings and employment by removing men with poor job prospects. Chapter 5 suggests that by the end of the 1990s, prison and jail among young black men raises observed average wages 8 percent as low-wage workers are removed from the lower tail of the distribution. On the other hand, men reentering society after leaving prison are likely to fare worse, so the effects of imprisonment on the labor market are approximately offsetting, at least in the short term.

69. Harrison (2000).

70. National Bureau of Economic Research (1979, 2000).

71. Bureau of Justice Assistance (1998), Ditton and Wilson (1999), Tonry (1996), and Wicharaya (1995).

72. Klarner (2003).

73. BJS (2002).

74. National Crime Victimization Survey (1983–1999).

CHAPTER 4

1. Newman (1999, xiii–xiv).

2. Shipler (2004, 11).

3. Harrington (1962, 10).
4. Harrington (1962, 13).
5. Massey and Denton (1991).
6. Wilkes and Iceland (2004).
7. Orwell (1937, 87).
8. Elder (1974), Hogan (1981).
9. Clogg (1974).
10. *Washington Post* (February 6, A1).
11. *New York Times* (December 13, 1998, C-4).
12. Butler and Heckman (1977).
13. Welch (1990, S42), Jaynes (1990).
14. Heckman (1989).
15. Blau and Beller (1992), Chandra (2003).
16. Francine Blau and Andrea Beller (1992), Chinhui Juhn (2003), and Amitabh Chandra (2003) assume that nonworkers would receive wage offers around 60 percent as large as those received by workers.
17. See, for example, Crouch (1985), Colbjørnsen and Kalleberg (1988), Korpi (1990), Kolberg and Esping-Andersen (1990), Hicks (1994), and Janoski, McGill, and Tinsley (1997).
18. Olson (1982), Lindbeck (1985), Giersch (1993), OECD (1994).
19. Western and Pettit (2005).
20. Blau and Beller (1992), Chandra (2003).
21. Blau and Beller (1992).

CHAPTER 5

1. Freeman (1999) describes the widening gap in incomes as the "new inequality."
2. Mishel, Bernstein, and Boushey (2003, 149).
3. Bruce Western, Jeffrey Kling, and David Weiman (2001) review the literature.
4. Robert Sampson and William Julius Wilson (1995) outline a theory of ghetto crime that builds on Clifford Shaw and Henry McKay's (1942) classic study of social disorganization. Sampson, Jeffrey Morenoff, and Thomas Gannon-Rowley (2002) review recent research.
5. Duster (1997), Sullivan (1989), Bourgois (1995).
6. Levitt and Venkatesh (2001, 770–71).
7. Freeman and Fagan (1999).
8. More information about the schooling of prison and jail inmates is provided by Caroline Harlow (2003).

9. Grogger (1995), Kling (1999), Lott (1990), Waldfogel (1994a).

10. Richard Freeman (1992) and Western and Katherine Beckett (1999) analyze the NLSY.

11. Boshier and Johnson (1974), Buikhuisen and Dijksterhuis (1971).

12. Holzer (1996, 59).

13. Pager (2003).

14. Office of the Pardon Attorney (1996).

15. Legal Action Center (2004).

16. Freeman (1992), Grogger (1995), Western and Beckett (1999).

17. Jeffrey Kling (1999), for example, finds that each additional year in prison has a negative effect on earnings.

18. Irwin and Austin (1997, 121). See also Haney (2003) on the behaviorial effects of supermax facilities and Maruna and Toch (2005) on imprisonment and criminal desistance.

19. See, for example, Jankowski (1991, 272–76), and Venkatesh and Levitt (2000).

20. Granovetter (1995, 173–74).

21. Studies of administrative data are reported by Kling (1999), John Lott (1990), Daniel Nagin and Joel Waldfogel (1998), Waldfogel (1994a, 1994b), Jeffrey Grogger (1992, 1995), Becky Pettit and Christopher Lyons (2004).

22. Rossi, Beck, and Lenihan (1980, 182–83). Robert Kornfeld and Howard Bloom (1999, 175, 194) find that male youth with a prior arrest understate their quarterly earnings by a third to a half in unemployment insurance records compared to survey reports.

23. Grogger (1992, 101).

24. The effects of incarceration have been analyzed by Grogger (1992), Freeman (1992), Western and Beckett (1999). Bushway (1996) analyzes the National Youth Survey.

25. Center for Human Resource Research (2004).

26. Western (2002) matches NLSY incarceration rates to imprisonment rates for men under age forty. Survey nonresponse does not appear to be a significant source of bias because response rates for those interviewed in prison are just as high as for those who never are.

27. LaLonde (1986).

28. Hirschi and Gottfredson (1983).

29. See, for example, Gottfredson and Hirschi (1990).

30. Tracy, Wolfgang, and Figlio (1990).

31. Doeringer and Piore (1971).

32. Kalleberg, Reskin, and Hudson (2000).

33. Akerlof (1982).

34. Granovetter (1995, 173–74).

35. Lott (1990), Waldfogel (1994a). Kling (1999) reports similar results for white-collar offenders.

36. Nagin and Waldfogel (1998).

37. Sampson and Laub (1993, 153–68).

38. Duneier (1999), Jankowski (1991, 281), Sullivan (1989). See also Hagan (1993).

39. Sullivan (1989, 64).

40. Sullivan (1989, 72).

41. Evans (1968, 208).

42. Consistent with slow wage growth among former inmates, a few studies find that the earnings penalty for arrest or conviction is larger among older workers. See Bushway (1996) and Nagin and Waldfogel (1998).

43. BJS (2004).

44. See, for example, Zimring and Hawkins (1995).

45. See Western (2002).

CHAPTER 6

1. Sampson and Laub (1993), Laub, Nagin and Sampson (1998).

2. See Warr (1998). Laub and Sampson (2004) also emphasize the routines of married life that constrain crime.

3. David Ellwood and Christopher Jencks (2004) detail trends in family structure for blacks and whites at different levels of education. Part of the decline in marriage from age twenty-five to thirty-four also reflects delays in marriage until after the mid-thirties.

4. Wilson (1987).

5. See, for example, Lichter, LeClere, and McLaughlin (1991), McLanahan and Casper (1995), and Blau et al. (2000).

6. Sampson and Laub (1993, 132).

7. See, for example, Farrington (1989), Baker and Mednick (1984).

8. DuBois (1899/1973, 67, 70, 72).

9. Frazier (1939), Myrdal (1944/1996, 930–35), Office of Policy Planning and Research (1965).

10. Liebow (1966, 131).

11. Liebow (1966, 135–36).

12. See for example, Zimring and Hawkins (1995) and chapter 7 this volume.
13. Edin, Nelson, and Paranal (2004, 54–55).
14. Nurse (2002, 83). See also Braman (2003, 50–51).
15. Edin, Nelson, and Paranal (2004, 57).
16. Braman (2003, 109).
17. Braman (2003, 110).
18. Braman (2003), Travis (2004, chap. IIIB).
19. Mumola (2000, 3).
20. Hairston (1995), Nurse (2002).
21. Braman (2003, 86).
22. Sabol and Lynch (2003).
23. Wilson (1987, 83–92).
24. Edin (2000).
25. Edin (2000, 29).
26. Anderson (1999, 153).
27. Edin (2000, 28).
28. Goffman (1963, 30).
29. Braman (2003, 170).
30. Nurse (2002, 109).
31. Nurse (2002). See also Edin, Nelson, and Paranal (2004, 62).
32. Braman (2003).
33. Nurse (2002, 57–61).
34. See chapter 1 this volume, Calculating Rates and Risks of Incarceration.
35. Edin (2000).
36. Nurse (2002), Sullivan (1989).
37. It would also be useful to study factors that are just related to incarceration, but not marriage. Some have suggested that state sentencing laws are strongly related to the risk of incarceration but should be unrelated to marriage rates. Chapter 3, however, showed that there is mixed evidence for the positive effects of determinate sentencing on incarceration rates. Indeed, sentencing guidelines may even have moderated prison growth.
38. Petersilia (2003, 41).
39. Travis (2004, 257).
40. For example, Tonry (1999), Mauer (2000).
41. Piehl and DiIulio (1995).
42. "The Fragile Families and Child Wellbeing Study (Survey of New Parents) Mother's 1-Year Follow-up Survey" (2003, 66).

43. Sampson and Laub (1993).

44. Other variables recording whether husbands were encouraging or critical were also available and they produced results similar to those reported. Reichman et al. (2001).

45. BJS (1993, 1994, 1997a, 1997b, 1997c, 1997d, 1999a), BJS and Federal Bureau of Prisons (2001).

46. Current Population survey (1980, 2000).

47. BJS and Federal Bureau of Prisons (2001) and BJS (1999a).

48. Western, Lopoo, and McLanahan (2004). The Fragile Families Survey is described by Reichman et al. (2001).

CHAPTER 7

1. The leading studies are by William Spelman (2000), Rosenfeld (2000), Steven Levitt (2004).

2. Blumstein (2000), Cork (1999).

3. Grogger (2000) and Levitt (2004) also express skepticism that the economic expansion contributed to the crime drop. The main arguments for the 1990s crime drop are excellently surveyed in the edited book by Alfred Blumstein and Joel Wallman (2000). Levitt (2004) and John Donohue and Levitt (2001) provide evidence for the effects of legalized abortion on crime.

4. Levitt (2004) and Spelman (2000) are the key studies, which I discuss in greater detail below.

5. William Sabol and James Lynch (2001, 11–12) report figures on program participation. Petersilia (2005) has called for a reinvestment in prison programs.

6. William Bennett, John DiIulio, and John Walters, for example, describe the effects of prison programming as "mixed, anemic, or nonexistent" (1996, 48).

7. Lipton, Martinson, and Wilks (1975).

8. See also Achen (1986).

9. Martinson (1974, 25).

10. Sechrest, White, and Brown (1979), Greenberg (1977a), Brody (1976).

11. Palmer (1975).

12. Lipsey (1992).

13. Gaes et al. (1999, 361).

14. Gaes et al. (1999, 370–71).

15. Saylor and Gaes (1997).

16. Saylor and Gaes (1999).

17. Tyler and Kling (2004).

18. Bureau of Justice Statistics (1997e, 1998).
19. Petersilia (1999), Travis (2005).
20. Wilson (1975, 22).
21. Spelman (1994, v).
22. Quoted in Piehl and DiIulio (1995, 23).
23. See, for example, Tracy, Wolfgang, and Figlio (1990), Visher (1986), DiIulio and Piehl (1991), Piehl and DiIulio (1995).
24. Tracy, Wolfgang, and Figlio (1990).
25. Visher (1986, 167).
26. Gottfredson and Hirschi (1990).
27. Zimring and Hawkins (1995, 43).
28. Piehl and DiIulio (1995, 25). See also DiIulio and Piehl (1991).
29. Wilson (1994, 38).
30. Nagin and Waldfogel (1998) provide an excellent review.
31. Nagin (1998).
32. Robinson and Darley (2004).
33. Anderson (2002).
34. Robinson and Darley (2004, 179).
35. BJS (1995, 5, 8).
36. Robinson and Darley (2004, 183).
37. Robinson and Darley (2004), Nagin (1998).
38. Levitt's (1996) most detailed analysis used data from 1971 to 1993, a period that preceded the crime drop. He extrapolated from those findings to reflect on the effects of prison on crime in the late 1990s (2004). Spelman (2000) augmented Levitt's original data to estimate the effect of imprisonment on murder and other serious crime from 1971 to 1997.
39. Spelman (2000, 108, 123).
40. Levitt (1996, 346–47).
41. Levitt (2004, 184).
42. Levitt (1996, 348).
43. See Marvell and Moody (1994) and Useem, Piehl, and Liedka (2001). Spelman (2000, 102) also lists several studies with imprisonment effects in the neighborhood of −.1.
44. Levitt (1996).
45. Nagin (1998).
46. Useem, Piehl, and Liedka (2001, 6).

47. The margin of error of plus or minus .02 indicates that the imprisonment effect is statistically significant.
48. See Analyzing Endogeneity later this chapter.
49. Piehl and DiIulio (1995), Wilson (1994).
50. Nagin (1998).
51. Sampson and Laub (1993), Laub and Sampson (2004). The impact of employment on desistance has also been studied by Christopher Uggen (2000). Mark Warr (1998) and Laub, Nagin, and Sampson (1998) have examined marriage and criminal desistance. Sampson and Laub (1993) and Laub and Sampson (2004) also emphasize the importance of military service for criminal desistance.
52. Levitt (1996).

CONCLUSION

1. Rothman (1980/2002, 49).
2. Marshall (1950/1992, 6).
3. Whalen and Whalen (1985, 234).
4. Bobo and Johnson (2004) report that in the Race, Crime, and Public Opinion Study, 34 percent of white respondents and 9 percent of blacks would be unlikely to vote for gubernatorial candidate who opposed the death penalty because of her concerns about wrongful conviction. When respondents are told that seventy-nine death row inmates have been exonerated since 1976, opposition drops to 31 percent for whites and 8 percent for blacks.
5. Furrillo (2004), Walters (2004).
6. Michael Jacobson (2005, 78–105) discusses the effects of state budget crises in 2002 and 2003 on correctional spending. Jacobson also reports that, though thirteen states reduced prison capacity, nine cut prison programs, and others introduced hiring freezes or delays on new prison construction.
7. Jeremy Travis (2005) and Joan Petersilia (2003) detail the key features of prisoner reentry programs, and describe a number of innovative programs across the country.
8. Bush (2004).

REFERENCES

Abramsky, Sasha. 2002. *Hard Time Blues: How Politics Built a Prison Nation*. New York: Dunne Books.

Achen, Christopher. 1986. *The Analysis of Quasi-Experiments*. Berkeley: University of California Press.

Akerlof, George A. 1982. "Labor Contracts as Partial Gift Exchange." *Quarterly Journal of Economics* 97: 543–69.

Albonetti, Celesta A. 1991. "An Integration of Theories to Explain Judicial Discretion." *Social Problems* 38: 247–66.

Allen, Walter R. and Joseph O. Jewell. 1996. "The Miseducation of Black America." In *An American Dilemma Revisited: Race Relations in a Changing World*, edited by Obie Clayton, Jr. New York: Russell Sage Foundation.

American Friends Service Committee. 1971. *Struggle for Justice. A Report on Crime and Punishment in America*. New York: Hill and Wang.

Anderson, David. 2002. "The Deterrence Hypothesis and Picking Pockets at the Pickpocket's Hanging." *American Law and Economics Review* 4: 295–313.

Anderson, Elijah. 1990. *Streetwise: Race, Class, and Change in an Urban Community*. Chicago: University of Chicago Press.

———. 1999. *Code of the Street: Decency, Violence, and the Moral Life of the Inner City*. New York: W. W Norton.

Ayers, Edward. L. 1986. *Vengeance and Justice: Crime and Punishment in the Nineteenth Century American South*. New York: Oxford University Press.

Baker, Robert L., and Birgitte R. Mednick. 1984. *Influences on Human Development: A Longitudinal Perspective*. Boston, Mass.: Kluwer.

Beaumont, Gustave de, and Alexis de Tocqueville. 1833/1964. *On the Penitentiary*

System in the United States and its Applications in France, translated by Francis Lieber. Carbondale: Southern Illinois University Press.

Beck, Allen, and Lauren Glaze. 2004. "Correctional Populations in the United States, 1980–2003." Washington: U.S. Department of Justice, Bureau of Justice Statistics. Available at: http://www.ojp.usdoj.gov/bjs/glance/sheets/corr2.wk1.

Becker, Gary S. 1968. "Crime and Punishment: An Economic Approach." *Journal of Political Economy* 76: 169–217.

Beckett, Katherine. 1997. *Making Crime Pay: Law and Order in Contemporary American Politics.* New York: Oxford University Press.

Beckett, Katherine, Kris Nyrop, Lori Pfingst, and Melissa Bowen. 2004. "Drug Abuse, Drug Possession Arrests, and the Question of Race: Lessons from Seattle." Manuscript. Seattle: University of Washington.

Beckett, Katherine, and Bruce Western. 2001. "Governing Social Marginality: Welfare, Incarceration, and the Transformation of State Policy." In *Mass Imprisonment: Social Causes and Consequences,* edited by David Garland. London: Sage.

Becsi, Zsolt. 1999. "Economics and Crime in the United States." *Economic Review of the Federal Reserve Bank of Atlanta* 84: 38–56.

Bennett, William J., John J. DiIulio, and John P. Walters. 1996. *Body Count: Moral Poverty. . . and How to Win America's War Against Crime and Drugs.* New York: Simon & Schuster.

Blau, Francine D., and Andrea H. Beller. 1992. "Black-White Earnings Over the 1970s and 1980s: Gender Differences in Trends." *Review of Economics and Statistics* 74: 276–86.

Blau, Francine D., Lawrence M. Kahn, and Jane Waldfogel. 2000. "Understanding Young Women's Marriage Decisions: The Role of Labor and Marriage Market Conditions." *Industrial and Labor Relations Review* 53: 624–47.

Blau, Judith R., and Peter M. Blau. 1982. "The Cost of Inequality: Metropolitan Structure and Violent Crime." *American Sociological Review* 47: 114–29.

Blomberg, Thomas G., and Karol Lucken. 2000. *American Penology: A History of Control.* New York: Aldine DeGruyter

Blumstein, Alfred. 1982. "On Racial Disproportionality of the United States' Prison Populations." *Journal of Criminal Law and Criminology* 73: 1259–81.

———. 1988. "Prison Populations: A System out of Control?" *Crime and Justice* 10: 231–66.

———. 1993. "Racial Disproportionality in the U.S. Prison Population Revisited." *University of Colorado Law Review* 64: 743–60.

———. 2000. "Disaggregating the Violence Trends." In *The Crime Drop in Amer-*

ica, edited by Alfred Blumstein and Joel Wallman. New York: Cambridge University Press.

————. 2002. "Prisons: A Policy Challenge." In *Crime: Public Policies for Crime Control*, edited by James Q. Wilson and Joan Petersilia. San Francisco: National Council on Crime and Delinquency.

Blumstein, Alfred, and Allen J. Beck. 1999. "Population Growth in U.S. Prisons, 1980-1996." In *Crime and Justice: Prisons*, vol. 26, edited by Michael Tonry and Joan Petersilia. Chicago: University of Chicago Press.

Blumstein, Alfred, and Elizabeth Graddy. 1981. "Prevalence and Recidivism Index Arrests: A Feedback Model." *Law and Society Review* 16: 265–90.

Blumstein, Alfred, and Joel Wallman, eds. 2000. *The Crime Drop in America*. Cambridge: Cambridge University Press.

Bobo, Lawrence C., and Devon Johnson. 2004. "A Taste for Punishment." *DuBois Review* 1(1): 151–80.

Bonczar, Thomas P., and Allen J. Beck. 1997. *Lifetime Likelihood of Going to State or Federal Prison*. Bureau of Justice Statistics Bulletin, NCJ 160092. Washington: U.S. Department of Justice.

Boshier, Roger, and Derek Johnson. 1974. "Does Conviction Affect Employment Opportunities?" *British Journal of Criminology* 14: 264–68.

Bourgois, Philipe I. 1989. "Crack in Spanish Harlem: Culture and Economy in the Inner City." *Anthropology Today* 5: 6–11.

Box, Steven, and Chris Hale. 1982. "Economic Crisis and the Rising Prison Population in England and Wales." *Crime and Social Justice* 17: 20–35.

Braman, Donald S. 2004. *Doing Time on the Outside: Incarceration and Family Life in Urban America*. Ann Arbor: University of Michigan Press.

Brody, S. R. 1976. *The Effectiveness of Sentencing: A Review of the Literature*. Home Office Research Report No. 35. London: HMSO.

Buikhuisen, Wouter, and Fokke P.H. Dijksterhuis. 1971. "Delinquency and Stigmatization." *British Journal of Criminology* 11: 185–87.

Bureau of Justice Assistance. 1998. *1996 National Survey of State Sentencing Structures*. Washington: U.S. Department of Justice.

Bureau of Justice Statistics (BJS). 1990. *Survey of Inmates of State Correctional Facilities and Census of State Adult Correctional Facilities, 1974*. [Computer file]. Conducted by U.S. Department of Commerce, Bureau of the Census. 3rd ICPSR ed. Ann Arbor, Mich.: Inter-university Consortium for Political and Social Research [producer and distributor].

————. 1993. *Survey of Inmates of State and Federal Correctional Facilities, 1991*.

[Computer file]. Conducted by U.S. Department of Commerce, Bureau of the Census. ICPSR ed. Ann Arbor, Mich.: Inter-university Consortium for Political and Social Research [producer and distributor].

———. 1994. *Survey of Inmates of State Correctional Facilities, 1986.* [Computer file]. Conducted by the U.S. Department of Commerce, Bureau of the Census. 2nd ICPSR ed. Ann Arbor, Mich.: Inter-university Consortium for Political and Social Research [producer and distributor],

———. 1995. *Drugs and Crime Facts, 1994.* Washington: Department of Justice. NCJ 154043.

———. 1997a. *Survey of Inmates of State Correctional Facilities, 1979.* [Computer file]. Conducted by the U.S. Department of Commerce, Bureau of the Census. 3rd ICPSR ed. Ann Arbor, Mich.: Inter-university Consortium for Political and Social Research [producer and distributor].

———. 1997b. *Survey of Jail Inmates, 1978.* [Computer file]. Conducted by U.S. Department of Commerce, Bureau of the Census. 5th ICPSR ed. Ann Arbor, Mich.: Inter-university Consortium for Political and Social Research [producer and distributor].

———. 1997c. *Survey of Inmates of Local Jails, 1983.* [Computer file]. Conducted by U.S. Department of Commerce, Bureau of the Census. 1st ICPSR ed. Ann Arbor, Mich.: Inter-university Consortium for Political and Social Research [producer and distributor].

———. 1997d. *Survey of Inmates of Local Jails, 1989.* [Computer file]. Conducted by U.S. Department of Commerce, Bureau of the Census. 1st ICPSR ed. Ann Arbor, Mich.: Inter-university Consortium for Political and Social Research [producer and distributor].

———. 1997e. *Census of State Adult Correctional Facilities, 1979.* [Computer file]. Conducted by the U.S. Department of Commerce, Bureau of the Census. 2nd ICPSR edition. Ann Arbor, Mich.: Inter-university Consortium for Political and Social Research [producer and distributor].

———. 1998. *Census of State Adult Correctional Facilities, 1995.* [Computer file]. Conducted by the U.S. Department of Commerce, Bureau of the Census. ICPSR edition. Ann Arbor, Mich.: Inter-university Consortium for Political and Social Research [producer and distributor].

———. 1999a. *Survey of Inmates of Local Jails, 1996.* [Computer file]. Conducted by U.S. Department of Commerce, Bureau of the Census. 1st ICPSR ed. Ann Arbor, Mich.: Inter-university Consortium for Political and Social Research [producer and distributor]

———. 1999b. *Truth in Sentencing in State Prisons*. NCJ 170032. Washington: U.S. Department of Justice.

———. 2002. *National Corrections Reporting Program, 1983–1999*. [Computer file]. Conducted by U.S. Department of Commerce, Bureau of the Census. 2nd ICPSR ed. Ann Arbor, Mich.: Inter-university Consortium for Political and Social Research [producer and distributor].

———. 2004. *State Prison Expenditures*. NCJ 20249. Washington: U.S. Department of Justice.

———. 2005. "FBI Uniform Crime Reports. Reported Crime in United States—Total." Available at: http://bjsdata.ojp.usdoj.gov/dataonline/search/crime/statebystaterun.cfm?stateid=52.

BJS and Federal Bureau of Prisons. 2001. *Survey of Inmates in State and Federal Correctional Facilities, 1997*. [Computer file]. Compiled by U.S. Department of Commerce, Bureau of the Census. ICPSR ed. Ann Arbor, Mich.: Inter-university Consortium for Political and Social Research [producer and distributor].

Bush, George W. 2004. "State of the Union Address." Available at: http://www.whitehouse.gov/news/releases/2004/01/20040120-7.html (accessed January 3, 2006).

Bushway, Shawn David. 1996. *The Impact of a Criminal History Record on Access to Legitimate Employment*. Ph.D. dissertation. Pittsburgh, Pa.: Carnegie Mellon University.

Butler, Richard, and James Heckman. 1977. "The Government's Impact on the Labor Market Status of Black Americans: A Critical Review." In *Equal Rights and Industrial Relations*, edited by Farrell E. Bloch et al. Madison, Mich.: Industrial Relations Research Association.

Button, James W. 1978. *Black Violence: The Political Impact of the 1960s Riots*. Princeton, N.J.: Princeton University Press.

Center for Human Resource Research. 2004. *National Longitudinal Study of Youth, 1979-2000* [computer file]. National Opinion Research Center, University of Chicago [producer]. Center for Human Resources, Ohio State University [distributor].

Chambliss, William. 2000. *Power, Politics, and Crime*. Boulder, Colo.: Westview Press.

Chandra, Amitabh. 2003. "Is the Convergence in the Racial Wage Gap Illusory." NBER Working Paper 9476. Cambridge, Mass.: National Bureau of Economic Research.

Chiricos, Theodore G., and Miriam A. Delone. 1992. "Labor Surplus and Punishment: A Review and Assessment of Theory and Evidence." *Social Problems* 39: 421–46.

Christie, Nils. 1993. *Crime Control as Industry: Towards Gulags Western Style*. London: Routledge.

———. 2000. *Crime Control as Industry: Towards Gulags Western Style*. 3rd edition. London: Routledge.

Clogg, Clifford C. 1974. *Measuring Underemployment: Demographic Indicators for the United States*. New York: Academic Press.

Colbjørnsen, Tom, and Arne L. Kalleberg. 1988. "Spillover, Standardization, and Stratification: Earnings Determination in the United States and Norway." *European Sociological Review* 4: 20–31.

Council of Europe. 1983. *Prison Information Bulletin*, no. 2.

———. 2002. *Prison Information Bulletin*, nos. 23–34.

Crouch, Colin. 1985. "Conditions for Trade Union Wage Restraint." In *The Politics of Inflation and Economic Stagnation: Theoretical Approaches and International Case Studies*, edited by Leon Lindberg and Charles Maier. Washington, D.C.: Brookings Institution.

D'Alessio, Stewart. J. and Lisa A. Stolzenberg. 2002. "A Multilevel Analysis of the Relationship Between Labor Surplus and Pretrial Incarceration." *Social Problems* 49: 178–93.

Davey, Joseph D. 1998. *The Politics of Prison Expansion: Winning Elections by Waging War on Crime*. Westport, Conn.: Praeger.

Dechter, Aimée R., and Glen H. Elder. 2004. "World War II Mobilization and Men's Work Lives: Continuity of Disruption for the Middle Class?" *American Journal of Sociology* 110: 761–94.

DiIulio, John J. 1987. *Governing Prisons: A Comparative Study of Correctional Management*. New York: Free Press.

DiIulio, John J., and Anne Morrison Piehl. 1991. "Does Prison Pay? The Stormy National Debate over the Cost Effectiveness of Imprisonment." *Brookings Review* 9: 28–35.

Ditton, Paula M., and Doris James Wilson. 1999. *Truth in Sentencing in State Prisons*. Bureau of Justice Statistics Special Report. NCJ 170032. Washington: U.S. Department of Justice.

Dodge, Calvert R. (ed.) 1975. *A Nation Without Prisons: Alternatives to Incarceration*. Lexington, Mass.: Lexington Books.

Doeringer, Peter B., and Michael Piore. 1971. *Internal Labor Markets and Manpower Analysis*. Lexington, Mass.: Heath.

Donohue, John J., and Steven D. Levitt. 2001. "The Impact of Legalized Abortion on Crime." *Quarterly Journal of Economics* 116: 379–420.

Donziger, Steven A. 1996. *The Real War on Crime: The Report of the National Criminal Justice Commission.* New York: Harper.

Dubber, Markus Dirk. 2001. "Policing Possession: The War on Crime and the End of Criminal Law." *Journal of Criminal Law and Criminology* 91: 829–996.

DuBois, W.E.B. 1899/1973. *The Philadelphia Negro.* Milwood, N.Y.: Kraus-Thomson.

Duneier, Mitchell. 1999. *Sidewalk.* New York: Farrar, Straus, and Giroux.

Duster, Troy. 1997. "Pattern, Purpose, and Race in the Drug War: The Crisis of Credibility in Criminal Justice." In *Crack in America: Demon Drugs and Social Justice,* edited by Craig Reinarman and Harry G. Levine. Berkeley: University of California Press.

Edin, Katherine. 2000. "Few Good Men: Why Poor Mothers Don't Marry or Remarry." *American Prospect* 11: 26–31.

Edin, Katherine, Timothy Nelson, and Rechelle Paranal. 2004. "Fatherhood and Incarceration as Potential Turning Points in the Criminal Careers of Unskilled Men." In *Imprisoning America: The Social Effects of Mass Incarceration,* edited by Mary Patillo, David Weiman, and Bruce Western. New York: Russell Sage Foundation.

Edsall, Thomas B., and Mary D. Edsall. 1991. *Chain Reaction: The Impact of Race, Rights, and Taxes on American Politics.* New York: W. W. Norton.

Elder, Glen H. 1974/1999. *Children of the Great Depression.* Chicago: University of Chicago Press.

———. 1986. "Military Times and Turning Points in Men's Lives." *Developmental Psychology* 22: 233–45.

———. 1987. "War Mobilization and the Life Course: A Cohort of World War II Veterans." *Sociological Forum* 2: 449–72.

Ellwood, David, and Christopher Jencks. 2004. "The Growing Differences in Family Structure: What Do We Know? Where Do We Look For Answers?" In *Social Inequality,* edited by Katherine Neckerman. New York: Russell Sage Foundation.

Evans, Robert. 1968. "The Labor Market and Parole Success." *Journal of Human Resources* 3: 201–12.

Fairlie, Robert W., and William A. Sundstrom. 1999. "The Emergence, Persistence, and Recent Widening of the Racial Unemployment Gap." *Industrial and Labor Relations Review* 52: 252–70.

Farrington, David P. 1989. "Early Predictors of Adolescent Aggression and Adult Violence." *Violence and Victims* 4: 79–100.

Federal Bureau of Investigation. 1993. *Age-Specific Arrest Rates and Race-Specific Ar-*

rest Rates for Selected Offenses 1965–1992. Washington: Uniform Crime Reporting Program, Federal Bureau of Investigation.

———. 2003. *Age-Specific Arrest Rates and Race-Specific Arrest Rates for Selected Offenses 1993–2001.* Washington: Uniform Crime Reporting Program, Federal Bureau of Investigation.

Federal Bureau of Prisons. 1994. *Survey of Inmates of Federal Correctional Facilities, 1991.* [Computer file]. Washington: U.S. Department of Commerce, Bureau of the Census [producer], 1991. Ann Arbor, Mich.: Inter-university Consortium for Political and Social Research [distributor].

"The Fragile Families and Child Wellbeing Study (Survey of New Parents) Mother's 1-Year Follow-up Survey." 2003. Princeton, N.J., and New York: Center for Research on Child Wellbeing, and Social Indicator Survey Center.

Frazier, E. Franklin. 1939. *The Negro Family in the United States.* Chicago: University of Chicago Press.

Freeman, Richard B. 1992. "Crime and the Employment of Disadvantaged Youth." In *Urban Labor Markets and Job Opportunity,* edited by George Peterson and Wayne Vroman. Washington, D.C.: Urban Institute.

———. 1995. "The Labor Market." In *Crime,* edited by James Q. Wilson and Joan Petersilia. San Francisco: ICS Press.

———. 1996. "Why Do So Many Young American Men Commit Crimes and What Might We Do About It?" *Journal of Economic Perspectives* 10: 25–42.

———. 1999. *The New Inequality: Creating Solutions for Poor America.* Boston: Beacon Press.

Freeman, Richard B., and Jeffrey Fagan. 1999. "Crime and Work." *Crime and Justice* 25: 225–90.

Frey, William H. 2004. "The New Great Migration: Black Americans' Return to the South, 1965-2000." Center on Urban and Metropolitan Policy. Washington, D.C.: Brookings Institution.

Furrillo, Andy. 2004. "Late Infusion of Cash Sank Proposition 66." *Sacramento Bee,* November 4, p. A3.

Gaes, Gerald, Timothy Flanagan, Lawrence Motiuk, and Lynn Stewart. 1999. "Adult Correctional Treatment." In *Prisons, Criminal Justice: A Review of Research,* edited by M. Tonry and Joan Petersilia. Chicago: University of Chicago Press.

Garland, David. 1990. *Punishment and Modern Society: A Study in Social Theory.* Chicago: University of Chicago Press.

———. 2001a. "Introduction: The Meaning of Mass Imprisonment." In *Mass Imprisonment: Social Causes and Consequences,* edited by David Garland. London: Sage Publications.

———. 2001b. *Culture of Control: Crime and Social Order in Contemporary Society.* Chicago: University of Chicago Press.

Gest, Ted. 2001. *Crime and Politics: Big Government's Erratic Campaign for Law and Order.* New York: Oxford University Press.

Giersch, Herbert. 1993. *Openness for Prosperity: Essays in World Economics.* Cambridge, Mass.: MIT Press.

Goffman, Erving. 1963. *Stigma: Notes on the Management of Spoiled Identity.* Englewood Cliffs, N.J.: Prentice Hall.

Gonnerman, Jennifer. 2003. *Life on the Outside: The Prison Odyssey of Elaine Bartlett.* New York: Farrar, Straus, & Giroux.

Gottfredson, Michael R., and Travis Hirschi. 1990. *A General Theory of Crime.* Stanford, Calif.: Stanford University Press.

Granovetter, Mark. 1995. *Getting a Job: A Study of Contracts and Careers,* 2nd ed. Chicago: University of Chicago Press.

Greenberg, David F. 1977a. "The Correctional Effects of Corrections: A Survey of Evaluations." In *Corrections and Punishment,* edited by David F. Greenberg. Beverly Hills, Calif.: Sage Publications.

———. 1977b. "The Dynamics of Oscillatory Punishment Processes." *Journal of Criminal Law and Criminology* 68: 643–51.

Greenberg, David F., and Valerie West. 2001. "State Prison Populations and Their Growth, 1971–1991." *Criminology* 39: 615–54.

Griset, Pamala. 1991. *Determinate Sentencing: The Promise and Reliability of Retributive Justice.* Albany: State University of New York.

Grogger, Jeffrey. 1992. "Arrests, Persistent Youth Joblessness, and Black/White Employment Differentials." *Review of Economics and Statistics* 74: 100–6.

———. 1995. "The Effect of Arrests on the Employment and Earnings of Young Men." *Quarterly Journal of Economics* 110: 51–71.

———. 2000. "An Economic Model of Recent Trends in Violence." In *The Crime Drop in America,* edited by Alfred Blumstein and Joel Wallman. Cambridge: Cambridge University Press.

Guetzkow, Joshua. 2004. *The Carrot and the Stick: An Inquiry into the Relationship Between Welfare and Criminal Justice.* Ph.D. dissertation. Princeton University.

Hagan, John. 1993. "The Social Embeddedness of Crime and Unemployment." *Criminology* 31: 465–91.

Hairston, Creasie Finney. 1989. "Men in Prison: Family Characteristics and Family Views." *Journal of Offender Counseling Services, and Rehabilitation* 14: 23–30.

———. 1995. "Fathers in Prison." In *Children of Incarcerated Parents,* edited by Katherine Gabel and Denise Johnston. New York: Lexington Books.

Hall, Stuart. 1978. *Policing the Crisis: Mugging, the State, and Law and Order.* London: Macmillan.

Haney, Chris. 2003. "Mental Health Issues in Long-Term Solitary and 'Supermax' Confinement." *Crime & Delinquency* 49: 124–56.

Harlow, Caroline Wolf. 2003. *Education and Correctional Populations.* Bureau of Justice Statistics Special Report. NCJ 195670. Washington: U.S. Department of Justice.

Harrington, Michael. 1962. *The Other America: Poverty in the United States.* New York: Macmillan.

Harrison, Paige M. 2000. "Total Number of Persons Under Local, State, or Federal Correctional Supervision, 1993, 1988, 1983." Bureau of Justice Statistics Spreadsheet. Available at: http://http://www.ojp.usdoj.gov/bjs/.

Harrison, Paige M., and Allen J. Beck. 2005. "Prison and Jail Inmates at Midyear 2004." *Bureau of Justice Statistics Bulletin.* NCJ 208801. Washington: U.S. Department of Justice.

Heckman, James. 1989. "The Impact of Government on the Economic Status of African Americans." In *The Question of Discrimination*, edited by Steven Shulman, William Darity, and Robert Higgs. Middletown, Conn.: Wesleyan University Press.

Hicks, Alexander M. 1994. "The Social Democratic Corporatist Model of Economic Performance in the Short- and Medium-run Perspective." In *The Comparative Political Economy of the Welfare State*, edited by Thomas Janoski and Alexander Hicks. New York: Cambridge University Press.

Hirsch, Amy E., Sharon M. Dietrich, Rue Landau, Peter D. Schneider, Irv Ackelsberg, Judith Bernstein-Baker, and Joseph Hohenstein. 2002. *Every Door Closed: Barriers Facing Parents with Criminal Records.* Washington, D.C.: Center for Law and Social Policy.

Hirschi, Travis, and Michael R. Gottfredson. 1983. "Age and the Explanation of Crime." *American Journal of Sociology* 89: 552–84.

Hogan, Dennis P. 1981. *Transitions and Social Change: The Early Lives of American Men.* New York: Academic Press.

Holzer, Harry J. 1996. *What Employers Want: Job Prospects for Less-Educated Workers.* New York: Russell Sage Foundation.

Hughes, Timothy A., Doris James Wilson, and Allen J. Beck. 2001. *Trends in State Parole, 1990–2000.* Bureau of Justice Statistics Special Report. NCJ 184735. Washington: U.S. Department of Justice.

Irwin, John James, and James Austin. 1997. *It's About Time: America's Imprisonment Binge,* 2nd. ed. Belmont, Calif.: Wadsworth.

Jacobs, David, and Jason T. Carmichael. 2001. "The Politics of Punishment Across Time and Space: A Pooled Time-Series Analysis of Imprisonment Rates." *Social Forces* 80: 61–91.

Jacobs, David, and Ronald E. Helms. 1996. "Toward a Political Model of Incarceration: A Time-Series Examination of Multiple Explanations for Prison Admission Rates." *American Journal of Sociology* 102: 323–57.

———. 2001. "Toward a Political Sociology of Punishment: Politics and Changes in the Incarcerated Population." *Social Science Research* 30: 171–94.

Jacobson, Michael. 2005. *Downsizing Prisons: How to Reduce Crime and End Mass Incarceration.* New York: New York University Press.

Jankowski, Martin Sanchez. 1991. *Islands in the Street: Gangs and American Urban Society.* Berkeley: University of California Press.

Janoski, Thomas, Christa McGill, and Vanessa Tinsley. 1997. "Making Institutions Dynamic in Cross-National Research: Time-Space Distancing in Explaining Unemployment." *Comparative Social Research* 16: 227–68.

Jaynes, Gerald D. 1990. "The Labor Market Status of Black Americans: 1939–1985." *Journal of Economic Perspectives* 4: 9–24.

Johnston, L.D., P.M. O'Malley, J.G. Bachman, and J.E. Schulenberg. 2004. *Monitoring the Future Survey Results on Drug Use, 1975–2003.* Bethesda, Md.: National Institute on Drug Abuse.

Juhn, Chinhui. 2003. "Labor Market Dropouts, Selection Bias, and Trends in the Wages of Black and White Men." *Industrial and Labor Relations Review* 56: 643–62.

Kalleberg, Arne, Barbara F. Reskin, and Ken Hudson. 2000. "Bad Jobs in America: Standard and Nonstandard Employment Relations and Job Quality in the United States." *American Sociological Review* 65: 256–78.

Klarner, Carl. 2003. "The Measurement of the Partisan Balance of State Government." *State Politics and Policy Quarterly* 3(3): 309–19.

Kling, Jeffrey R. 1999. "The Effect of Prison Sentence Length on the Subsequent Employment and Earnings of Criminal Defendants." Woodrow Wilson School Discussion Papers in Economics No. 208. Princeton, N.J.: Princeton University Press.

Kluegel, James R. 1990. "Trends in Whites' Explanations of the Black White Gap in SES." *American Sociological Review* 55: 512–25.

Kolberg, Jon Eivind, and Gøsta Esping-Andersen. 1990. "Welfare States and Employment Regimes." *International Journal of Sociology* 20: 3–36.

Kornfeld, Robert, and Howard S. Bloom. 1999. "Measuring Program Impacts on

Earnings and Employment: Do Unemployment Insurance Wage Reports from Employers Agree with Surveys of Individuals?" *Journal of Labor Economics* 17: 168–97.

Korpi, Walter. 1990. "Political and Economic Explanations for Unemployment: A Cross-National and Long-Term Analysis." *British Journal of Political Science* 21: 315–48.

LaFree, Gary, and Kriss A. Drass. 1996. "The Effect of Changes in Intraracial Income Inequality and Educational Attainment on Changes in Arrest Rates for African Americans and Whites, 1957 to 1990." *American Sociological Review* 61: 614–34.

LaLonde, Robert J. 1986. "Evaluating Econometric Evaluations of Training Programs with Experimental Data." *American Economic Review* 76: 604–20.

Land, Kenneth C., Patricia McCall, and Lawrence E. Cohen. 1990. "Structural Covariates of Homicide Rates: Are There Any Invariances Across Time and Space?" *American Journal of Sociology* 95: 922–63.

Laub, John H., Daniel S. Nagin, and Robert J. Sampson. 1998. "Trajectories of Change in Criminal Offending: Good Marriages and Desistance Processes." *American Sociological Review* 63: 225–38.

Laub, John H., and Robert J. Sampson. 2003. *Shared Beginnings, Divergent Lives: Delinquent Boys to Age 70.* Cambridge, Mass.: Harvard University Press.

Leamer, Edward E. 1993. "A Bayesian Perspective on Inference from Macroeconomic Data." *Scandinavian Journal of Economics* 93: 225–48.

Legal Action Center. 2004. *After Prison: Roadblocks to Reentry: A Report on State legal barriers Facing People with Criminal Records.* New York: Legal Action Center.

Levitt, Steven D. 1996. "The Effect of Prison Population Size on Crime Rates: Evidence from Prison Overcrowding Litigation." *Quarterly Journal of Economics* 111: 319–51.

———. 2004. "Understanding Why Crime Fell in the 1990s: Four Factors that Explain the Decline and Six that Do Not." *Journal of Economic Perspectives* 18: 163–90.

Levitt, Steven D., and Sudhir Venkatesh. 2001. "The Financial Activities of Urban Street Gang." *Quarterly Journal of Economics* 115: 755–89.

Lichter, Daniel T., Felicia B. LeClere, and Diane K. McLaughlin. 1991. "Local Marriage Markets and the Marital Behavior of Black and White Women." *American Journal of Sociology* 96: 843–67.

Liebow, Elliott. 1966. *Tally's Corner: A Study of Negro Streetcorner Men.* Boston, Mass.: Little, Brown.

Lindbeck, Assar. 1985. "What Is Wrong with the West European Economies?" *World Economy* 8: 153–70.

Lipsey, Mark W. 1992. "Juvenile Delinquency Treatment: A Meta-Analytic Inquiry into the Variability of Effects." In *Meta-Analysis for Explanation: A Casebook*, edited by Thomas D. Cook, Harris Cooper, David S. Cordray, Heidi Hartmann, Larry V. Hedges, Richard J. Light, Thomas A. Louis, and Frederick Mosteller. New York: Russell Sage Foundation.

Lipton, Douglas S., Robert Martinson, and Judith Wilks. 1975. *The Effectiveness of Correctional Treatment: A Survey of Treatment Evaluation Studies.* New York: Praeger.

Lott, John R. 1990. "The Effect of Conviction on the Legitimate Income of Criminals." *Economics Letters* 34: 381–85.

Maguire, Kathleen, and Ann L. Pastore. 1996. *Sourcebook of Criminal Justice Statistics, 1995.* Washington: U.S. Department of Justice.

———, eds. 2001. *Sourcebook of Criminal Justice Statistics.* Available at: http://www.albany.edu/sourcebook/.

———. 2002. *The Sourcebook of Criminal Justice Statistics.* Washington: U.S. Department of Justice.

Manza, Jeff, and Clem Brooks. 1999. *Social Cleavages and Political Change: Voter Alignments and U.S. Party Coalitions.* Oxford: Oxford University Press.

Marshall, Thomas H. 1950/1992. *Citizenship and Social Class.* London: Pluto Press.

Martinson, Robert. 1974. "What Works? Questions and Answers about Prison Reform." *Public Interest* 35: 22–54.

Maruna, Shadd, and Hans Toch. 2005. "The Impact of Imprisonment on the Desistance Process." In *Prisoner Reentry and Crime in America*, edited by Jeremy Travis and Christy Visher. New York: Cambridge University Press.

Marvell, Thomas B. 1996. "Sentencing Guidelines and Prison Population Growth." *Journal of Criminal Law and Criminology* 85: 696–709.

Marvell, Thomas B., and Carlisle E. Moody. 1994. "Prison Population Growth and Crime Reduction." *Journal of Quantitative Criminology* 10: 109–40.

———. 1996. "Determinate Sentencing and Abolishing Parole: the Long-Term Impacts on Prisons and Crime." *Criminology* 34: 107–28.

Massey, Douglas S., and Nancy A. Denton. 1991. *American Apartheid: Segregation and the Making of the Underclass.* Cambridge, Mass.: Harvard University Press.

Mauer, Marc. 1999. *Race to Incarcerate.* New York: The New Press.

———. 2003. "Comparative International Rate of Incarceration: An Examination of Causes and Trends." Paper presented to the U.S. Commission on Civil Rights. Washington, D.C.: The Sentencing Project.

McLanahan, Sara, and Lynne Casper. 1995. "Growing Diversity and Inequality in the American Family." In *State of the Union, America in the 1990s: Social Trends,* edited by Reynolds Farley. New York: Russell Sage Foundation.

Merton, Robert K. 1968. *Social Structure and Social Action.* Enlarged ed. New York: Free Press.

Messner, Steven F., Lawrence E. Raffalovich, and Richard McMillan. 2001. "Economic Deprivation and Changes in Homicide Arrest Rates for White and Black Youths." *Criminology* 39: 591–613.

Mishel, Lawrence, Jared Bernstein, and Heather Boushey. 2003. *The State of Working America, 2002/2003.* Ithaca, N.Y.: Cornell University Press.

Modell, John, Frank F. Furstenberg, and Theodore Hershberg. 1976. "Social Change and Transitions to Adulthood in Historical Perspective." *Journal of Family History* 1: 7–32.

Mumola, Christopher J. 2000. "Incarcerated Parents and Their Children." *Bureau of Justice Statistics Special Report.* NCJ 182335. Washington: U.S. Department of Justice.

Murakawa, Naomi. 2004. *Electing to Punish: Congress, Race, and the Rise of the American Criminal Justice State.* Ph.D. dissertation. New Haven, Conn.: Yale University.

Myers, Martha A. 1998. *Race, Labor, and Punishment in the New South.* Columbus: Ohio State University Press.

Myrdal, Gunnar. 1944/1966. *An American Dilemma: The Negro Problem and Modern Democracy,* vol. 2. New Brunswick, N.J.: Transaction Publishers.

Nagin, Daniel, and Joel Waldfogel. 1998. "The Effect of Conviction on Income Through the Life Cycle." *International Review of Law and Economics* 18: 25–40.

National Bureau of Economic Research. 2002. *CPS Labor Extracts: Merged Outgoing Rotation Group Files 1979–2000.* [Computer file]. Compiled by U.S. Department of Commerce, Bureau of the Census. Cambridge, Mass.: National Bureau of Economic Research [producer and distributor].

Newman, Katherine S. 1999. *No Shame in My Game: The Working Poor in the Inner City.* New York: Alfred A. Knopf and the Russell Sage Foundation.

Nicholson-Crotty, Sean. 2004. "The Impact of Sentencing Guidelines on State-Level Sanctions: An Analysis Over Time." *Crime and Delinquency* 50: 395–411.

Niemi, Richard, John Mueller, and Tom Smith. 1989. *Trends in Public Opinion: A Compendium of Survey Data*. New York: Greenwood Press.

Nurse, Ann M. 2002. *Fatherhood Arrested: Parenting from Within the Juvenile Justice System*. Nashville, Tenn.: Vanderbilt University Press.

OECD. 1994. *The OECD Jobs Study: Part II - The Adjustment Potential of the Labor Market*. Paris: Organization for Economic Cooperation and Development.

Office of Applied Studies, SAMHSA, Drug Abuse Warning Network. 2003. "Table 4.4.0—Emergency Department Drug Mentions by Patient Demographic Characteristics: Estimates for the Coterminous U.S. by Year." Available at: http://dawninfo.samhsa.gov/old_dawn/pubs_94_02/pickatable/2002/4.4.0.xls (accessed January 20, 2006).

Office of the Pardon Attorney. 1996. *Civil Disabilities of Convicted Felons: A State-by-State Survey*. Washington: U.S. Department of Justice.

Office of Policy Planning and Research. 1965. *The Negro Family: The Case for National Action*. Washington: U.S. Department of Labor.

Olson, Mancur. 1982. *The Rise and Decline of Nations: Economic Growth, Stagflation, and Social Rigidities*. New Haven, Conn.: Yale University Press.

Orwell, George. 1937. *The Road to Wigan Pier*. London: Gollancz.

Oshinsky, David M. 1996. *Worse than Slavery: Parchman Farm and the Ordeal of Jim Crow Justice*. New York: Free Press.

Pager, Devah. 2003. "The Mark of a Criminal Record." *American Journal of Sociology* 108(5): 937–75.

Palmer, Ted. 1975. "Martinson Revisited." *Journal of Research in Crime and Delinquency* 12: 133–52.

Pastore, Ann L., and Kathleen Maguire, eds. 2003. *Sourcebook of Criminal Justice Statistics*. Washington: Bureau of Justice Statistics.

———. 2005. *Sourcebook of Criminal Justice Statistics* [online]. Available at: http://www.albany.edu/sourcebook/ (accessed December 2005).

Petersilia, Joan. 1999. "Parole and Prisoner Re-Entry in the United States." *Crime and Justice* 21: 479–530

———. 2003. *When Prisoners Come Home: Parole and Prisoner Reentry*. New York: Oxford University Press.

———. 2005. "Hard Time: Ex-Offenders Returning Home After Prison." *Corrections Today* 67: 66–71, 155.

Pettit, Becky and Christopher Lyons. 2004. "Status and the Stigma of Incarceration: The labor Market Effects of Incarceration by Race, Class, and Criminal Involvement." Unpublished manuscript. Seattle: University of Washington.

Pettit, Becky, and Bruce Western. 2004. "Mass Imprisonment and the Life Course: Race and Class Inequality in U.S. Incarceration." *American Sociological Review* 69: 151–69.

Piehl, Anne Morrison, and John J. DiIulio. 1995. "Does Prison Pay? Revisited." *Brookings Review* 13(Winter): 21–25.

Quinney, Richard. 1974. *Criminal Justice in America: A Critical Understanding.* Boston, Mass.: Little, Brown.

Reichman, Nancy E., Julien O. Teitler, Irwin Garfinkel, and Sara S. McLanahan. 2001. "Fragile Families: Sample and Design." *Children and Youth Services Review* 23: 303–26.

Rennison, Callie. 2002. *Criminal Victimization 2001, Changes 2000–01 with Trends 1993–2001.* NCJ 194610. Washington: Department of Justice.

Robinson, Paul H., and John M. Darley. 2004. "Does Criminal Law Deter? A Behavioral Science Investigation." *Oxford Journal of Legal Studies* 24: 173–205.

Rosenfeld, Richard. 2000. "Patterns in Adult Homicide: 1980–1995." In *The Crime Drop in America,* edited by Alfred Blumstein and Joel Wallman. Cambridge: Cambridge University Press.

Rossi, Peter H., Richard A. Berk, and Kenneth J. Lenihan. 1980. *Money, Work, and Crime: Experimental Evidence.* New York: Academic Press.

Rothman, David. 1980/2002. *Conscience and Convenience: the Asylum and its Alternatives in Progressive America.* New York: Aldine DeGruyter.

Rotman, Edgardo. 1995. "The Failure of Reform: United States 1865–1965." In *The Oxford History of the Prison,* edited by Norval Morris and David J. Rothman. New York: Oxford University Press.

Rusche, Georg. 1933/1978. "Labor Market and Penal Sanction." *Crime and Justice* 10: 2–8.

Rusche, Georg, and Otto Kirchheimer. 1939/2003. *Punishment and Social Structure.* New Brunswick, N.J.: Transaction Books.

Ruth, Henry, and Kevin R. Reitz. 2003. *The Challenge of Crime: Rethinking Our Response.* Cambridge, Mass.: Harvard University Press.

Sabol, William J., and James P. Lynch. 2001. "Prisoner Reentry in Perspective." *Crime Policy Report,* vol. 3. Washington, D.C.: Urban Institute.

———. 2003. "Assessing the Longer-run Consequences of Incarceration: Effects on Families and Employment." In *Crime Control and Social Justice: The Delicate Bal-*

ance, edited by Darnell Hakins, Samuel L. Myers Jr., and Randolph Stone. Westport, Conn.: Greenwood Press.

Sampson, Robert J. 1987. "Urban Black Violence: The Effect of Male Joblessness and Family Disruption." *American Journal of Sociology* 93: 348–82.

Sampson, Robert J., and John H. Laub. 1993. *Crime in the Making: Pathways and Turning Points Through Life*. Cambridge, Mass.: Harvard University Press.

———. 1996. "Socioeconomic Achievement in the Life Course of Disadvantaged Men: Military Service as a Turning Point, Circa 1940–1965." *American Sociological Review* 61: 347–67.

Sampson, Robert J., Jeffrey D. Morenoff, and Thomas Gannon-Rowley. 2002. "Assessing 'Neighborhood Effects': Social Processes and New Directions for Research." *Annual Review of Sociology* 28: 443–78.

Sampson, Robert J., and Stephen W. Raudenbush. 1999. "Systematic Social Observation of Public Spaces: A New Look at Disorder in Urban Neighborhoods." *American Journal of Sociology* 105: 603–51.

Sampson, Robert J., and William Julius Wilson. 1995. "Toward a Theory of Race, Crime, and Urban Inequality." In *Crime and Inequality*, edited by John Hagan and Ruth D. Peterson. Stanford, Calif.: Stanford University Press.

Saylor, William G., and Gerald G. Gaes. 1997. "Training Inmates Through Industrial Work Participation and Vocational and Apprenticeship Instruction." *Corrections Management Quarterly* 1: 32–43.

———. 1999. "The Differential Effect of Industries and Vocational Training on Post Release Outcome for Ethnic and Racial Groups." Office of Research and Evaluation. Washington: Federal Bureau of Prisons.

Scholz, John Karl, and Kara Levine. 2002. "U.S. Black-White Wealth Inequality: A Survey." Working Paper. Madison: University of Wisconsin, Department of Economics and Institute for Research on Poverty.

Sechrest, Lee, Susan O. White, and Elizabeth D. Brown, eds. 1979. *The Rehabilitation of Criminal Offenders*. Washington, D.C.: National Academy of Sciences Press.

Shaw, Clifford Robem, and Henry D. McKay. 1942. *Juvenile Delinquency and Urban Areas*. Chicago: University of Chicago Press.

Shipler, David. 2004. *The Working Poor: Invisible in America*. New York: Alfred A. Knopf.

Singh, Gopal K., and Stella M. Yu. 1995. "Infant Mortality in the United States: Trends, Differentials, and Projections, 1950 Through 2010." *American Journal of Public Health* 85: 957–64.

Smith, Herbert L., S. Philip Morgan, and Tanya Koropeckyj-Cox. 1996. "A Decomposition of Trends in the Nonmarital Fertility Ratios of Blacks and Whites in the United States, 1960–1992." *Demography* 33: 141–51.

Smith, Kevin B. 2004. "The Politics of Punishment: Evaluating Political Explanations of Incarceration Rates." *Journal of Politics* 66: 925–38.

Somer, Robert. 1976. *The End of Imprisonment.* New York: Oxford University Press.

Spelman, William.1994. *Criminal Incapacitation.* New York: Plenum Press.

———. 2000. "The Limited Importance of Prison Expansion." In *The Crime Drop in America*, edited by Alfred Blumstein and Joel Wallman. New York: Cambridge University Press.

Spitzer, Steven. 1975. "Toward a Marxian Theory of Deviance." *Social Problems* 22: 638–51.

Spohn, Cassia, and David Holleran. 2000. "The Imprisonment Penalty Paid by Young, Unemployed Black and Hispanic Male Offenders." *Criminology* 38: 281–306.

Steffensmeier, Darrell, Jeffery Ulmer, and John Kramer. 1998. "The Interaction of Race, Gender, and Age in Criminal Sentencing: The Punishment Cost of Being Young, Black, and Male." *Criminology* 36: 763–97.

Stephan, James J. 1997. *Census of State and Federal Correctional Facilities, 1995.* Washington: Bureau of Justice Statistics.

Sullivan, Mercer. 1989. *"Getting Paid": Youth Crime and Work in the Inner City.* Ithaca, N.Y.: Cornell University Press.

Sutton, John. 2000. "Imprisonment and Social Classification in Five Common-Law Democracies, 1955-1985." *American Journal of Sociology* 106: 350–96.

Tittle, Charles R., and Debra A. Curran. 1988. "Contingencies for Dispositional Disparities in Juvenile Justice." *Social Forces* 67: 23–58.

Tonry, Michael. 1995. *Malign Neglect.* New York: Oxford University Press.

———. 1996. *Sentencing Matters.* New York: Oxford University Press.

Tracy, Paul M., Marvin E. Wolfgang, and Robert M. Figlio. 1990. *Delinqunecy Careers in Two Birth Cohorts.* New York: Plenum Press.

Travis, Jeremy. 2005. *But They All Come Back: Facing the Challenges of Prisoner Reentry.* Washington, D.C.: Urban Institute.

Turner, R. 1995. "Black-White Infant Mortality Differential has Grown in Recent Decades and Will Persist into Next Century." *Family Planning Perspectives* 27: 267–68.

Tyler, John H., and Jeffrey R. Kling. 2004. "Prison-Based Education and Re-Entry into the Mainstream Labor Market." Unpublished manuscript. Providence, R.I.: Brown University.

Uggen, Christopher. 2000. "Work as a Turning Point in the Life Course of Criminals: A Duration Model of Age, Employment and Recidivism." *American Sociological Review* 65: 529–46.

Uggen, Christopher, and Jeff Manza. 2002. "Democratic Contraction? Political Consequences of Felon Disenfranchisement in the United States." *American Sociological Review* 67: 777–803.

Uggen, Christopher, and Sara Wakefield. 2005. "Young Adult Reentering the Community from the Criminal Justice System: The Challenge of Becoming an Adult." In *On Your Own Without a Net: The Transition to Adulthood for Vulnerable Populations,* edited by Wayne Osgood, Mike Foster, and Connie Flanagan. Chicago: University of Chicago Press.

U.S. Bureau of the Census. 1964–1999. *Statistical Abstracts of the United States.* Washington: U.S. Department of Commerce.

———. 1971. *Census of Population and Housing, 1970: Public Use Samples.* [Computer file]. Washington: U.S. Department of Commerce, Bureau of the Census [producer]. Ann Arbor, Mich.: Inter-university Consortium for Political and Social Research [distributor], 1991.

———. 1985. *Census of Population and Housing, 1980: Public Use Microdata Sample (C SAMPLE): 1-Percent Sample.* [Computer file]. Washington: U.S. Dept. of Commerce, Bureau of the Census [producer]. Ann Arbor, Mich.: Inter-university Consortium for Political and Social Research [distributor], 1994.

———. 1995. *Census of Population and Housing, 1990: Public Use Microdata Sample: 1-Percent Sample.* [Computer file]. 4th release. Washington: U.S. Department of Commerce, Bureau of the Census [producer]. Ann Arbor, Mich.: Inter-university Consortium for Political and Social Research [distributor], 1998.

Useem, Bert, Anne Morrison Piehl, and Raymond V. Liedka. 2001. "The Crime Control Effect of Incarceration: Reconsidering the Evidence." Final Report to the National Institute of Justice. Washington: U.S. Department of Justice.

Venkatesh, Sudhir A., and Steven D. Levitt. 2000. "'Are We a Family or a Business?' History and Disjuncture in the Urban American Street Gang." *Theory and Society* 29: 427–62.

Visher, Christy A. 1986. "The Rand Inmate Survey: A Re-Analysis." In *Criminal Careers and Career Criminals,* vol. 2, edited by Alfred Blumstein, Jacqueline Cohen, Jeffrey Roth, and Christy Visher. Washington, D.C.: National Academy Press.

Wacquant, Loïc. 2000. "The New 'Peculiar Institution:' On the Prison as Surrogate Ghetto." *Theoretical Criminology* 4: 377–89.

———. 2001. "Deadly Symbiosis: When Ghetto and Prison Meet and Mesh." In

Mass Imprisonment: Social Causes and Consequences, edited by David Garland. London: Sage Publications.

Waldfogel, Joel. 1994a. "The Effect of Criminal Conviction on Income and the Trust 'Reposed in the Workmen.'" *Journal of Human Resources* 29: 62–81.

———. 1994b. "Does Conviction Have a Persistent Effect on Income and Employment?" *International Review of Law and Economics* 14: 103–19.

Walters, Dan. 2004. "Voter turnaround on Proposition 66 was a Dramatic Campaign Event." *Sacramento Bee*, November 16, p. A3.

Warr, Mark. 1998. "Life-Course Transitions and Desistance From Crime." *Criminology* 36: 183–216.

Welch, Finnis. 1990. "The Employment of Black Men." *Journal of Labor Economics* 8: S26–S74.

Western, Bruce. 2002. "The Impact of Incarceration on Wage Mobility and Inequality." *American Sociological Review* 67:477–98.

Western, Bruce, and Katherine Beckett. 1999. "How Unregulated is the U.S. Labor Market: The Penal System as a Labor Market Institution." *American Journal of Sociology* 104: 1030-60.

Western, Bruce, Meredith Kleykamp, and Jake Rosenfeld. 2004. "Crime, Punishment, and American Inequality." In *Social Inequality*, edited by Katherine Neckerman. New York: Russell Sage Foundation.

Western, Bruce, Jeffrey R. Kling, and David F. Weiman. 2001. "The Labor Market Consequences of Incarceration." *Crime & Delinquency* 47: 410–27.

Western, Bruce, Len Lopoo, and Sara McLanahan. 2004. "Incarceration and the Bonds Between Parents in Fragile Families." In *Imprisoning America: the Social Effects of Mass Incarceration*, edited by Mary Patillo, David Weiman, and Bruce Western. New York: Russell Sage Foundation.

Western, Bruce, and Sara McLanahan. 2000. "Fathers Behind Bars: The Impact of Incarceration on Family Formation." In *Families, Crime, and Criminal Justice: Charting the Linkages*.

Western, Bruce, and Becky Pettit. 2005. "Black-White Wage Inequality, Employment Rates, and Incarceration." *American Journal of Sociology* 111: 553–78.

Western, Bruce, Becky Pettit, and Josh Guetzkow. 2002. "Black Economic Progress in the Era of Mass Imprisonment." In *Collateral Damage: The Social Cost of Mass Incarceration*, edited by Meda Chesney-Lind and Marc Mauer. New York: Free Press.

Whalen, Charles W., and Barbara Whalen. 1985. *The Longest Debate: A Legislative History of the 1964 Civil Rights Act*. Washington, D.C.: Seven Locks Press.

Wicharaya, Tamasak. 1995. *Simple Theory, Hard Reality: The Impact of Sentencing Reforms on Courts, Prisons, and Crime.* Albany: State University of New York Press.

Wilkes, Rima, and John Iceland. 2004. "Hypersegregation in the Twenty-first Century." *Demography* 41: 23–36.

Wilson, James Q. 1968. *Varieties of Police Behavior; The Management of Law and Order in Eight Communities.* Cambridge, Mass.: Harvard University Press.

———. 1975. *Thinking About Crime.* New York: Basic Books.

———. 1994. "Prisons in a Free Society." *The Public Interest* 11: 37–40.

Wilson, William Julius. 1987. *The Truly Disadvantaged: The Inner City, the Underclass and Public Policy.* Chicago: University of Chicago Press.

———. 1996. *When Work Disappears: The World of the New Urban Poor.* New York: Alfred A. Knopf.

Windelsham, Lord. 1998. *Politics, Punishment and Populism.* New York: Oxford University Press.

Xie, Yu. 1992. "The Socioeconomic Status of Young Male Veterans, 1964–1984." *Social Science Quarterly* 73: 379–96.

Zimring, Franklin E., and Gordon Hawkins. 1992. *Search for Rational Drug Control.* New York: Cambridge University Press.

———. 1995. *Incapacitation: Penal Confinement and the Restraint of Crime.* New York: Oxford University Press.

Zimring, Franklin E., Gordon Hawkins, and Sam Kamin. 2001. *Punishment and Democracy: Three Strikes and You're Out in California.* New York: Oxford University Press.

INDEX

Boldface numbers refer to figures and tables.